The Beats:
Essays in Criticism

edited by

Lee Bartlett

McFarland 1981

Jefferson, N.C., & London

also by Lee Bartlett

William Everson, A Descriptive Bibliography (with Allen Campo)
Benchmark and Blaze: The Emergence of William Everson
Karl Shapiro: A Descriptive Bibliography
Earth Poetry: Selected Essays and Interviews of William Everson
*Letters to Christopher: Stephen Spender's Letters to Christopher Isher-
    wood, 1929-1939*

Library of Congress Cataloging in Publication Data

Main entry under title:

The Beats.

Bibliography: p.
Includes index.
CONTENTS: Holmes, J.C. Unscrewing the locks: the
beat poets — Stull, W.L. The quest and the question:
cosmology and myth in the work of William S. Burroughs,
1953-1960. — Peterson, R.G. A picture is a fact:
Wittgenstein and Naked lunch. — [etc.]

    1. American literature — 20th century — History and
criticism — Addresses, essays, lectures. 2. Bohemianism —
United States — Addresses, essays, lectures. I. Bartlett,
Lee, 1950-   .
PS228.B6B48   810'.9'0054   80-28179

ISBN 0-89950-026-9

Manufactured in the United States of America

for William Everson

And the sudden Eye will swell with the gift of sight
And split the tomb.

Contents

Acknowledgments

The editor would like to thank Jack Hicks for introducing him to Kerouac's fiction, and Peter L. Hays for a very great favor which has nothing to do with either this collection or the Beats. All but one of the essays gathered here have been previously published; thanks go to both their authors and the books and journals where they first appeared for permission to reprint.

"Unscrewing the Locks: The Beat Poets," in *Poets of the Cities* (New York: Dutton, 1974).

"The Quest and the Question: Cosmology and Myth in the Work of William S. Burroughs, 1953-1960," *Twentieth Century Literature*, 24 (May, 1974).

"A Picture Is a Fact: Wittgenstein and *Naked Lunch*," *Twentieth Century Literature*, 12 (July, 1966).

"Everson/Antoninus: Contending with the Shadow," afterword to William Everson, *The Veritable Years* (Santa Barbara, Calif.: Black Sparrow Press, 1978).

"Lawrence Ferlinghetti's Fourth Person Singular and the Theory of Relativity," *Wisconsin Studies in Contemporary Literature*, 8 (© 1967 by the Board of Regents of the University of Wisconsin System).

"Allen Ginsberg: The Origins of *Howl* and *Kaddish*," *Iowa Review*, 8 (1977).

"Allen Ginsberg's *Reality Sandwiches*," in Thomas Merrill, *Allen Ginsberg* (Boston: Twayne, 1969).

"Whatever Happened to Bob Kaufman" *Black World*, 21 (1972).

"The Delicate Dynamics of Friendship: A Reconsideration of Kerouac's *On the Road*," *American Literature*, 46 (May, 1974).

"The Poetry of Gary Snyder," *The Southern Review*, 4 (Summer 1968).

"Clearing the Ground: Gary Snyder and the Modernist Imperative," *Criticism*, 19 (Spring 1977).

"The Development of the New Language: Michael McClure, Philip Whalen, and Gregory Corso," in Geoffrey Thurley, *The American Moment* (London: St. Martin's, 1978).

"Dionysus and the Beat Generation," in William Everson, *Earth Poetry* (Berkeley, Calif.: Oyez, 1980).

"Dionysus & The Beat: Four Letters on the Archetype," *Sparrow 63*, December, 1977.

Introduction

When Allen Ginsberg arrived in San Francisco in 1953 with a letter of introduction from William Carlos Williams to Kenneth Rexroth, *Howl* had not been written and Whitman's stock was low. If for the country at large Eisenhower was president and golf the national sport, for the literati Eliot was god and New Criticism the national creed. Following I.A. Richards' lead, Brooks and Warren's *Understanding Poetry* (the standard anthology textbook for freshman literature courses since its publication in 1938), argued that "Literature in general—poetry in particular—also represents a specialization of language for the purpose of precision." And in a culture preparing itself with the New Mathematics to enter the space race against increasingly more refined Russian technology, precision—the objective correlative in life as well as art—was the order of the day.

Yet there are many versions of cultural reality, and in San Francisco another was operative. In his Introduction to D.H. Lawrence's *Selected Poems*, published by New Directions in 1947, Kenneth Rexroth had already flung down the gauntlet before the New Critical academies. "Any bright young man can be taught to be artful," he wrote. "It is always the lesser artists who are artful, they must learn their trade by rote." And again, "I suppose it is the absolutism which has swept over popular taste in the wake of Cubism which has encouraged the ignorant to expect a canzone of Dante's in each issue of their favorite little magazine, a School of Athens in every WPA mural." And the final blast, "Modern man is terribly afraid of sex, of pain, of evil, of death. Today childbirth, the ultimate orgiastic experience, has been reduced to a meaningless dream.... Men and women torture each other to death in the bedroom, just as the dying dinosaurs gnawed each other as they copulated in the chilly marshes.... When we show signs of waking, another cocktail instead of the Wine of God."

Robert Duncan, William Everson, and Philip Lamantia—in the mid-forties all three were part of a still amorphous literary rebellion drawn together by "the long honorable San Francisco tradition of Bohemian-Buddhist-Wobbly-mystical-anarchist social involvement." The

1

rabble was preparing to storm the universities and the quarterlies, with Rexroth at the lead. According to Everson, Rexroth's strategy was simple — to replace what he saw as a life-denying, hyperartificial, worn-out literary classicism with "the combination of Lawrentian passionate eroticism, populist-anarchist-collective surge and American precisionist adhesion through Bill Williams." Everson was to be Rexroth's "Lincolnesque populist pacificist — the 'pome-splitter,' Duncan a celebrative dionysian asthete with formalist adhesions to the precisionists, Lamantia a dionysian surrealist." But because of "personality problems and the women," the revolution fizzled at the gates.

So a few years later when Ginsberg arrived in San Francisco things were pretty quiet. After a stint as a market-researcher, he took a job as a busboy to finance a course in prosody at Berkeley. In the meantime, in an apartment on Market Street, he had completed the first part of *Howl*, a poem "typed out madly in one afternoon, a tragic custard-pie comedy of wild phrasing, meaningless images for the beauty of abstract poetry of mind running along making awkward combinations like Charley Chaplin's walk, long saxaphone-like chorus lines I knew Kerouac would hear *sound* of — Taking off from his own inspired prose line really a new poetry." And to get that new poetry some public attention, Rexroth suggested to the young poet that he rent a hall and organize a reading.

Ginsberg did just that. He enlisted his friends Gary Snyder, Philip Whalen, Philip Lamantia, and Michael McClure to read with him at an artists' cooperative called the Six Gallery, with Rexroth acting as master of ceremonies. Jack Kerouac was in the audience, as were Neal Cassady and Lawrence Ferlinghetti. In his advertisements, Ginsberg had promised a "Happy Apocalypse," and if we can believe the poet writing in retrospect, no one was disappointed. "Like this was the end of the McCarthy scene.... The evening ended up with everybody absolutely radiant and happy, with talk and kissing and later on big happy orgies of poets." Ginsberg took Whitman's "Unscrew the locks from the doors!/ Unscrew the doors themselves from their jambs!" as the epigraph to *Howl and Other Poems*, and it was apt; as the long apocalyptic poem unscrewed the New Critical locks from their precisionist jambs, the Six Gallery reading heralded the Beat Generation.

The Beat Generation. Kerouac used the term in 1948, and four years later John Clellon Holmes wrote a piece for the *New York Times* called "This Is the Beat Generation." In the aftermath of the publication of *Howl and Other Poems* and *On the Road*, critics and reviewers tended to choose sides, either seeing the Beats as "fragmentary, febrile, pretentious, confused," or seeing them in the tradition of Twain, Melville, and Thoreau, as "purely American." There have been numerous anthologies of Beat writing, and much criticism and biography — Bruce Cook's *The Beat Generation*, Ann Charters' *Kerouac*, and Dennis McNally's recent

Desolate Angel: Jack Kerouac, the Beat Generation, and America come immediately to mind. Even so, attempting to delineate the characteristics shared by those writers we associate with the Beat Generation has remained a difficult task. William Burroughs himself (certainly a central figure in and for the Generation), when asked by Daniel Odier whether or not he considered himself a part of the Beats, replied, "I don't associate myself with [them] at all, and never have, either with their objectives or their literary style." He goes on to suggest that while Kerouac, Ginsberg, and Corso "are all personal friends of many years standing," one "couldn't really find four writers more different, more distinctive. It's simply a matter of juxtaposition rather than any actual association of literary styles or overall objectives."

"Beat," John Clellon Holmes wrote in his *New York Times* piece, "implies the feeling of having been used, of being raw. It involves a sort of nakedness of mind, and, ultimately, of soul; a feeling of being reduced to the bedrock of consciousness." And yet the response to this "rawness" by those writers we tend to think of as emerging with the Beat Generation differed more widely than is popularly supposed. All of them, for example, evinced broad political concerns, though there was hardly a Beat "party line." Gary Snyder was, at least for a time, a communist, Allen Ginsberg a sort of anarchist; during the sixties, both poets were profoundly and vocally opposed to America's involvement in Vietnam. Jack Kerouac, however, always conservative in his political beliefs, died a Republican and an admirer of William F. Buckley. Like Kerouac, Gregory Corso supported Americ's role in Vietnam; in 1965, he wrote to Ginsberg, attacking his stand on Vietnam: "My kid brother saw action in Santa Domingo—goes to Vietnam—me I'm all for the Marines now by god—fuck all you pacifist abusers."

Again, the Beats were certainly concerned with spiritual matters, but aside from the fact of the spiritual quest itself, can we find a common thread running through their work? Snyder spent many years in a Zen Buddhist monastery and he looks to a combination of Zen and American Indian philosophy to bring about a spiritual transformation in America. While Kerouac was also interested in Zen, he was raised a Catholic and remained loyal to the Church throughout his life. William Everson converted to Catholicism in 1949, and as Brother Antoninus spent the next eighteen years working through a philosophy of erotic mysticism grounded in Catholic faith. Ginsberg's spiritual interests have manifested themselves in his preoccupation with Hinduism, most especially mantras and Tantric yoga, while for Burroughs the grail seems buried somewhere in the hinterland of linguistics.

Although it seems to me that there may be a certain stylistic and thematic cohesion to the Beat Generation (this is the subject of William Everson's piece and, by implication at least, Albert Gelpi's essay on Everson and my own essay on Kerouac), its definition is not really the purpose of this collection. Rather, this book more modestly attempts to bring together some fairly recent criticism on several writers frequently associated under the rubric Beat. Thomas Parkinson's *Casebook on the Beat* has remained the central work on the Generation since its publication in 1961. The present collection may be seen as an extension and updating. When Parkinson's book appeared, these writers were just beginning to emerge (which explains the exclusion of Rexroth here; by the time of the Six Gallery reading he was already a poet and essayist of reputation, and is better seen as a presiding figure than as a member of the Beat Generation); now, almost twenty years later, they have each produced a large, and I think often significant, body of work. Criticism has attempted to keep pace. Because the Beats have been as much a social as a literary force in America, much of the writing about them has been of necessity polemical, often focusing on biography. Still, as John Clellon Holmes commented in "The Game of the Name," the "Beat Generation, like to the Lost Generation before it, was primarily a literary group, and not a social movement." Many fine literary critics have been drawn to one or another of the Beats — if for no other reason than to dissociate their particular author from the rest of the group. In editing this book I have tried as nearly as possible to choose pieces dealing with the members of the Generation as writers rather than simply social or political figures.

Lee Bartlett

September 25, 1980
Pikeville, Kentucky

Unscrewing the Locks:
The Beat Poets

by John Clellon Holmes

> *Free verse is, or should be direct utterance from the instant, whole man. It is the soul and the mind and body surging at once, nothing left out. They speak all together. There is some confusion, some discord. But the confusion and the discord only belong to the reality, as noise belongs to the plunge of water.* —D.H. Lawrence.

1 Queries

Indifference to history is as American as the built-in obsolescence of our automobiles. Heirs of the past, we ignore it out of lust for the future—to the despair of our artists, marooned in the unfinished present, and thereby speaking in a language that is often unintelligible to their countrymen, who are bewitched by tomorrow or captive to yesterday.

For the so-called Beat Poets of the 50's and early 60's, dissertation-time, retrospective-time has come. Who were they? Where did they come from? Were they significant? Did they make any difference?

Above all, have they become *safe* enough — back there a decade or more ago — for us to confront what they were saying so insistently?

2 Groups

I take this movement to include all those poets and writers who would agree, either whole-heartedly or with minor reservations, with William Carlos Williams' reaction to T.S. Eliot's *The Wasteland*. Williams felt that it would set American poetry back by twenty years, and

5

by the late-40's those twenty years were over, and the prophecy redeemed. I take this movement to embrace all those writers who rejected the formalism, conservatism and "classicism" that Eliot's influence grafted on American writing; who went back to essential sources — in our national experience and in our earlier literature — to be renewed.

The New York group, which included Allen Ginsberg, Jack Kerouac, Gregory Corso and others, became officially known as the Beats. There was the so-called Black Mountain group, loosely including Charles Olson, Robert Creeley, Robert Duncan and others. In San Francisco, there was Lawrence Ferlinghetti, Gary Snyder, Philip Whalen, and Michael McClure. Another New York enclave, centered around the art scene there, was composed of Frank O'Hara, John Ashbery and Kenneth Koch.

No artist, I suspect, is ever completely at ease finding himself shoved into a category. But I believe that all these writers more or less instantly recognized a similarity of life-attitude and aesthetic-direction in each other, and felt less alone, and drew fresh energy, from that recognition. Most of them found their ancestors in Melville and Whitman, rather than James and Hawthorne. Most of them believed that Ezra Pound and Hart Crane held out more hope for a new and vital American poetry than T.S. Eliot or W.B. Yeats. And most of them felt a fraternal kinship with William Carlos Williams that signalized the victory of his long struggle to establish a new poetics here.

3 Origins

The roots of the attitudes that are peculiar to these writers are as random and diverse as American life in the last forty years. There are taproots in the movies, comic books, radio and jazz-music of the 30's that formed the images of the youth-mythos of that period before it was educated-out of such trivia to higher "cultural" concerns. Think of such epiphanies as Chaplin eating his shoe, the sacred and profane dada of Harpo and Groucho, the lift towards ecstacy in a Basie riff, the princely cape beneath Clark Kent's plebeian suit. Think of football twilights, the erotic secrecies of boys' rooms, the carnival of neighborhood streets, sad Huck Finn rivers — followed by the disintegrative uprootings of the war, death and euphoria kissing in a Kansas convertible, angels of excess haunting Terre Haute. Later, roots as well in the exegetical twitter of G.I. Bill classrooms, asphalted-pages of explication in the critical journals — all those sestinas and objective correlatives and analogies-to-myth and privileged moments — those suitcases-full of academic stones the young Sisyphuses of the time were forced to haul up Morningside Heights, and elsewhere.

More on-going origins in the secret excitement of reading Blake,

Lawrence, Rimbaud, Céline, Miller, Whitman—having no way to make them *respectable* to the New Critics, and thus long thoughts about the veracity of that "respectability." At one point in 1949, for instance, *everyone* (as they later learned with astonishment) was reading Melville's *Pierre*, just re-published then for the first time in more than half a century, everyone's separate mind moving towards the same sources at some mysterious behest. Also, there was the eruptive, mobile, fluctuating nature of American postwar life—streets, bars, pads, bop, drugs, hipsters, sexual breakthroughs, urgings towards any Unknown.

Outrageous and unsettling questions started to shape themselves towards words. What did a sonnet really have to do with Hiroshima, Charlie Parker upheavings in the spirit? Could you structure an account of cross-the-country-on-your-thumb by the old, mechanical psychologies? Was poetic form simply an overlay you scissored the raw edges of content to fit? Could 17th century meter and rhyme contain the syncopated accelerations of the actual reality of blaring radios and jackhammers and pavement-crowds and bomb-reverberations? Was John Donne the most reliable guide to past-midnight, cold-water-flat illuminations? How write about real death, under the bitter bridges, in the accents of madrigal? Was art no more than an afternoon teacup, after all?

Charles Olson wrote, dismantling Eliot's "classicism" in a sentence, "Verse now, 1950, if it is to go ahead, if it is to be of *essential* use, must, I take it, catch up and put into itself certain laws and possibilities of the breath, of the breathing of the man who writes as well as of his listenings." To go ahead. To be of essential use. The breathing of the man. One perception leading directly to a further perception. Spontaneous prose. First thought best thought. Literature made by the whole man, writing. Rather remain silent than cheat the language.

Ultimate origins, there. A flowering, possible.

4 Histories

The dismal early 50's, which Nelson Algren best characterized by saying that if *The Man in the Grey Flannel Suit* and *Marjorie Morningstar* were being married down the block he wouldn't go to the wedding, were "woodshed" years—a jazz musician's term for going off, and getting out of sight, and honing his axe alone.

In New York, Jack Kerouac wrote *On the Road*, and couldn't get it published, and set off back into America, freed by failure to write the books he himself would like to read. Ferlinghetti migrated "overland" to San Francisco, going westward as Thoreau had long ago divined the American intuitive direction, to eventually open *City Lights Bookstore*, the *Shakespeare and Company* of its generation. Ginsberg gave up writing murderously-compacted imitations of the

Metaphysicals, and went to school to Williams, and then off to Yucatan to brood on prosody and invite new visions. Ex-streetboy Corso's *Wander-jahr* took him to Harvard, Harvard-man Creeley's to Mallorca, and Snyder's to logging camps and mountain-lookouts.

Poets were composing everywhere, most still unknown to each other, in that buried isolation of soul in which U.S. artists have immemorially labored, deprived even of the company of their fellow-exiles, with no place to publish in the *Sewanee, Kenyon, Partisan* reviews of Academy America. So, a gradual budding of small presses and now-and-again little magazines — *Origin* in Boston, *Black Mountain Review* in North Carolina, the *Pocket Poets Series* in Frisco, and countless other fugitive blossoms appearing stubbornly between the paving stones of the "official" literature. There was general movement away from traditional centers, and realignment in chance locations where the climate and vibrations were congenial, there to discover brother-scriveners also on the move, writing the poems of actual, living-meat experience in Late Empire America, in our own true speech, and in forms as organic and mysterious as the seed-become-tree. All this ferment and innovation and creative flow not surfacing into the slumberous upper air until mid-decade.

As propitiously as the conjunction of Hawthorne, Emerson, Thoreau, Alcott and Melville in the Massachusetts of a hundred years before (that first flowering of indigenous American writing), an astounding spectrum of writers converged in San Francisco by the felicities of chance, the breadth of that Bay, perhaps, corresponding to some enlargement within them — last margin of the continent, white clapboarded city of bridges that flung themselves, more audaciously than all of Crane's imaginings, in the direction of the Buddha-lands the Transcendentalists had been, themselves, an early bridge towards. It was the place, the time. Natural to these poets, for whom the life of the poem was the man breathing, was the urge to read in public — the wine-rich voice, the living people listening, the sound of streets as an antiphonal, and sometimes the skirl of sax or stutter of drum for punctuation.

At the Six Gallery, in late 1955, Allen Ginsberg got up, after others, and began,

> I saw the best minds of my generation destroyed by madness,
>   starving hysterical naked,
> dragging themselves through the negro streets at dawn
>   looking for an angry fix,
> angelheaded hipsters burning for the ancient heavenly
>   connection to the starry dynamo in the machinery of night —

raising his *Howl* against the cautious murmur of the times, and despite the bewilderment and outrage, it was clear (even to the *New York Times*) that something was happening: the first audible rumble of an immense underground river that had been building in volume and force for years. Whitman had said: "Unscrew the locks from the doors! Unscrew the doors themselves from their jambs!," and suddenly through the literature's doorless jambs the breath of whole men, writing, blew like a prairie wind.

It was as if the Indians were off the reservation, and the first instinct of the Cowboys of the Media and the Academy was an attempt to corral them into a category, to stone them with epithets or bury them in non sequiturs. Following fast: *Partisan Review's* "no-nothing bohemians," *Life Magazine's* "only rebellion around," Kerouac's prose described as "typing not writing," and countless other idiocies that seemed to ironically acknowledge, by their very vehemence, the cultural wasteland in which these writers seemed so much more vivid. Following faster: public readings as scandalous, thronged and disruptive as protest-rallies; obscenity trials that were the start of the long dismantling of American censorship laws; ugly and beautiful secrets about money, God, war and sex let out of the psychic bag at last; and the discovery, as well, of the "great audiences" for which Whitman had called so long ago. But following fastest of all, the new literature itself: Ferlinghetti's *Coney Island of the Mind*, Olson's *The Maximus Poems*, Corso's *Gasoline*, Kerouac's *On the Road* (and thereafter a steady flow of all the other books he had written during his personal Diaspora). Levertov's *Here and Now*, Snyder's *Riprap*, Burroughs' *Naked Lunch*, and books by Duncan, Creeley, McClure, Weiners, Whalen, O'Hara and a dozen others. And finally, to plant a flag on the mountain and claim it as national territory, Don Allen's landmark anthology, *The New American Poetry* (1960), making apparent that, despite early obscurity and later notoriety, it had been a *decad mirabilis*, after all — its meanings and influences still, then, to be assessed.

5 Continuities

Most essentially, these poets were *American* poets, eschewing both the forms and attitudes that had characterized verse in English heretofore, and from which even Dickinson, Pound, Jeffers and Frost had never wholly gotten free. They used American rhythms of speech, which, as Williams knew, were profoundly different from the British. They linked up again with the oldest American literary tradition — the rolling combers of Melville, the bardic inclusiveness of Whitman, the October tang of Thoreau, the lapidary apothegms of Emerson. And the westward-looking, open-souled, who-reads-this-encounters-a-man stance of these ancestors was *their* stance too. They shared, with Pound, a certain native crankishness and village-scholar erudition. Olson studied Mayan heiroglyphics, Ginsberg delved into mystical and pharmacological lore,

Kerouac transliterated the Sutras, Snyder and Whalen became Zen acolytes. Nothing undehumanized was alien to them, and they wrote out of a passionate awareness of the unity of all knowledge, and that awe before undifferentiated nature that the presence of this continent, still untamed by thought, must have aroused in the earliest colonists.

They had connections, too, if looser, with Existential ideas of being and becoming, of locating yourself (in the instant between breaths) and starting from there, of the freedom always imminent in on-going time, the freedom to become free once you know you are, to transcend the Determined Ego into the Organic Self. "I am free: there is absolutely no more reason for living, all the ones I have tried have given way and I can't imagine any more of them. I am still fairly young, I still have enough strength to start again. But do I have to start again?" The Kerouac of *Desolation Angels*? No, Jean-Paul Sarte.

There was, as well, the powerful appeal of Oriental modes of thought, and these writers probably came closer to apprehending, across the mapless cultural Pacifics, the unique genius of the Eastern Mind than any Westerners since Blythe and Fenollosa. Zen Buddhism, particularly, seemed to describe the fix they had perceived we were in, trapped in the absurdity of time-consciousness, only able to point at things, waiting for the sudden blissful silly flash to come. Both Zen and Existentialism are ultimately concerned with the true nature of reality, which the formulating intelligence obscures. The purpose of *haiku*, to blow the mind; *satori*, perfect apprehension of what is *there*.

> Sweet is the swamp with its secrets,
> Until we meet a snake;
> 'Tis then we sigh for houses ...

Basho? Buson? Gary Snyder? No, Emily Dickinson. It is an old way of seeing among us.

Innovators? Yes. But, like all the most consequential innovators, these writers were concerned with the re-connection of broken circuits, insisting that body, mind and soul are enmeshed, that corporeality is the "field" from which spirit emanates like the weather that is the protagonist in Turner's paintings. And so they were affirming older continuities against contemporary relativisms, trying to annul alienation by passing through it to the other side, where (their faith implied) we all might enter into Blake's "lineaments of gratified desire." For which they were called nihilists, obscurantists, dope & sex-fiends, and corrupters of literary values. Another hoary American tradition that American literature has always somehow survived.

6 Technics

A few glancing words about the nature of this writing—its tone, imagery, rhythm, and literary stance.

Gregory Corso writes: "O I would like to break my teeth/by means of expressing a radiator!" To comprehend, you must envision the iron-ribbed radiator, and the enamel-ribbed teeth, and the poet's mad need to *become* the radiator if he would seize it in his words. "I would like to drive a car/but I must *drive* it!" How often do people realize, in this way, that it is human intention that makes inert machinery go? The poem is called *Discord*, and moves forward towards the question: "Look—there must be a firing squad, yes,/but why a wolf?" And the discord clearly lies between what we automatically do, and what we intuitively know. One perception leading directly to a further perception, without the deadening losses that result from beaver-logic building dams against the flow. Instead, keep the mind and senses connected, and let them go. Then the movement will be natural, the way the consciousness actually works, with a consequent gain in richness, immediacy, and verisimilitude.

The image, "Fried shoes" (also from Corso), seems meaningless, arbitrary, and merely surrealistic, if you hold back and think about it. But if you let it enter your consciousness as effortlessly as butter in the mouth, further images and associations surface—charmingly different for everyone. I variously see Chaplin in his Arctic *Gold Rush* cabin, inferno-sidewalks of the city, leathery steaks in which you taste the real sole of life, and the actual shoe that comes to assume something of the *mana* of the wearer along the miles he has walked in it. Take your frying pan, melt your meager grease; fry up the shoe, and eat it—such are the secular communions of the starved, contemporary heart.

Of rhythm: most often staccato as the piano-chords changing beneath a bop-sax solo (the pianist acknowledging the soloist's shift of mind), or long and exfoliating like that soloist's try to contain everything, a *gloss* of his entire sentience, in a single unbroken line of melody. But, above all, *organic*—growing as natural things grow at the behest of their nature. Iambic? Trochee? Yes, for sometimes we have emotions best expressed in the old, solemn rhythms, so let them come. But rhythm seen as the instantaneous concatenation of blood-pulse, heartbeat, and eye-ear apprehension of the whole moment.

The old questions—How do we know what we know? Is the table really there? Am I a butterfly dreaming I'm a man?—are no longer merely intellectual conundrums in our time. Awareness of the precarious connection between sense-data and the reality "out there" is the common-ground of most contemporary literary work. And these poets say: Cleanse the senses in the morning and jog them in the evening, or vice versa—but always begin at the point of their intersection with a moment in time, in your world. Most aesthetic problems are solved the minute you vow never to lie about yourself seeing the gull fly.

7 Aftermaths

It's difficult to assess how many of the lifestyles, artforms, and attitudes of the 60's, both on-going and counter-productive, proceeded directly from a kind of *contact-high* between these writers and the generation that matured after them. But rock-lyrics show the distinct influences of this poetry in their insistence of reflecting more than just the callow insipidities of Moon-and-June, and Bob Dylan might never have come out of his fantasy of the hobo-30's but for Allen Ginsberg, or the Beatles (their very name an indication) ever become more than just another Liverpool whiffle-band without ex-Beatnik John Lennon. Also, of course, there were roses in the butts of rifles, beards and beads and jeans, Make Love Not War (a Beat one-liner), Throw Money at the Stock Exchange, Don't be Chicken Talk Turkey, If it Feels Good Do It, and so many of the other first principles that motivated young people a little while ago.

Most knowledges that are worth their cost must be earned, not learned, and some of the behavior of these same young people smacked of rote. There were dirty needles, conversational impoverishment, minds blown to smithereens by the careless ingestion of psychic and chemical overkill, and nerves ruined by continual decibel-feedback. There was, also, the violence that grows out of impatience and disappointment, campus Chés riffing on revolution like zapped-out guitarists who can only play two chords, the dumb romanticism of hitching with thirty dollars in your pocket, the parent-hatred, system-putdown, and square-baiting that were so often a pointless and debilitating irrelevance.

Some responsibility for all of this must end up at the doorstep of the Beats, and perhaps the immediate effects of the movement will turn out to be (as Lawrence said) "post-mortem effects." But literature for the next few years will probably never become the kind of cul-de-sac out of which these writers made their way. It is impossible to keep wind in burst balloons, or to back off from certain difficult admissions once made, or to forget the heady sniff of free air in the lungs. It will be no easier to write the truth, or even to appreciate it, but some obstacles, some hangovers from the past, have been cleared away.

Last year, an issue of the *New York Times Book Section*, which, on the front page, reviewed Ginsberg's *The Fall of America* (later to win half the National Book Award), stated about a biography of Kerouac, "This is a book about the men who changed everything." Only time will tell about that. But assuredly these writers left things different than they found them. They did honest work in the face of incomprehension and neglect, and they persisted in the name of their unique vision, as all true poets have.

That work, that vision, remains.

The Quest and the Question: Cosmology and Myth in the Work of William S. Burroughs, 1953-1960

by William L. Stull

In the years since the publication of *Naked Lunch* in 1959, critics have almost unanimously praised or blamed Burroughs for the "newness" of his message and style. Marshall McLuhan early hailed him as the novelist of the Electronic Age, and the very word "new" pervades the articles on Burroughs written in the 1960s. William Phillips placed Burroughs and Genet at the head of "The New Immoralists" who "have broken almost completely with the past"; Tony Tanner explored "The New Demonology" in Burroughs' work, contending that "he has been creating a mythology appropriate to the new age and environment which has been brought about by modern inventions." In a BBC interview with Eric Mottram, Burroughs himself called his work "a new mythology for the space age," while in *William Burroughs: The Algebra of Need* Mottram summed up Burroughs' message as a rejection of the gods of the past finally aiming at "freedom from mythology—what Edward Dahlberg calls freedom from living mythologically."[1]

If Burroughs and his critics are right about this obsessive novelty, he is, indeed, a novelist for a new age, and it is no wonder that his detractors are violently repelled or thoroughly baffled by his books. In the light of the insights of Freud and Jung, someone who has actually managed to reject the fundamental patterns of mythology would be, psychologically if not physically, a mutant, out of touch with the patterns of unconscious life that have informed our literature and history, as different from most of us as those extraterrestrial monsters that float in and out of *The Soft Machine, The Ticket That Exploded,* and *Nova Express.* But is Burroughs' "newness" actually this extreme? Even those who praise him for rejecting everything they know still can respond to his work and understand his characters, however strange they may appear at first sight. More importantly, critics such as Eric Mottram find a purposiveness and pattern in Burroughs' novels that is hardly unfamiliar to us or unprecedented. While Tony Tanner calls Burroughs' "a private mythology," he finds similarities to it in the "private mythology" of Blake's *The Four Zoas*. Mottram, while he argues that "Burroughs' waste land is not redeemable by resurrecting old gods," calls to mind a comparison with T.S. Eliot such as Burroughs himself drew in his comment that "The Waste Land" was "the first great cut-up collage." Most telling is Tanner's passing observation that *Junkie* is a "sort of inverted Holy Grail search."[2] On close inspection, the "newness" of Burroughs' vision fades and the stronger lines of a familiar pattern appear: the quest. Since the appearance of Tennyson's "The Holy Grail" (1869) and Wagner's *Parsifal* (1882) this motif has been in the mainstream of modern thought and writing, whether inverted, cut up, incomplete, tentative, or failed, and it reaches back into medieval romance and, finally, ancient ritual. Criticism has kept pace with literature here, and it is not difficult to account for Burroughs' appeal beyond his "novelty" when one considers the general acceptance of the theories of myth critics such as J.G. Frazer, Jessie L. Weston, and Joseph Campbell. Burroughs himself did graduate work in comparative anthropology, and he has admitted that, however exotic his imagery, he is "quite deliberately" addressing himself "to the whole area of what we call dreams."[3] Far from radically breaking with the past, psychological or literary, Burroughs has tapped a primordial source of vitality. Like Eliot and Joyce, he sets himself to the task of "rendering the modern world spiritually significant," in Joseph Campbell's phrase. His adherence to the basic quest pattern much outweighs his variations on it, even in his early work, where the positive results of the adventure are still provisional.

The quest, the motif Jessie L. Weston traced in *From Ritual to Romance* (1920), is itself a species of what Joseph Campbell has termed "the monomyth" or adventure in *The Hero with a Thousand Faces* (1949).[4] The basic pattern is one of separation, initiation, and return — the stages paralleling in small the cosmic cycle of emanation, transformation, and dissolution — as well as the stages of psychological maturation. Campbell's chapter "The Keys" provides a diagram and summary of the adventure, while Part I of the book describes the pattern in detail, the most important aspects being "The Call to Adventure," "The Road of Trials," "The Ultimate Boon" (symbolized by the Holy Grail in medieval romance), and "The Return." Burroughs' early work, *Junkie*, "In Search of Yage," and *Naked Lunch*, is structured as a quest first for "the final fix" and later for what Campbell calls "the freedom to live" and "the ultimate boon" that can revive the dying world. The remainder of the tetralogy, as well as shorter works such as *Minutes to Go* and *The Exterminator* (both 1960), shows the power of the boon in action against the enemies of freedom, the individualism that closes *Naked Lunch* gradually reaching cosmic proportions as the "Break through in Grey Room" of *Nova Express*.[5]

Burroughs, however, noted that there is an important difference between *Naked Lunch* and the books that follow in his interview with Daniel Odier, published as *The Job*: his adaptation of the cut-up method of Brion Gysin. *The Soft Machine* develops out of the quest in the early novels, but the question that boldly opens the "Atrophied Preface" at the end of *Naked Lunch* is perhaps more important than the complex answers to it in the later works. "Wouldn't You?" triggers an elaborate program of anarchic individualism aimed at revitalizing the junk universe. As in the medieval romances, almost immediately after the hero asks the magical question the waters of life begin to flow.

Along with the myth, however, goes a cosmology, "a vision of the creation and destruction of the world that is vouchsafed to the successful hero."[6] Here gods and demons will symbolize the forces at work inside and outside the hero's psyche which aid and distract him in his quest for the very source of the life force. This is the dimension of Burroughs' work that has most pleased and perplexed his critics and gained his work a reputation for "newness." Even here, however, novelty fades into familiarity when we see the basic outlines of a cosmogonic cycle involving good and evil, heaven and hell, emerging in the early books.

For Thales, it was water; for Anaximander, "the Boundless"; and in Christian cosmology, the *arche*, the basic element of life and matter, is the Word. Burroughs' *Urstoff* is junk — chaotic, self-consuming power — and the expansion of this principle informs his early work with a malign and enervating dreariness. In *Junkie* he presents the world of addiction in an impersonal style he has since called "journalistic," but the autobiographical facts recorded there become the cosmic metaphors of the tetralogy.[7] The transformation of junk from fact to symbol is by far the most important result of this movement toward higher levels of abstraction in *Naked Lunch*.

Burroughs has commented extensively on the function of the junk metaphor in his writing, most recently in "Playback from Eden to Watergate," but his first formulation of it appeared in "Deposition: Testimony Concerning a Sickness," an essay arising directly out of the experiences described in *Junkie* and "In Search of Yage." This piece is now included as a preface to the Grove Press edition of *Naked Lunch*, but it was written after the novel and first appeared in *Evergreen Review* (Jan.-Feb. 1960). The fundamental laws of Burroughs' universe are nearly codified there:

> Junk yields a basic formula of "evil" virus: *The Algebra of Need*. The face of "evil" is always the face of total need. A dope fiend is a man in total need of dope. Beyond a certain frequency need knows absolutely no limit or control [p. vii].

A situation of total need, constant crisis, and addiction has rendered the world of the early novels stagnant: "Thermodynamics has won at a crawl.... Orgone balked at the post.... Christ bled.... Time ran out" (p. 224). But by this time Burroughs has envisioned an alternative:

> A mathematical extension of the Algebra of Need beyond the junk virus. Because there are many forms of addiction I think that they all obey basic laws. In the words of Heiderberg: "This may not be the best of all possible universes but it may well prove to be one of the simplest." If man can *see* [pp. xii-xiii].

This is the "great vision" of the hero that is concomitant with "the ultimate boon" which revives the waste land. But without delving into the elaborations on this in the later novels, it is possible to gloss the "basic laws" Burroughs had grasped by 1960.

The transformations of the junk metaphor through the "many forms of addiction" include heroin itself, control, sex, bureaucratic power, technology, and even time. Burroughs is obsessed with control systems—from Mayan codices to Scientology—and control and sex begin to fuse more and more in his later novels. "Bureaucracy is wrong as a cancer, a turning away from the human evolutionary direction of infinite potentials and differentiation and independent spontaneous action, to the complete parasitism of a virus," he wrote in *Naked Lunch* (p. 134). His position on technology is ambivalent. In the early parts of the tetralogy he seems to regard gadgets and machinery as literal "junk" (with a McLuhanesque pun). Later, however, he proposes alternative uses for technology, and in the *Paris Review* interview echoed Flaubert's dictum that literature would become more scientific. Despite his admiration for Einstein's relativity theory, Burroughs regards time and space as moral opposites. In both "Seven Years Later" and *The Job* he calls time man's prison, space his new frontier. The most pernicious form of addiction, though, is the word: Reichian engrams, Aristotelian either/ or logic, and the declarative sentence itself. This manifestation becomes the number one enemy in Burroughs' work after 1960, and he personifies it in the "Atrophied Preface":

> Gentle Reader, the Word will leap on you with leopard man iron claws, it will cut off fingers and toes like an opportunist land crab, it will hang you and catch your jissom like a scrutable dog, it will coil round your thighs like a bushmaster and inject a shot glass of rancid ectoplasm ... [p. 230].

Tony Tanner's essay, "Rub Out the Word" (the title taken from one of Gysin's permutated poems in *The Exterminator*), follows out Burroughs' campaign on "the human virus" in the tetralogy. By 1960 Burroughs and his personae had gained enough insight into the junk cosmology to take action.

Thus junk, the *arche*, spread through the cosmos, permeating nearly every life process. The "politics" of contamination are fairly clear in *Naked Lunch*, although the author has since called them "a crude and tentative classification." Eric Mottram has outlined "the Algebra of Need" in the later novels, describing Burroughs' "myth of power": "The scheme finally reaches into the metaphysics of dependence at the point where addiction to authority is seen to be addiction to the idea of an ultimate authority, and the origin of that totalitarian trauma is the idea of a god."[8]

This rejection of monotheism may in part account for the "newness" critics have seen in Burroughs' work. When Conrad Knickerbocker asked him whether his universe involved a god, he replied, "I think there are innumerable gods. What we on earth call God is a little tribal god who has made an awful mess." More recently, however, Burroughs has drawn analogies between Christian cosmology and his own, as in "Playback from Eden to Watergate," where he finds the "origins and history of this word virus" analogous to original sin.[9] Although he did not diagnose the spread of the "basic form of 'evil' " as a viral process until *Naked Lunch*, as early as 1953 his vision of the later cosmology was sharpening, and he could preface *Junkie* by saying, "I have learned the junk equation. Junk is not, like alcohol or weed, a means to increased enjoyment of life. Junk is not a kick. It is a way of life" (p. 11). His first novel clearly anticipates the final viral theory, abounding with images of ominous parasites invading passive hosts: "The live human being has moved out of these bodies long ago. But something moved in when the original tenant moved out" (p. 73).

Oppressed by the junk equation on every level of existence in *Naked Lunch* from economics — "How much $? How much junk?" — to psychology, Burroughs is nonetheless optimistic when he concludes the "Islam Incorporated and the Politics of Interzone" section with an assertion that "*The Human Virus can now be isolated and treated*" (p. 169). Isolation of the problem, the first step in scientific treatment, may be as far as he can go in *Naked Lunch*, but he considers this enough of a milestone to merit declaring it in an italicized authorial voice.

In terms of a cure for the viral infection, a boon that will revive the blighted waste land, both *Junkie* and "In Search of Yage" have little to offer, representing wrong turns on Burroughs' quest. The first describes the contemporary world of drug addiction (junk at a low level of abstraction) failing to transcend the bourgeois values Burroughs/Lee fled; the second shows the impossibility of cracking the junk equation by means of drugs, however exotic. It is only in the postscript to *The Yage Letters*, "Seven Years Later" (1960), after *Naked Lunch* and the adaptation of the cut-up method, that Burroughs can boldly write to Allen Ginsberg:

> WHAT SCARED YOU INTO TIME? INTO BODY? INTO SHIT? I WILL TELL
> ~~YOU. THE WORD. THE THEE-WORD. IN THE BEGINNING WAS THE~~
> WORD. SCARED YOU ALL INTO SHIT FOREVER. COME OUT FOREVER
> [....] ACROSS ALL YOUR SKIES SEE THE SILENT WRITING OF BRION
> GYSIN HASSAN SABBAH. THE WRITING OF SPACE. THE WRITING OF
> SILENCE.
> LOOK LOOK LOOK [pp. 61-62]

These last three words echo the challenge that closes the "Deposition," and promise that visual imagery need not always be as horrific as it has been in the early works.

By 1960 Burroughs had attained a vision of the way out of the junk equation; he was increasingly to share Conrad's goal for the novelist: "to make you *see*": "Naked Lunch is a blueprint, a How-To Book[....] How-To extend levels of experience by opening the door at the end of a long hall.... Doors that only open in *Silence...*" (p. 224). The "long hall" is the quest that has led Burroughs and his personae to a vision of "freedom to live" that may lift the blight from the land: "Cure is always: *Let Go! Jump!*" (p. 222). If the vision of how the world works is tentative in *Naked Lunch* — the last "Quick" section shows Lee nodding after his breakthrough — it still anticipates what Burroughs later agreed was "the principle of freedom" in the "last words" of Hassan i Sabbah, "Nothing is true. Everything is permitted."[10] After this point in his adventure the hero is transformed from victim to warrior, wielding the power of his great vision against the enemies of freedom. A fragment from the original manuscript of *Naked Lunch* not included in the Olympia edition but reprinted as "The Conspiracy" in *Kulchur* 1 (1960) reveals how much this insight meant to Burroughs:

> The addict has glimpsed the formula, the bare bones of life, and this knowledge has destroyed for him the ordinary sources of satisfaction that make life endurable. To go a step further, to find out exactly what tension is, and what relief, to discover the means of manipulating these factors.... The final key always eluded me, and I decided that my search was as sterile and misdirected as the alchemist's search for the philosopher's stone [....] But I was wrong. There is a secret now in the hands of ignorant and evil men. A secret beside which the atom bomb is a noisy toy ... [pp. 6-7].

If a cosmology represents the way the world works in the abstract, a mythology dramatizes how men must act in relation to that system. In the BBC interview, Burroughs explained his own conception of myth:

> In *The Naked Lunch* and *The Soft Machine* I have diagnosed an illness, and in *The Ticket That Exploded* and *Nova Express* is suggested a remedy. In this work I am attempting to create a new mythology for the space age. I feel that the old mythologies are definitely broken down and not adequate at the present time. In this mythology I have Nova conspiracies, Nova Police, Nova criminals. I do definitely have heroes and villains with respect to overall intentions with regard to this planet. Love plays little part in my mythology, which is a mythology of war and conflict[....] Heaven and hell exist in my mythology. Hell consists of falling into enemy hands, into the hands of the virus power, and heaven consists of freeing oneself from this power, of achieving inner freedom, freedom from conditioning.[11]

Admittedly, the Nova conspiracy seems light years away from the blighted waste lands of medieval romance, but the power of the "monomyth" is in its flexibility, accommodating new details into the basic pattern of the adventure. Just as the "newness" of Burroughs' cosmology veils such ancient concerns as the *arche* of existence, the basic laws of the cosmogonic cycle, heaven and hell, good and evil, so the plots of his early novels, abstracted out of the space age context and grotesque details, follow the outline of departure, initiation, and return that Campbell describes.

Before delving into *Junkie*, "In Search of Yage," and *Naked Lunch*, however, it is important to note a built-in ambiguity about any quest that may partially account for some of the emphasis critics have placed on Burroughs' "newness." Any quest *for* something is also a flight — with varying degrees of urgency — *from* something. Since Burroughs early grasped "the junk equation," a strong element of persecution and pursuit suffuses his work. Both Mottram and Tanner have stressed this, the latter in fact placing Burroughs in the forefront of American novelists because of his extreme dread of being " 'taken over' by some external force."[12] Still, the "inner freedom" Burroughs calls heaven is at least as much a long-sought ideal as it is an escape. The part of the adventure leading to this "freedom to live" which Tanner calls "inverted" proves, in the long run, to be a series of wrong turns, later acknowledged, such as earlier failure motifs in medieval and modern quest literature readily account for. The best known of the medieval grail romances, Chrétien de Troyes' *Perceval* or *Conte del Graal*, considered in its unfinished state, is exactly such a record of a hero's failure to ask the right questions at the right time on the first leg of his "road of trials," while for Tennyson the questers' wanderings after false fires hasten the destruction of the already blighted land. That Burroughs has been able to follow the quest he began in *Junkie* through partial failure to a final vision of "the ultimate boon" that informs his work after *Naked Lunch* is perhaps his greatest achievement, and it is proof that even if he considers older myths "definitely broken down and not adequate at the present time," the basic "monomyth" is still vital in the space age.

Junkie (1953) shows Burroughs' earliest persona, the largely autobiographical "William Lee," responding to the call to adventure and entering the dreamlike road of trials leading into the unknown, beginning his initiation and education in the laws of the junk universe. Here the call is much less clear than in the "last words" of Hassan i Sabbah that open *Nova Express*, but Lee chooses to leave his comfortable home behind voluntarily: "The environment was empty, the antagonist hidden, and I drifted into solo adventures" (p. 8). Like Gawain in the early "Bleheris" version of the grail romance, Lee heads into the waste land not knowing exactly what he seeks, aware only that the land is sterile and something amiss. In several of the medieval romances a revenge motif parallels the quest (Manissier adds this element to Chrétien's story in his continuation), and Burroughs himself has expressed a hatred for matriarchal power in *The Job* that recalls Orestes' mission against an evil female usurper who has upset the order of society and polluted the kingdom. The world of

drugs and homosexuality offers a "symbol system" that provides a sem-
blance of vitality and orderliness: "You become a narcotics addict because
you do not have strong motivations in any other direction. Junk wins by
default" (p. 10).

What Lee is seeking at this point is summed up in the word "kick,"
which Burroughs defines in the "Glossary" to *Junkie* as "a special way of
looking at things" (p. 15). Both the meaning and phrasing here anticipate
his later emphasis on vision, seeing the "basic laws" of the junk universe in
action and attacking the source of evil directly. The conclusion Burroughs
reaches — and here it is important to separate him from his persona, who
is still wholeheartedly after "the final fix" — is that, far from being a
special angle on life, "Junk is not a kick. It is a way of life," and it is one
which leads to stasis rather than freedom. The preface to *Junkie*
acknowledges that the quest has not yet passed beyond the land of the
Lotus Eaters, and this acknowledgment promises that the journey is far
from finished. Once Burroughs/Lee has crossed the threshold into the
underworld (the dreamlife Campbell has discussed as "The Belly of the
Whale" and "The Womb of Redemption"), the act of seeing becomes
crucial to his development, and the book transcends the limits of confession or autobiography because of its almost hallucinatory clarity in
describing dreamy, archetypal images analogous to those in "The Waste
Land" and the grail romances. The city, here New York, but, as Tanner
argues, potentially Babylon, is desiccated and dying. Small-time hoods
and addicts scurry through its labyrinths, described in animal and insect
images worthy of Interzone's monstrous inhabitants. Burroughs focuses
on a detail in his characters while allowing the rest of the description to
retain a dreamlike formlessness. Significantly, it is Mary's *eyes* that first
draw his attention and trigger a fantasy: "Her eyes were cold fish-eyes
that looked at you through a viscous medium she carried with her. I could
see those eyes in a shapeless, protoplasmic mass undulating over the dark
sea floor" (p. 28). "Junk" is personified, "a ghost in daylight on a crowded
street" (p. 40), and long before the appearance of Hassan i Sabbah as "The
Exterminator" Burroughs has linked the source of evil, mythically, with
the lands of early Aryan and Arabic culture, the lands near Eden:

> There is a type of person occasionally seen in these neighborhoods who
> has connections with junk, though he is neither a user nor a seller. But
> when you see him the dowser wand twitches. Junk is close. His place of
> origin is the Near East, probably Egypt[....] He looks as if he nourished
> himself on honey and Levantine syrups that he sucks up through a
> proboscis [pp. 99-100].

Like the questers of Greek mythology, Odysseus and Theseus, Lee
spends part of this stage of his adventure literally underground, in the
realm of the dead. He enters the underworld first through subway tunnels
where, with the help of an experienced thief, Roy, he learns how to survive by victimizing the bourgeois world he fled. He is finally arrested and

taken to "The Tombs," and it is a mark of his having passed through the first part of his initiation successfully that he keeps his head even among the disembodied voices around him. When Lee returns from the underworld he is a new person, no longer the private-school boy, but a tough thief and pusher, a man who knows the junk equation and can sense when it is time to move on.

Lee heads south, still dissatisfied with himself, heading for what would seem more fertile country. He is by this time aware that addiction is a dead end and junk "an inoculation of death that keeps the body in a condition of emergency" (p. 108). Still, his insight is not yet developed to allow him to escape the junk equation; he tries in vain to break the cycle by means of flight and more exotic drugs. In Texas he finds that crops grow only because of artificial irrigation, and the Rio Grande is stagnant and polluted: "All the worst features of America have drained down to the Valley and concentrated there" (p. 98). As Frazer and Weston showed, the quest ultimately derives from prehistoric vegetation rituals, and it is sure proof of the hero's failure in *Junkie* that even in the tropics the world remains essentially a waste land. Nevertheless, if the novel is a detailed map of a mistake, the closing paragraphs show Lee more aware of what he is seeking:

> What I look for in any relationship is contact on the non-verbal level of intuition and feeling, that is, telepathic contact[....] Maybe I will find in yage what I was looking for in junk and weed and coke. Yage may be the final fix [p. 126].

The error in the second sentence does not, in the long run, obscure the truth in the first; as the later novels show, "other level experience" was to emerge more and more as a primary value for Burroughs. The hero of *Junkie*, despite his cool, is not mature. The book is a *Bildungsroman* where Burroughs/Lee gets a thorough education in the laws of the junk universe and barely survives his testing. Despite what at first seem great differences, its closest contemporary analogue is Salinger's *The Catcher in the Rye* (1951), another record of initiation and partial success in a quest for freedom that ends with a balance of self-doubt and hope: "How do you know what you're going to do till you do it? The answer is, you don't."

"In Search of Yage," the 1953 section of the Burroughs-Ginsberg correspondence over ten years collected as *The Yage Letters*, documents a stage of the quest in Central and South America, shortly after the period covered in *Junkie*. Here Burroughs and his persona "Willy Lee" move through a land blighted with fascist cons and homosexual boy-hustlers, where people look like "the end result of atomic radiation" (p. 14). If the water in this region is tentatively drinkable, the oily black yage infusion is not, leading to nausea and immediate vomiting. Instead of "the final fix" Burroughs/Lee anticipated, yage produces "an uncontrollable mechanical silliness" and "hebephrenic meaningless repetitions" that put him through yet another dark night of the soul, beset by visions of mocking insects (pp. 29-30). Again, psychologically and mythically, he has proved his stamina, endured another test, but the boon is not forthcoming. Moving farther south, he is still gripped by "the stasis horrors" in Peru and writes to Ginsberg: "Did you ever read H.G. Wells' *The Country of the Blind?* About a man stuck in a country where all the other inhabitants had been blind so many generations they had lost the concept of sight. He flips" (pp. 43-44). As earlier, the emphasis on *seeing* anticipates the "Deposition" and later works. If a continent-long chase has led the hero nearly to madness, it has also helped him mature, as the hardboiled defiance of *Junkie* turns gradually into the satirical humor of *Naked Lunch*. This episode closes with a sudden awakening to another leg of the journey that recalls the sense of urgency the medieval questers Gawain and Perceval felt after their hallucinations in the Chapel Perilous:

> Suddenly I wanted to leave Lima right away. This feeling of urgency has followed me like my ass all over South America[....] Where am I going in such a hurry? Appointment in Talara, Tingo Maria, Pucallpa, Panama, Guatemala, Mexico City? I don't know. Suddenly I have to leave right now [p. 46].

For Burroughs and his personae, as for Gawain and Perceval, the next appointment was to prove decisive, confronting him with the "secret" he had long been seeking.

With the first line of *Naked Lunch* (1959), "I can feel the heat closing in" (p. 1), Lee seems to have been transported back to the world of *Junkie* where he "could feel the Federals moving steadily closer" (p. 60). Still, the difference in abstraction between "the heat" and "the Federals" symbolizes the difference between the two books. Here only the essential element remains, searing the landscape, and a cluster of images associated with the quest and the waste land give *Naked Lunch* a unity beneath its fragmented panorama of the gone world. As in "The Waste Land," what water remains in the city is filled with the rubbish of a dying culture. The Rube chases his boy

> right into the East River, down through condoms and orange peels, mosaic of floating newspapers, down into the silent black ooze with gangsters in concrete, and pistols pounded flat to avoid the probing finger of prurient ballistics experts [p. 4].

The Rube's own situation, "the blond God has fallen to untouchable vileness" (p. 10), recalls the Tammuz-Adonis motif Weston found as "the possible ultimate source from which the incidents and *mise-en-scène* of the Grail stories were derived" (p. 51). The presence of his atonement motif becomes more obvious when Burroughs speculates that the Sollubis in the market might well be the descendents of "a fallen priest caste[....] taking on themselves all human vileness" (pp. 118-19); more than ever, junk is surrounded with "magic and taboos, curses and amulets" (p.5). Before he heads west, retracing the path in *Junkie,* Lee comments on the waste land ahead: "America is not a young land: it is old and dirty and evil before the settlers, before the Indians. The evil is there waiting" (p. 11). Like Gawain in the German romance *Diu Crône,* the hero knows what is before him now.

The characters, too, are refined from the addicts and pushers who helped Lee enter the underworld in *Junkie.* Bradley the Buyer, later Mr. Bradley/ Mr. Martin, embodies the essential parasitism of the pusher and control addict, himself caught in the junk equation. Lee's insight into the situation qualifies him for more esoteric lessons by various mentors. His assignment with Dr. Benway is especially valuable in view of the hero's later transformation into healer, both literally in his diagnosis of "the human virus" and metaphorically in his revival of the land itself.[13] The key point in Lee's encounter with Benway, one that prevents him from being overwhelmed, is that both characters are individualists even in the context of "Islam Inc." and the collective parties of Interzone. Even a psychopath like Benway, because of his anarchic zeal, has some value for Burroughs; Hassan i Sabbah, based on the historical head of the Assassins and traditionally associated with hashish-induced frenzy, heads the campaign against the Nova conspiracy later in the tetralogy. Benway's unreliability as a narrator comes from his advocacy of "pure" science with no ethics beyond the repeated dictum "Be just and if you can't be just, be arbitrary," and no purpose other than creating "one all-purpose blob" to replace mankind (p. 131). Nevertheless, he gives Lee more insight into the junk equation: "The naked need of the control addicts must be decently covered by an arbitrary and intricate bureaucracy so that the subject cannot contact his enemy direct" (p. 21). This very covering is, of course, Benway's profession, and Burroughs satirizes it throughout the novel.

The scene shifts with apparent randomness, from the Reconditioning Center to the sanitarium, but a common grayness deadens the landscape. A gray haze hangs over the city and seeps into men's eyes and skin. As in *Junkie,* the eyes are an index of the state of the mind; always they are gray, "cancelled," "undersea," or otherwise suggestive of devolution, all this in contrast to the value placed on sight as insight in the "Deposition" and later works. When the panorama comes from the point of view of the mock-hero Carl Peterson, who is later — unlike Lee — trapped by Benway, stream of consciousness images underscore the regression of the land, recalling Eliot's "tumid river":

> erect wooden phallus on the grave of dying peoples plaintive as leaves in the wind, across the great brown river where whole trees float with green snakes in the branches and sad-eyed lemurs watch the shore out over a vast plain (vulture wings hush in the dry air) [p. 50].

Instead of seeing, the world is busy feeding. The book's title fuses the two images, and in "The Black Meat" Burroughs shows the logical extension of this compulsion after a tainted food which is "overpoweringly delicious and nauseating so that the eaters eat and vomit and eat again until they fall exhausted" (p. 55). Capital punishment on stage in "Hassan's Rumpus Room" and the image of the wasted orgasm of a hanged man symbolize the death and infertility brought on by the all-encompassing junk equation. The New York of *Junkie* has become "The City," "a waste of raw pink shame to the pastel blue horizon where vast iron mesas crash into the shattered sky" (p. 118). Despite this abstraction and universalizing, however, Burroughs is careful to link the images to "the basic American rottenness" with sections like "Ordinary Men and Women," where housewives fight off mixmasters and a man is taken over by his anus.

Burroughs and his persona are isolating the problem in these middle episodes, finding a common element in all manifestations of the junk equation. "The notorious Merchant of Sex," A.J., is Lee's next mentor, and the hero learns about the ultimate consumer organization first hand in "Islam Incorporated and the Parties of Interzone." Lee again proves himself by supporting the Factualists in opposition to the Liquifactionists, Divisionists, and Senders, who threaten man's individuality. If by the time he reaches the end of the "long hall" the hero is still not fully aware of what his quest for freedom finally involves, he is at least able to take decisive action and break the stasis that held him prisoner in the earlier works. Isolation of "the human virus" promises that treatment through direct attack can begin, and it is significant that from this point on Lee is in the full sense of the word an "agent" rather than a victim. In "The County Clerk" he outwits the bureaucrats hampering his mission. His increased strength contrasts with Carl Peterson's weakness in the face of Benway's psychological warfare, the conventional hero being no match for the evil powers in Burroughs' junk universe.

Before his last, decisive encounter with the agents of the status quo, however, Lee fades momentarily into an avatar of the hero of the later novels, the Exterminator. During this apotheosis he knows the magic question that can unleash "the ultimate boon" against the evil virus blighting the land. The Exterminator fully understands his present assignment: "Find the live ones and *exterminate*. Not the bodies but the 'molds,' you understand" (p. 205). Still, there is a catch—"but I forgot that you cannot understand"—Lee's apotheosis can only be temporary if he is to finish his quest as a representative *man*, since as Campbell observes, "if the monomyth is to fulfill its promise, not human failure or superhuman success but human success is what we shall have to be shown" (p. 207). The Exterminator knows how much "defecting agents" threaten the mission, agents who succumb to the evil forces or linger on in the dreamworld, and at this point the author seems to concur that "all Agents defect and all Resisters sell out" (p. 205). Burroughs clarified his

position here in the BBC interview: "I may add that none of the characters in my mythology are free. If they were free they would not still be in
the mythological system, that is, the cycle of conditioned action."[14] Since
the author later admitted that the "last words" of Hassan i Sabbah contained "the principle of freedom," it seems reasonable to consider his
position in *Naked Lunch* a tentative one. This distrust of the central
character, however, accounts for the abrupt shifts in persona and point of
view as the novel closes.

Granted these restrictions, Lee's final actions nevertheless result in
positive effects not found in the failed quests, *Junkie* and "In Search of
Yage." As in the last section of "The Waste Land," the images of drought
and decay in the closing chapters of *Naked Lunch* become frenzied:

> The Mississippi rolls great limestone boulders down the
> silent alley....
> "Clutter the glind!" screamed the Captain of Moving Land
> ....
> Distant rumble of stomachs.... Poisoned pigeons rain from
> the Northern Lights.... The reservoirs are empty.... Brass
> statues crash through the hungry squares of the gaping city ... [p. 199].

Voice, imagery, and setting all link the "Hauser and O'Brien" section
before the "Atrophied Preface" with the first scenes of the book in the
Hotel Lamprey. In a sense the journey has been a dream, an adventure in
a landscape Campbell describes as "curiously fluid" and ambiguous,
populated with figures "dissolving, transcending, or transmuting the in-
fantile images of our personal past" (pp. 97, 101). In the medieval quests,
both the continuations of Chrétien and the *Queste* Malory translated, the
heroes endure their final trials and receive illumination while dreaming in
a perilous chapel filled with apparitions.

Whatever the route, Lee has reached the end of the line when
detectives Hauser and O'Brien walk in on him. Significantly, they are not
after narcotics alone. They have orders to "bring in all books, letters,
manuscripts. *Anything* printed, typed, or written" (p. 209). The Bureau is
after the knowledge Lee has acquired, fearful lest he put it to use. In contrast to his earlier passivity, Lee takes decisive action. Violence promises
him a last chance at freedom, and he opts to save himself. On the pretext
of taking a last shot, he fills his syringe with alcohol and uses it to blind
Hauser. He methodically shoots both agents, picks up his notebooks,
shells, and junk, and walks out into a beautiful Indian Summer day, his
long journey having taught him to remain calm:

> Americans have a special horror of giving up control, of letting things
> happen in their own way without interference[....] Your mind will an-
> swer most questions if you learn to relax and wait for the answer [p. 215].

This acceptance of his destiny is itself proof of Lee's maturity, and it links
him with the Exterminator, the warrior hero of the later novels:

NO ONE IS HIS SENSES WOULD TRUST "THE UNIVERSE." SWEPT WITH

CON THE MILLIONS STOOD UNDER THE SIGNS. WHO EVER PAID OFF A
MARK A GOOK AN APE A HUMAN ANIMAL? NO BODY EXCEPT HASSAN
SABBAH ["Seven Years Later," p. 62].

Lee has learned the value of the silence Burroughs demands from his
readers in the "Atrophied Preface" that follows. After spending the night
in the Ever Hard Baths (Campbell points out that "the magic flight" is often treated comically), Lee telephones the Narcotics Bureau and discovers
that his violent act has tossed Hauser and O'Brien completely out of
existence. He has crossed the final threshold, at least tentatively cracked
the junk equation: "The Heat was off me from here on out ... relegated
with Hauser and O'Brien to a landlocked junk past[....] Far side of the
world's mirror" (p. 217). For a moment, Lee is what Campbell terms "the
master of the two worlds," standing on a path between heaven and hell,
the past and the future.

　　"The Conspiracy," that section of the original *Naked Lunch*
manuscript not included in the first edition, was clearly intended to fit into "Hauser and O'Brien," and it amplifies the meaning of both Lee's
escape and his quest as a whole, explicitly stressing the mythic dimension
of Burroughs' earlier work. Here Lee excitedly flees to "Mary's flat" after
killing the agents, and he tells her of "the anti-dream drug" he has
discovered the authorities use to keep control, through which "contact
with the myth that gives each man the ability to live alone and unites him
with all other life, is cut off. He becomes an automaton, an interchangeable quantity in the political and economic equation" (p. 6). He
also tells her of his own discoveries since the yage search which promise to
increase "the symbolizing or artistic faculty": "We can all be artists infinitely greater than Shakespeare or Beethoven or Michelangelo" (p. 6).
But Lee is getting ahead of himself, and Burroughs may well have sup-
pressed "The Conspiracy" from *Naked Lunch* because he was not yet
ready for such optimism. After Mary verifies that Hauser and O'Brien
have become non-persons, Lee more calmly brings her up to date on the
events that led to his discovery of "the secret," revealing that the quest
myth had long been the guiding force in his life:

> What was the beginning? Since early youth I had been searching for some
> secret, some key with which I could gain access to basic knowledge, an-
> swer some of the fundamental questions. Just what I was looking for, what
> I meant by basic knowledge or fundamental questions, I found it difficult
> to define. I would follow a trail of clues [p. 6].

Burroughs' early works follow this trail across America, and the "basic
knowledge" proves to be the insight into the cosmology of the junk universe the author and his personae had gathered by 1960, knowledge which
was to call for "Break through in Grey Room" with growing urgency.

　　In *Naked Lunch* as we have it, however, the breakthrough is more
mythological than polemical. Lee has only momentarily broken out of the

junk equation, "occluded from space-time" (p. 217). After the "Atrophied Preface" the final "Quick" section shows him stunned after crossing the threshold, nodding and mumbling absently, "No good ... no bueno ... hustling myself" (p. 235). The voice that reiterates the magic question at the end of the quest is authorial: "WOULDN'T YOU?" calls forth the anarchic individualism that can free the world from "random insect doom." Just as the medieval heroes questioned the very source of life, asking "What is the Grail?" or "Whom does it serve?" Burroughs and Lee find that to tap the power of the life source, gain the boon that can revive the land, "you feed in the question, sit back, and wait..." (p. 215). First there is a last vision of the blighted world: "The black wind sock of death undulates over the land, feeling, smelling for the crime of separate life" (pp. 223-24). Like Orestes, the "exterminator" in Sartre's *Les Mouches*, Burroughs/Lee now knows that this "crime" is man's last chance for freedom. The "word horde" unlocks with a promise of change in the landscape:

> I, William Seward, captain of this lushed up hash-head subway, will quell the Loch Ness monster with rotenone and cowboy the white whale. I will reduce Satan to Automatic Obedience, and sublimate subsidiary friends. I will banish the candiru from your swimming pools [p. 226].

Mythologically, "the river is served," and a new sense of vitality and innocence spreads over the waste land:

> My Viking heart fares over the great brown river where motors put put put in jungle twilight and whole trees float with huge snakes in the branches and sad-eyed lemurs watch the shore, across the Missouri field (The Boy finds a pink arrowhead) out along distant train whistles, comes back to me hungry as a street boy don't know to peddle the ass God gave him ... [p. 230].

[1] Marshall McLuhan, "Notes on Burroughs," *The Nation*, 28 Dec. 1964, pp. 517-19; William Phillips, *Commentary*, Apr. 1965, p. 66; Tony Tanner, *Partisan Review*, 33 (Fall 1966), pp. 547-72, reprinted as "Rub Out the Word" in *City of Words* (New York: Harper & Row, 1971), p. 109. The March 1964 BBC interview is partially transcribed in "Rencontre avec William Burroughs," *Les Langues Modernes*, 59 (1965), p. 80. Eric Mottram, *William Burroughs: The Algebra of Need* (Buffalo: Intrepid Press, 1971), p. 60.

[2] Tanner, pp. 109, 113; Mottram, p. 32. Burroughs' comment is from "The Art of Fiction XXXVI," an interview by Conrad Knickerbocker in *Paris Review*, vol. 9, no. 34 (Fall 1965), p. 24.

[3] *Paris Review*, p. 21.

[4] *From Ritual to Romance* (rpt. Garden City: Doubleday, 1957); *The Hero with a Thousand Faces* (New York: Bollingen, 1949).

[5] New York: Grove Press, 1964, p. 60. All my references are to Grove Press editions of the tetralogy. My text of *Junkie* is the 1964 reprint of the 1953 Ace Books edition, and I follow *The Yage Letters* (San Francisco: City Lights, 1963).

[6] Campbell, p. 40.

[7] *Paris Review*, p. 15.

[8] Mottram, p. 88.

[9] *Paris Review*, p. 46. "Playback" is reprinted in *The Job* (New York: Grove Press, 1974), p. 13.

[10] *The Job*, p. 97. The dictum appears in "Seven Years Later" in *Yage*, p. 60, as well as in *The Exterminator* and later works.

[11] *Les Langues Modernes*, p. 80.

[12] Tanner, p. 109.

[13] See Weston's Chapter 8, "The Medicine Man."

[14] *Les Langues Modernes*, p. 80.

A Picture Is
a Fact: Wittgenstein
and *Naked Lunch*

by R.G. Peterson

That the heat closing in at the beginning of William S. Burroughs's *Naked Lunch* could as well be from the refiner's fire of Ludwig Wittgenstein as from the proximity of the narcotics dick might seem yet another example of critical obscurantism. But the *Naked Lunch* could hardly be made more obscure than it seems, and the suggestion, in such a case, that the maze does have a plan and a purpose may not be entirely vain. Although it is obvious that philosophy can shed some light on some literature, it is nevertheless surprising that a philosophical system (or parts of one) can illuminate even such a pointless, disorderly, and pornographic (to use the language of its detractors) book as the *Naked Lunch*. It is the very outrageousness of so much in the *Naked Lunch* that distracts the reader from the serious purpose fulfilled by it. When fascination conquers revulsion, and the reader finishes his *Naked Lunch*, he is left (as he should be) horrified and disturbed but he does not know at what vision he has recoiled, nor why. "Somehow," he wants to say with Alice, "it seems to fill my head with ideas — only I don't exactly know what they are!" But the ideas become much clearer when he realizes that the world of the *Naked Lunch* takes its shape from certain views expressed or implied in Ludwig Wittgenstein's *Tractatus Logico-Philosophicus*. This work, by its powerful analysis, called into question the validity of philosophical discourse and, indeed, philosophy itself. Even before its translation in 1922 it had begun to exert a heavy pressure on British and American philosophy; and we are not surprised to find some of its ideas passing now into imaginative literature. The world of the *Tractatus*, disturbing enough to its creator and other philosophers, is even more disturbing to the layman; and this is the world which the *Naked Lunch* reflects or, more precisely, demonstrates. The main symbol (junk), the incoherence, and the lack of a point-of-view may all be explained by reference to Wittgenstein's *Tractatus*. And just as the ideas in the *Tractatus* prepared Wittgenstein and his readers for the construction of a more

30

correct view of language and the old problems of philosophy, so the *Naked Lunch* should force us to a truer vision of our world and to a new understanding of the work of art in that world.

Pornographic, obscene, and scatological (I use these words in their most literal senses) the *Naked Lunch* undoubtedly is, but it is not prurient; chaotic in structure, disorderly in style, and fragmented in imagery the *Naked Lunch* is, but it is not pointless. The *Naked Lunch* belongs to a recognizable tradition and is moralistic in its final effect: it is a drugtaker's confession in which the sex and sadism, the anatomy and physiology, suggest an almost medieval contempt for the body and in which the apparent strangeness springs not from the diseased mind's explosion into a chaos of violence and obscenity but from the major conventions of a literary *genre* and from the world-view suggested by the procedures of philosophical analysis and implied in the early work of Wittgenstein. The *Naked Lunch* is a junky's confession, but it is also a sustained comment on and illustration of the fabric of twentieth-century life.

Although the *Naked Lunch* was finished in 1959, it was not published in complete form in the United States until 1962; and its subject matter, primarily sex and dope, assured it of a considerable *succès de scandale*. The mixed reception the book got from serious reader and critics is now literary history.[1] But it is easy to understand both the scorn and the praise—for junk is the hero of the book and junk enables the speaker-narrator and, through him, the reader to recognize some painful facts about himself and the world. Junk is at once inspirer and hero and, at last, symbol of life itself. "Not the opium-eater," says Thomas DeQuincey in *Confessions of an English Opium-Eater*, "but the opium, is the true hero of the tale, and the legitimate centre on which the interest revolves."[2] And DeQuincey, who seems to have established the conventions of the drug-taker's confession, can be of some help to the reader of the *Naked Lunch*. The drug, in both DeQuincey and Burroughs, is the energizing force, the inspiration: it produces the *furor poeticus* in which the author is enabled to deliver the true message life has spelled upon his imagination. In the Introduction Burroughs describes his method of writing: "Most survivors do not remember the delirium in detail. I apparently took detailed notes on sickness and delirium. I have no precise memory of writing the notes which have now been published..."[3] The *Naked Lunch*, like the *Confessions*, is a factual record of experience.

But even though the availablity of the message is due to the drug, the terms in which this message is conveyed come, according to DeQuincey, from what the author knows: "If a man 'whose talk is of oxen' should become an opium-eater, the probability is, that ... he will dream about oxen," but if one "boasteth himself to be a philosopher" (p. 16), his dreams are more elaborate. DeQuincey was steeped in German philosophy of Romanticism, in travel books, and in a very wide range of literature; his world was a world of varied figures, desirable and threatening, but always related to transcendental ideas vaguely evident through the Romantic mist. In the twentieth century, on the other hand, it is not only impossible to transcend the material world but it is also impossible to take refuge in it. Both idealistic and materialistic escapes from the ego-centric predicament (the inability of the self to find convincing proof of the independent existence of an external world) have been finally closed. Even the "objective reality" of scientific method has been recognized as nothing more than a convenient presupposition; and the more the individual thinks about such matters, the more certainly he is forced to conclude that he is trapped within his own self, that there is nothing outside the self: he becomes a solipsist. The *Naked Lunch*, I believe, gets its strange power from its ability to make the reader feel the terrors of solipsism. Its dreamlike movement and its blending of literary realism and fantasy suggest that the speaker-narrator (he is both mindless reproducer and creating organizer; he is, as will become obvious, one who *demonstrates* a state of affairs) has found himself back in the ego-centric predicament. In several passages central to the *Tractatus* (e.g. 5.63ff.)[4] we must confront solipsism as an intellectual problem; in the *Naked Lunch* we meet it as an emotional one.

The hint that Wittgenstein may be able to explain the *Naked Lunch* appears in Burroughs's Introduction. After a slighting reference, in the form of a "quotation" from one "Heiderberg" (presumably a combination of Heidegger and Heisenberg), to existentialist philosophy and theoretical physics (both popularly supposed to offer Ways Out), Burroughs introduces, with appropriate fanfare, a pretended quotation from Wittgenstein: "The razor belonged to a man named Occam and he was not a scar collector. Ludwig Wittenstein [sic] *Tractatus Logico-Phlilosophicus* [sic]: 'If a proposition is NOT NECESSARY it is MEANINGLESS and approaching MEANING ZERO' " (p. xiv). The only important razor for the twentieth century is Occam's razor, i.e. the Law of Parsimony, which requires that unnecessary assumptions be "cut out" of any explanation and which is, of course, basic both to modern science and to Wittgenstein's ruthless criticism of traditional philosophical method. Although the "quotation" does not appear in the *Tractatus,* it represents what could well be a layman's recollection of Wittgenstein's two explicit comments on Occam: "If a sign is *not necessary* then it is meaningless" (3.328). And: the point of Occam's maxim "is that *unnecessary* elements in a symbolism mean nothing" (5.-47321). Burroughs follows his "quotation" with this rhetorical question: "And what is More UNNECESSARY than junk if You Don't Need it?" Whatever "junk" might be (although it could not be a proposition, it might, in the context of the book, be a symbol or an element in a symbolism), the reader is led to conclude that it is meaningless: it is symbol of nothing and everything, of the life of the speaker-narrator and the world (which is *his* world, the solipsist's world), a world where nothing is necessary and everything is possible (the *Tractatus*, as we shall see, disposed of the principle of causation). It is, in a sense, both symbol and thing symbolized. It *is* the *Naked Lunch*.

But Burroughs's rhetorical question can do more than unlock the main symbolism of the book. It can provide a key to our understanding of the relationship between the speaker-narrator and junk. By removing from the question the aspects of interrogation and negation we can produce the statement that nothing is more necessary than junk if one does need it. In this case one *must* use junk. If we discount for a moment the physiological need, we have left a hypothetical imperative: one *must* use junk if he desires to bring about a particular state of affairs. With regard to the situation within the book we cannot say that the speaker-narrator *must* use junk in order to obtain the complete apathy (see p. ix) which is the goal of the junky in life (for then there would be no book); the goal of the junky as speaker-narrator is to discover the ultimate nature of the world, and he uses junk in order to become aware of the symbolic value of that same junk. The junk dreams reveal the solipsistic world of which junk is symbol or picture. A picture is a fact (*Tractatus*, 2.141) and must have something in common with "reality" (2.022, 2.151ff.). What can be pictured, symbolized, named, or even imagined, Wittgenstein suggests, is, to some extent, "real." The dream-like, solipsistic world of the *Naked Lunch* seems real because it is real. Junk is not necessary if we do not need it; and as long as we do not want its revelation, it is also meaningless. There is nothing to compel assent to the imperative, "Use junk," or to any other imperatives. But men are only human and do give their assent to societies, institutions, and systems of belief. The true nature of these (things to which most men have given their assent) is revealed in the *Naked Lunch*; these become the objects of the satire. Only if one is content with things as they seem does he not need junk or does he not need junk or does he reject the record of its revelation: one refuses, as it were, to eat his naked lunch.

Based on the solipsistic world (see *Tractatus*, 5.62: "The world is *my* world," etc.) and designed to reflect a system of metaphysics hinted at in Wittgenstein, the *Naked Lunch* cannot be considered a novel in any accepted or useful sense of the term. It is a drug-addict's confession, and the confession, the most personal of literary *genres*, is ideally suited to describe a world which is, in the fundamental and dangerous way suggested above, absolutely personal. The structural similarity between DeQuincey's *Confessions* and the *Naked Lunch* is evident to any reader of both: there is, in each, the prefatory material describing the genesis of the book and the nature of the drug, the dreams themselves, and the appendix on dosages and the nature of addiction and withdrawal symptoms. I do not know whether or not Burroughs had read the *Confessions*, but his assertion that he has "no precise memory of writing the notes which have now been published" (p. v) sounds not unlike DeQuincey's explanation that he gives his "notes disjointed" as he finds them because to organize them into a "regular narrative" (pp. 101-102) would tax too heavily his emotional resources. Both works are disorderly; but the disorder in the *Naked Lunch* is the more significant because it is an essential part of a picture of the world.

This world is the very substance (i.e. form and content) of the *Naked Lunch*, and the substance is what the reader takes into his mind, making his world the solipsistic world of the *Naked Lunch*. And although he may be tempted to classify the *Naked Lunch* as another stream-of-consciousness novel, he finds he cannot because he cannot say *whose* consciousness he has taken into his own. It is certainly not Burroughs's; nor is it that of any of the characters in the book. There is nothing to suggest a single, clearly definable personality for the speaker-narrator; there is no point-of-view and no *persona* (in the sense that this term implies the intervention of another personality between author and reader).

The *Naked Lunch* thus illustrates Wittgenstein's understanding of the nature of the "subject" or the "I" (the pun that follows is accidental in English): "And from nothing *in the field of sight* can it be concluded that it is seen by an eye" (5.633). We would not expect a clear self or personality to emerge from the *Naked Lunch*, and none does. For Wittgenstein in the *Tractatus*, the truth of solipsism lay in the fact that the self cannot be inferred from the world of which that self is aware. The self is the limit of the world (as the number 2 is the limit of the series, $1\frac{1}{2}$, $1\frac{3}{4}$, $1\frac{7}{8}$, $1^{15}/_{16}$, etc.) but not part of it. If the *Naked Lunch* is to be a true representation of the world it cannot, thus, include a self. What self there is is outside the book: it is the self of the speaker-narrator or the reader. It is the "I" of solipsism shrunken to a "point without extension" (*Tractatus*, 5,64).

The "things" in the book (excluding the Introduction and Appendix) are presented as a discontinuous collection of perceptions. A few are causally connected in short or long series, but most are totally isolated; there is, in general, no causal nexus between events. And this too we find in the *Tractatus:* making up one comment are the statements that "the events of the future *cannot* be inferred from those of the present" and that "superstition is the belief in the causal nexus" (5.1361). There is no general plot; and there are no characters as we usually understand them: there are only what seem to be figments or impressions but what are more probably supposed to be sense-data, each of a particular shade (something like the "atomic facts" of Wittgenstein and other modern philosophers). Junk is, in one of its aspects, the inspirer, the hero of the tale, because it is the universal metaphysical solvent to dissolve the world into its basic units.

The "characters" are, therefore, fragmented and incomplete, as the world of the speaker-narrator (which becomes also the world of the reader) really is. And these "atomic facts" within one perceptional field (i.e. the world) are *recognized* as such: "Sooner or later," the various characters (a list of eleven follows) "are subject to say the same thing in the same words to occupy, at that intersection point, the same position in space-time. Using a common vocal apparatus complete with all metabolic appliances that is to be the same person—a most inaccurate way of expressing *Recognition: the junky naked in sunlight....*" (pp. 222-223). The emphasis in this quotation is the author's, and I take it to mean not only that the characters are meant to be recognized as fragments, projections from one junk-inspired mind, but also that the recognition of this fact is one of the important purposes of the *Naked Lunch.* It has taken place in the mind of the speaker-narrator and does in the reader's.

The events and the quasi-characters involved in them are organized only insofar as they exist in one mind; and their world is totally *inside* the speaker-narrator. The chaotic nature of the book, the absolute suspension of over-all order, of time and space, means that those tags by which men hang on to external reality have been recognized as fundamentally subjective. And in the new relation that is established between reader and book (the reader engulfs, as it were, the book, the speaker-narrator's mind, and the world), this solipsistic recognition is forced upon the reader. Completely isolated within his own consciousness, he is forced to doubt not only his own sanity but the meaning of the term itself. Out of this conception come the disconnected "notes" which make up the bulk of the *Naked Lunch.* There are twenty-two of these "notes" or sections, varying in length and degree of internal coherence, of which all but the first have names connected in some way with their contents. The last section is an "Atrophied Preface" of sixteen pages where the method is again described—this time by the speaker-narrator: "There is only one thing a writer can write about: *what is in front of his senses at the moment of writing* [author's emphasis and ellipsis throughout].... I am a recording instrument.... I do not presume to impose 'story' 'plot' 'continuity' ... In sofaras [sic] I succeed in *Direct* recording of certain areas of psychic process I may have limited function.... I am not an entertainer...." (p. 221).

If it is a particular view of mind and reality which has produced the structure of the *Naked Lunch*, it is this moralistic aim which lies behind the style—a style, alternately telegraphic and chaotic, which reinforces the picture of a world materialistic on the one hand and illusory on the other. The descriptive language of the physical and social sciences only *seems* to represent actuality; but there is, in fact, nothing that is not subjective or illusory. The parties of Interzone (the Factualists, the Liquefactionists, the Divisionists, and the Senders) are, thus, trying in

vain to create out of a subjective world-stuff some kind of Social Life or
General Will (pp. 162-169). And Burroughs's prose, designed to reflect
this unpleasant situation, is the prose of the satirist who, as he speaks,
parodies the styles characteristic of the objects of his satire. The usual
model is probably the tape-recorded case-history, told in the patient's
own words and mingled with the investigator's comments: "So I put it on
him for a sawski and make a meet to sell him some 'pod' as he puts it,
thinking, 'I'll catnip the jerk.' (Note: Catnip smells like marijuana when it
burns. Frequently passed on the incautious or uninstructed.)" (p. 4). But
at other times the prose assumes, from the jargon of reform, a deliberate
flatness: "Benway's first act was to abolish concentration camps, mass
arrest and, except under certain limited and special circumstances, the
use of torture" (p. 21). The qualifying phrase slides in so as to allow (in the
service, doubtless, of an important societal function) the greatest of all the
enormities supposedly abolished. As Swift parodied sometimes scientific
projects, the various hypocrisies of most of the self-deluding writers of his
age, so Burroughs parodies most of the *clichés* of modern sociological,
psychological, and scientific writing. Doc Benway explains things to a
young man accused of an at first unspecified sexual deviation: "On the
other hand you can readily see that *any* [author's emphasis and ellipsis
throughout] illness imposes certain, should we say *obligations*, certain *necessities* of a prophylactic nature on the authorities concerned with public
health, such necessities to be imposed, needless to say, with a minimum of
inconvenience and hardship to the unfortunate individual who has, through
no fault of his own, become uh infected.... That is to say, of course, the
minimum hardship compatible with adequate protection of other indivduals
who are not so infected..." (p. 188). This is the tone of sweet reason; and if
the style of this passage seems to become the style parodied, it may be
because the models themselves are beneath parody.

  The world satirized in the *Naked Lunch* is the world built upon
the twin pillars of science and pragmatism, the former to cope with
physical problems and the latter to settle philosophical ones. And since
the personal consciousness cannot separate appearance and reality, each
man relies upon and, at last, lives in the consensus. Mechanical devices,
Benway explains, give us the best grip on the only reality we have: "The
study of thinking machines teaches us more about the brain than we can
learn by introspective methods. Western man is externalizing himself in
the form of gadgets" (p. 24). The greatest gadget of all is the body and its
brain—except, the *Naked Lunch* suggests, when we force ourselves, or
are forced, to recognize that the consensus is a solution for a group, for
society and not for the separate personality.

  The sex and cruelty, the fantastic mechanical devices, the monstrous caricatures of psychology and biology, the endless succession of
orgies and orgasms, the whole Bosch-like canvas of the junk-dreams is

only an exaggeration of a world amply documented in the history of this century. It is a world of undistorted, unthwarted human life, physicalistic in its assumptions and Dionysiac (see Norman O. Brown's *Life Against Death*, where the Dionysiac is recommended) in its expression. The speaker-narrator responds with savage indignation: "Gentle reader, I fain would spare you this, but my pen hath its will like the Ancient Mariner. Oh Christ what a scene is this! Can tongue or pen accommodate these scandals?" (p. 40). The pen does have its will, and the scandals happen on nearly every page, often in surroundings the reader will almost recognize: There is the hotel room, the hospital, the convention room, New York, Mexico, Interzone, Freeland, etc. In most cases, as when the "horde of lust-mad American women" (p. 82) appear in Hassan's rumpus room, the satirical point if obvious enough; in other cases, as when democracy and the scientific welfare state are under attack, the criticism is even more direct. Democracy is "cancerous," ending in bureaucratic totalitarianism (p. 134); and the welfare state is one in which "enveloping benevolence" destroys the very "concept of rebellion" (p. 186). Tyrants of the past deprived men of their liberty; the technocrats of the present deprive them of both their liberty and their ideas. But in most of the *Naked Lunch* the germ of truth in the satirical, and often bitterly amusing, exaggeration is sufficient: the exaggeration itself is the word to those who would be wise about the world.[5]

And the sex that is virtually dominant in the world of the *Naked Lunch* is the sex that Freud, Lawrence, and the marriage manual have revealed as ultimate cause, means, and end. Proud modernism boasts of sexual freedom and sexual fulfillment; both are abundantly evident in the *Naked Lunch*. Anything goes in Freeland, Interzone, or New York: sex is there, in all the glorious varieties its expression can take. No version or perversion is unrepresented, and, in the universal search for sexual gratification, the very distinction between man and woman disappears. Men and women show the undifferentiated eroticism of Freudian babies. They are transformed by their lust into grotesque animals and plants and, at last, into masses of tissue or blobs of protoplasm. As the speaker-narrator needlessly points out, "the ugliness of that spectacle buggers [sic] description" (p. 39). Scientific method and pragmatic thinking have eliminated the old and troublesome dichotomy between mind and body — by eliminating mind.

It is junk in the *Naked Lunch* which sufficiently separates the speaker-narrator from the group consciousness to let him have this vision of things as they are. Junk has its literal importance as stimulus for the *furor poeticus;* but it is also important as a symbol. It is in general a symbol of meaninglessness, or life itself as be-all and end-all of an evolving world. Only by coming into ultimate contact with junk, by knowing it as thing or symbol, can one realize the separate life. But the risk is great, and "the black wind sock of death undulates over the land, feeling, smelling for the crime of separate life, movers of the fear-frozen flesh shivering under a vast probability curve" (pp. 223-224). Although (as has often been asserted about literature) a writer cannot represent chaos by reproducing it, Burroughs, by making his *picture* a *fact*, has both represented and reproduced it. Like DeQuincey's, the junk-dreams of Burroughs are recognizable in their details, the more painfully because his dreams have the added truth of being dreams in a world of dreams. They are as valid as anything else in the reader's experience; and the most important recognition in the *Naked Lunch* is the one from which scientific and pragmatic modernism has recoiled in horror, *viz.* that each man remains in the ego-centric predicament. For all of its seemingly powerful material presence, the world is still each man's world, limited by his language and his self (*Tractatus*, 5.6ff). The language of the *Naked Lunch* becomes the reader's language; and its world, his world. Junk in the *Naked Lunch* is a sign or symbol; Wittgenstein's *Tractatus* suggests both that an unnecessary sign is meaningless and that if a sign can be made at all it must signify some truth about the world. Junk is unnecessary and hence meaningless, as a drug; but as a symbol or sign, it has significance because it must: it signifies, in the most general sense, the meaninglessness of a world subjective, fluid, and made up ultimately of nothing but disconnected atomic facts. Without the *Tractatus*, the *Naked Lunch* could be understood as growing out of traditional solipsism; but with the *Tractatus*, it must, I think, be understood as embodying and illustrating that mysterious and frightening Wittgensteinian solipsism in which the self, the personality, the ego, is the least comprehensible element, not the world but the world's limit.

Just as the analysis in the *Tractatus* destroyed traditional philosophy and finally the *Tractatus* itself (it recognizes that its own propositions are nonsensical), so the *Naked Lunch* is a work of art that destroys the traditional understanding of art as the conscious product of human effort and the reader's stubborn notion that the *Naked Lunch* must itself be a work of art. The last proposition in the *Tractatus* consigns what cannot be said of silence; and near the end of the *Naked Lunch* we are told how to respond to the book: "*Naked Lunch* demands Silence from The Reader" (p. 224). Others may try to reconstruct art or philosophy or the world — "They are rebuilding the City" (p. 235) — but, because the fires of Wittgenstein and Burroughs burn away old values and new, the rebuilding will do "No good" (p. 235). Junk or a *Naked Lunch* or the *Tractatus* plunges each man back into the separate life, or death — if not now ... "C'lom Fliday" (p. 235). "*Naked Lunch* is a blueprint, a How-To book" (p. 224), and what it pictures is clear and a fact. At least we have the blueprint to shore against our ruins; at most we may learn "How-To extend levels of experience by opening the door at the end of a long hall" (p. 224). The *Naked Lunch* should be, like the *Tractatus Logico-Philosophicus*, a ladder (6.54) we must throw away after we have "climbed up on it."

[1] Something of the range of critical opinion is suggested by the difference between John Wain's condemnation ("The Great Burroughs Affair") in *The New Republic*, December 1, 1962, pp. 21-23, and by Ihab Hassan's careful and generally favorable evaluation ("The Subtracting Machine: The Work of William Burroughs") in *Critique*, VI (Spring 1963), 4-23. To assert, as Wain does, that the *Naked Lunch* is negative, life-denying, and an attempt to "Keep the reader's nose down in the mud" and therefore bad is only to make an unjustified assumption that a book *cannot* have certain themes or treat its subject in certain ways. Although I do not agree entirely with Hassan's view about the significance of junk or with his suggestion that it is lack of "love" that keeps Burroughs from equalling such masters as Mann, Kafka, and Faulkner (what recent writer does?), I recommend his essay to anyone who does not know what there is in the *Naked Lunch* to have called forth the praise of some of the best modern critics (e.g. Mary McCarthy at the Edinburgh Festival in 1962).

[2] *Confessions of an English Opium-Eater and Kindred Papers* (Boston, 1876), p. 125.

[3] *Naked Lunch* (New York: Grove Press, [1962]), p. v.

[4] *Tractatus Logico-Philosophicus* (London: Kegan Paul, Trench, Trubner & Co., 1947). I refer to the numbered (in order of logical importance) propositions into which Wittgenstein organized the *Tractatus*. Because the wording of this reprint of the 1922 translation is slightly closer to the wording of the *Naked Lunch*, I shall quote from it rather than from the new translation of Pears and McGuinness (London, 1961).

[5] Serious though its theme is, the *Naked Lunch* is not without humor. The bitter laughter of the savage satirist is laughter none the less, and there are numerous funny episodes in the *Naked Lunch*. Dr. Berger's Mental Health Hour (pp. 136-139) and many of the exploits of Doc Benway are good examples. The practical jokes of A.J., the "last of the big time spenders" (p. 154) provide several others. What connection there may be between A.J. and Terry Southern's Guy Grand, another "last of the big spenders," I do not presume to suggest. Cf. especially chapter XII of *The Magic Christian* (New York: Random House, 1960) and pp. 153-155 in the *Naked Lunch*.

Everson / Antoninus:
Contending with the Shadow

by Albert Gelpi

In a review almost a decade ago, I hailed *The Rose of Solitude* as the most significant volume of religious poetry since Robert Lowell's *Lord Weary's Castle* twenty years before, and argued that Brother Antoninus' poetry was more profoundly Christian than Lowell's because it was more Incarnational, whereas Lowell's lapse from Catholicism stemmed from his difficulty in accepting the awesome, violent paradoxes of the central Christian mystery. Now Lowell seems caught in the ambiguities of agnosticism, revising and adding to his random *Notebook* in the same, confined fourteen-line conventions. Now, too, with Antoninus' early, pre-Catholic poetry, written as William Everson, available again in the collection *The Residual Years*, and with a new collection, again as Everson, since his leaving the Dominican Order, I would venture the judgment that if T.S. Eliot is the most important religious poet in English in the first half of the twentieth century, Everson/Antoninus is the most important religious poet of the second half of the century.

The extreme contrasts between those two poets point to a symptomatic tension in the religious commitment. The differences are less doctrinal than temperamental: Eliot the conservative classicist submitting the weaknesses of the individual to the reasonable authority of tradition and institutional structures in order to absolve him from the exigencies of personality; and Everson, the romantic individualist, trusting reason less than the undertow of passion and instinct to write out a life-long poem, as Whitman did a century ago, of the struggles with himself to realize himself.

Many would argue that authentic religious experience must be distinguished from intellectual commitment to an ecclesiastical structure, and that the great religious poetry of the first half of the century came not from Eliot but from such figures as Ezra Pound, D.H. Lawrence, Robinson Jeffers. Such a statement is not fair to Eliot, since the philosophical meditations of *Four Quartets* do derive from genuine religious experiences. However, the distinction between *modes* of religious sensibility postulated bluntly above is fundamental and revealing.

40

For what links the other three poets and Everson together, for all their admitted differences, is precisely what Eliot shrank back from as from the devil: a sourcing of self in the Dionysian unconscious rather than Apollonian consciousness; a faith in the forces — pre-rational, irrational, supra-rational, what you will — instinct in nature and emergent in the human psyche. Their poetry functions in good part to articulate the eruption into consciousness of the unconscious energies which are for them the source and secret of life. Pound recovered such primal experiences in the Greek myths and the mysteries of the occult; Lawrence, like Whitman, in the divine carnality of the sexual drive; Jeffers, in the pantheism which sees in the sea and rocks and creatures of the shore "the brute beauty of God" beyond the predatory violences of the egotistic mind and will. And in the poetry of each such psychological and spiritual exploration led to open form and free verse, as the poem discovered its definition.

By contrast, the explicitly Christian poets of the twentieth century have, by and large, tended to stress the constraining limits of a radically flawed creation through which the refractions of the Spirit penetrate at best tenuously and elusively, and they have generally insisted on working within the limitations of formal conventions as a way of testing and fixing "hints and guesses," as Eliot described our experience of the Incarnation. The means and the meaning, the norms and the measure have therefore been ruminative, guarded, Apollonian in the main. The elaborated patterning of the *Quartets* conveys not just the timeless moments which have transformed Eliot's life, but also the abiding disillusionment with temporal existence which qualifies and survives the moments of transcendence. Marianne Moore's intricately artful syllabics are a discipline to verify and regulate the allegorist's reading of natural experience in moral and religious terms. The virtuosity of Richard Wilbur's carefully maintained poise and symmetry epitomizes his conviction that the Incarnation calls us to attend to "things of this world" for "their difficult balance" of body and spirit. The religious pieces which conclude Allen Tate's long spiritual travail are written in Dante's *terza rima* in aspiration towards a faith that seems all but beyond his grasp. In Robert Lowell's Catholic poems, alternately stretched and clenched on their metrical and metaphorical designs till they threaten to wrench themselves apart, the Spirit moves to save human nature in death, which saves it from natural corruption; for him, the advent of the Incarnation spells apocalypse. John Berryman enacted his religious anxiety through the knotted syntax and studied cadences of Anne Bradstreet and of Henry, and even after his late return to the Church his poems vacillate between prayers for patience and impatient anticipation of breaking free of the human tragedy.

It is the very history of religious, especially Christian, poetry in the twentieth century, with its fixation on human fallibility and its consequent insistence on necessarily prescribed forms, that makes Everson's poetry seem radical, original, transformative. Most of the Dionysians in recent poetry—Allen Ginsberg, Jack Kerouac, Lawrence Ferlinghetti, like Hart Crane in the twenties—have used alcohol or drugs for release into vision, but Ralph Waldo Emerson, who opened the way for Whitman and all the later Dionysian poet-prophets, was the first to condemn such "*quasi*-mechanical substitutes for the true nectar," which would end in "dissipation and deterioration." The distinctiveness of Everson's achievement springs, rather, from the Dionysian character of his Christianity. This has evolved in two complementary phases: from the beginning, his surrendering to primal experience until at last it yielded him the Christian mystery; and his surrendering, then, to the Christian mystery so unreservedly that it enflamed and illuminated, below and above structured rational consciousness, that dark area, at once the center and circumference of psyche, where passion and spirit reveal themselves as personhood incarnate.

* * *

How did this transpire through more than sixty years of living and forty of poetry? William Everson's life has been punctuated again and again by interruptions, abrupt changes and seeming reversals. What has been the continuity?

Born in 1912 in Sacramento, growing up in California's San Joaquin Valley, his grandfather the founder of an evangelical sect in Norway, his stern father an agnostic, his mother a Christian Scientist, Everson was a dreamy, withdrawn young man, but in 1934 he discovered the master whose work made him a poet: Robinson Jeffers. Jeffers represented an "intellectual awakening and the first religious conversion, all in one." "When Jeffers showed me God in the cosmos, it took and I became a pantheist," and "that pantheism was based on a kind of religious sexuality," a sense of the universal life-force compelling all things in the sexual rhythm. Reading Lawrence a few years later confirmed for him the sacredness, even divinity, of natural life, but stylistically his lines adapted the expansive free-verse of Jeffers to his own verbal movement and timbre. Everson married Edwa Poulson in 1938 and began cultivating his own vineyard in the valley. "August" is characteristic of much of the early poetry in its identification with the female earth as so deep that masculine intellect relinquishes sovereignty and the virginal poet yields to the God of Nature:

> Smoke-color; haze thinly over the hills, low hanging;
> But the sky steel, the sky shiny as steel, and the
>   sun shouting.
> The vineyard: in August the green-deep and

heat-loving vines
Without motion grow heavy with grapes.
And he in the shining, on the turned earth, loose-lying,
The muscles clean and the limbs golden, turns to
    the sun the lips and the eyes;
As the virgin yields, impersonally passionate,
From the bone core and the aching flesh, the offering.
He has found the power and come to the glory.
He has turned clean-hearted to the last God, the
    symbolic sun.
With earth on his hands, bearing shoulder and arm
    the light's touch, he has come.
And having seen, the mind loosens, the nerve lengthens,
All the haunting abstractions slip free and are gone;
And the peace is enormous.

That peaceful harmony was shattered by the Second World War.
Everson's pantheism made him a pacifist; death and destruction in nature
were part of the ecological cycle, but in the human order were violational
because egoistic and malevolent. The figure of the bloody warrior from
his Nordic ancestry stalks the poetry of the late 30's as the *shadow-*
inversion of the feminine pacifist-pantheist. But when the holocaust
broke, Everson retreated to nature and spent the years 1943 to 1946 as a
forester in an Oregon camp for conscientious objectors. "The Raid"
describes war as rape, and "The Hare" acknowledges the shadow in himself with the awareness, "fathered of guilt," that we are all killers. Still,
fascinated as he was and remained with assertive masculinity (Jeffers was
similarly ambivalent), he chose the C. O. camp in the name of his
feminine susceptibilities.

But only at great cost. "Chronicle of Division" recounts the personal crisis in the global disorder: the breakup of his marriage and the
dissolution of his previous life. In 1946 he came to San Francisco to join
the pacifist-anarchist group around Kenneth Rexroth who as writers were
opposing the established academic poets and critics in the cause of open
form and spontaneity. There he met and married the poet-artist Mary
Fabilli. The sequences *The Blowing of the Seed* and *The Springing of the
Blade* hymn their union and move the nature mysticism of the earlier
poetry more explicitly into the area of human sexuality. But she was a lapsed
Catholic undergoing a rebirth of faith, and through her ordeal Everson found his own life unexpectedly altered and clarified:

"It was my time with Mary Fabilli that broke both my Jeffersian pantheism and my Lawrencian erotic mysticism. She personalized this, her
whole touch was to personalize, to humanize.... Also the intuition to
which her course led me is that my mystical needs, my religious needs,
which had not really been met in my pantheism, could only find their
solution in the more permeable human context, and in a ritual and a rite,
and in a mythos that was established in a historical continuity."

At a midnight mass, Christmas 1948, Everson was overwhelmed, psychologically, almost physically, by the divine presence in the tabernacle, and that mystical encounter led directly to his conversion the next year. However, the previous marriages of both partners and the prevailing Church procedures at the time made it impossible for them to remain husband and wife. *The Falling of the Grain* deals with the wrenching ironies and the overriding commitment which underlay their decision to separate. Two years later he entered the Dominicans as a lay brother and served for almost nineteen years, during which time the poems written as Brother Antoninus made him a figure in the San Francisco Renaissance and the Beat Generation and a charismatic presence at readings on campuses around the country.

In fact, Everson's conversion and Antoninus' monasticism did not so much "break" his pantheism and erotic mysticism, as break them into a new set of circumstances and a new psychological and spiritual dimension. Now his life was centered on the Incarnation. Not an isolated historical event, but a daily miracle: the ongoing infusion of Creator into creation, supremely expressed in Jesus, the god-man. The individual hangs on that cross, where all the contradictions of the human condition take on new consequence. The natural and the supernatural, soul and body, sexuality and spirituality — the Incarnation means that those seeming polarities, often vehemently at cross purposes, are meshed at the point of tension.

From the human point of view the Incarnation canceled out original sin, so that God could redeem man from the sinfulness which was part of his freedom. Everson had seen the killer and ravager in himself; he knew that the fallible will needed to be curbed by ethical retraints and external norms lest creative freedom become oppression or anarchy; and his penitential bent sought the stricter discipline of monasticism. But from God's perspective the Incarnation *is* the completion of the creative act. On the one hand, God could be seen as driven to descend into flesh to save soul from body: the vision of Lowell's Catholic poems. But on the other hand God could be seen as having saved man in his human condition: no Spirit changing into flesh but Spirit embodied; not sinful flesh but transfigured body. The implications of this mystery were tremendous and dangerous, and Everson was driven to search them out. For when God became man, did He not submerge himself in the sexual element? In fact, was not sexuality the manifestation of that submersion? Had He not chosen from eternity to move in and through the sexual polarity, so that our sexual natures disclose their divine impulsion? Then in the heart-beat, pulse-throb, sex-urge, the Incarnation unfolds the contingencies of time and space, and subsumes them. Now Antoninus found himself confronting these paradoxes in exactly the situation which would test them most severely: separated from the wife who was the saint of his conversion, bound by his own election to a vow of celibacy.

Consequently the poetry of Brother Antoninus is almost obsessively concerned with the feminine—that is, not only women, but his own sexuality and the feminine component in his psyche which mediates his passional, instinctual and poetic life. Decades before he had read Jung's psychology his poetry was recording his own often conflicted encounter with the major archetypes: in the psyche of a man, the *shadow*, who represents his dark, repressed, even violent aspects; the *anima*, the woman within, who is his soul and leads him into engagement with his erotic and spiritual potentialities; and, most dimly, the *self*, that achieved and transcendent personhood realized through the resolution of polarities, who reveals himself as the God within and of whom, Jung says, Jesus is the symbol and reality. Everson's poetry through the war had enacted an initial rejection of the shadow; now the anima became the primary archetypal focus in the struggle toward transcendence.

In the Fictive Wish, written in 1946 before meeting Mary Fabilli, is a marvelous evocation of what Everson was already recognizing as "the woman within":

> Wader,
> Watcher by wave,
> Woman of water;
> Of speech unknown,
> Of nothing spoken.
>
> But waits.
>
> And he has,
> And has him,
> And are completed.
>
> So she.

But what was the monk to make of her? Often she came to him as the dark temptress, allied with his own lustful shadow and luring him on to what must now be sexual sin. Many of the poems in *The Crooked Lines of God*, written soon after converting and becoming a Dominican, excoriate the flesh, and the poems in the first half of *The Hazards of Holiness* churn in the frustration not just of lust but of his passionate nature. They recount, Everson has said, his own "dark night." "A Savagery of Love" makes Mary Magdalene, the patroness of the Dominicans, the image of the purified anima, redeemed from whoredom into "a consummate chasteness," her passion focussed on the passion of the Incarnated God.

Still, even in that transfiguring focus the anima could express her passionate nature. In "The Encounter" and several other remarkable poems towards the end of *Crooked Lines* Antoninus becomes the woman before God, his/her whole being called into activity by His totally mastering love. "Annul in Me My Manhood" opens with the prayer:

> Annul in me my manhood, Lord, and make
> Me woman-sexed and weak,
> If by that total transformation
> I might know Thee more.
> What is the worth of my own sex
> That the bold possessive instinct
> Should but shoulder Thee aside?

"A Canticle to the Christ in the Holy Eucharist" translates the meditation into graphic imagery: the doe seized by the buck's wounding love on the slopes of Tamalpais, the woman-shaped mountain north of San Francisco:

> In my heart you were might. And thy word was
>   the running of rain
> That rinses October. And the sweetwater spring
>   in the rock. And the brook in the crevice.
> Thy word in my heart was the start of the buck
>   that is sourced in the doe.
> Thy word was the milk that will be in her dugs,
>   the stir of new life in them.
> You gazed. I stood barren for days, lay fallow
>   for nights.
> Thy look was the movement of life, the milk in
>   the young breasts of mothers.

However, by 1954 the stresses of the monastic life had dried up the inspiration, and it could resume again in 1957 only after a profound, shattering "breakthrough into the unconscious" the previous year, made possible by Antoninus' association with the Dominican Jungian Victor White, and by saturating himself in archetypal psychology. The result was a long narrative poem called *River-Root*, which is the most sustained orgasmic celebration in English, perhaps in all literature. Amongst the Antoninus poems collected into *The Veritable Years*, *River-Root* can be seen as a watershed: the turning away from the austere asceticism of the years just after conversion back down again to primal nature, now transfigured in the mystery of the Incarnation. The narrative objectivity of the poem permitted Antoninus, while still under the vow of chastity, to render the intercourse between the husband and wife with a candor that, far from detracting from its sacramentality, climaxes in a vision of the Trinity. God's entry into flesh locates the sexual mystery, its source and activity and end, in the very Godhead.

River-Root, then, represented at once a recovery and synthesis and turning point. It opened the way back to poetry—and to the world. In *The Hazards of Holiness* the ascetic Antoninus struggled with and against the drift that had already begun to carry him, unaware, back to Everson. The last section of that divided volume expresses the full range of his ex-

perience of the feminine archetype: from the sexual force leading men to
their death in the title poem (whether demonically, like Salome and the
Baptist, or heroically, like Judith and Holofernes) to the virgin mother
and spiritual wisdom of "A Canticle to the Great Mother of God."

Two crucial poems here state the paradox in personal terms. "The
Song the Body Dreamed in the Spirit's Mad Behest" extends the erotic
imagery of bride and bridegroom from *The Canticle of Canticles* to allow
the plunge of God into corporeal existence in blunt sexual expression
possible only after Freud and Jung in this century and possible for Antoninus only through access to the unconscious:

> He is the Spirit but I am the Flesh.
> Out of my body must He be reborn,
> Soul from the sundered soul, Creation's gout
> In the world's bourn.
>
> Mounted between the termals of my thighs
> Hawklike He hovers surging at the sun,
> And feathers me a frenzy ringed around
> That deep drunk tongue.

And the counterthrust of the Incarnation lifts our straining sexuality until
we too are reborn, borne at last to Godhead:

> Proving what instinct sobs of total quest
> When shapeless thunder stretches into life,
> And the Spirit, bleeding, rears to overreach
> The buttocks' strife.
>
> ...
> Born and reborn we will be groped, be clenched
> On ecstacies that shudder toward crude birth,
> When his great Godhead peels its stripping strength
> In my red earth.

"God Germed in Raw Granite" spells out the same reciprocating
movement: God descending into the curves and folds of the female landscape; thence the "woman within" awakening the man erotically to the
call of Spirit; and finally the synthesis of masculine and feminine twinned
into a trinity by and with God:

> I am dazed,
> Is this she? Woman within!
> Can this be? Do we, His images, float
> Time-spun on that vaster drag
> His timelessness evokes?
> In the blind heart's core, when we
> Well-wedded merge, by Him
> Twained into one and solved there,

> Are these still three? Are three
> So oned, in the full-forthing
> (Heart's reft, the spirit's great
> Unreckonable grope, and God's
> Devouring splendor in the stroke) are we —
> This all, this utterness, this terrible
> Total truth — indubitably He?

Could "she" remain merely the "woman within," the anima arousing the monk to rapturous response to God? But if he is to find God not in some disembodied heaven but in the crucible of the heart, must he not run the risks, trusting in Him Whom the unconscious aches to disclose, and the passions burn to attain? "In Savage Wastes," the concluding poem of *Hazards*, makes the decision to reenter the world; the way out of agonized self-absorption, like the way out of pantheism, was "the more permeable human context."

The Rose of Solitude tells of an encounter which moved him to his most exalted realization of the feminine. The highest recognition that I can give the book, the final validation of poetry which refuses to distinguish between art and life, is the fact that it will leave the reader, too, shaken and transformed. The plot is not remarkable: Antoninus falls in love with a Mexican-American woman, breaks his vow of chastity with her, is led by her to repentance and confession; in the end they part. The remarkable quality stems from the character of the Rose herself. The sequence gradually reveals her and extols her as the apotheosis of the feminine. Beyond the divisions which split body from soul, beyond the mental abstractions which man invents to cope ineffectually with those divisions, beyond his pity and self-pity, his hesitations, and recriminations, she emerges — all presence and act, all physical and spiritual beauty in one — spontaneous yet resting in herself, drawing him not by her will but by her being what she is. The sequence is so densely and intricately woven that it is difficult to excerpt passages, but "The Canticle of the Rose," "The Rose of Solitude" and "The Raging of the Rose" are prodigious feats of rhetoric, the poet pitching language to the extremes of articulation (the prolonged compounding of multisyllabic philosophical concepts in the "Canticle," the wild incantation and imagery of "Solitude," the synthesizing of the two modes in "Raging") in order to express the inexpressible fact that, in her, sexual sin becomes *felix culpa* and the Incarnation is accomplished. Accomplished in her, and, through his realization of her, in himself. "The Raging of the Rose" concludes with an affirmation of selfhood sourced in the "I Am Who Am" of Genesis:

> Rose!
> Reality unfolded!

On the four wings of the Cross,
In the ecstasy of crucifixion,
In the blood of being,
In the single burn of beauty

BE!

So that
In you,
The consummate
Vision of Other:

In you
I AM!

But the relationship ends in separation: the monk returning to his cell, releasing her to her own life and to another relationship. The end of the book is muted — necessarily so, since the Rose has had to be experienced, for all her glory, as forbidden, alien finally to his chosen existence.

* * *

Thus, after all the years as Brother Antoninus, he still had not recovered, except in exalted moments, that unquestioned oneness which he had felt with nature in the mid-thirties. During the war his refusal of the shadow-role of warrior had cast him, reciprocally, in a shadow-relationship with the patriarchal institutions which said that he should fight. In middle age his commitment to the monastic ideal had made him similarly ambivalent about "the woman within," though she was the source of his religious experience as well as his muse.

It could be no simple duality. Everson had experienced Christianity "as a Dionysian phenomenon" at the time of his conversion and in subsequent moments of mystical transcendence; and, as he later recalled it, "this same movement took me into the monastery — to exclude everything from the ecstatic Dionysian core" in the life of Brother Antoninus. Dionysus symbolizes the *anima*-dominated man, whose creative energy comes from his feminine affinities. In the myth Dionysus' opponent is Pentheus, the repressive law-giver, the chaste soldier-king. Dionysus is Pentheus' *shadow*, but is it not true that Pentheus is Dionysus' shadow as well, driving him to furious reprisals? What, then, of Everson and Antoninus? The situation is different because Antoninus is not Pentheus any more than Everson is simply Dionysus. If Everson and Antoninus are shadows to each other, they are needed so within the single personality. Between them, even if we can distinguish twin aspects of the living person, lies no fight to the death, as with Pentheus and Dionysus, but a grappling toward accommodation, begun long before Everson became Antoninus. "The Sides of a Mind" in the late thirties is only one testimonial to how generic the struggle has been.

Thus, as psychic entity, the formative "Antoninus" had embodied a reflective, scrupulous, perfectionist dimension of character which got voiced in the earlier work mostly in his concern for revision and crafted statement. Later the monastically realized "Antoninus" brought to the work an emotional spiritual clarity and an intellectual subtlety that made for the most powerfully achieved poems. Hence "Antoninus," whether craftsman or monk, was no extraneous imposition but constituted an inherent reality. As Everson's becoming Antoninus represented an extension and integration of identity, not a denial, so his departure from the monastery would not affect the alchemy of his character.

Still, the tension persisted. He could be a Dionysian Christian, but could he remain a Dionysian monk? In the late sixties he moved toward taking final vows, even while sounding more emphatically the erotic basis of spirituality. *Who Is She That Looketh Forth as the Morning* redresses the previous image of Mary as Wisdom in "A Canticle to the Great Mother of God" by retrieving for her, at the moment of conception by the Spirit, the erotic and chthonic powers of a goddess like Venus. *Tendril in the Mesh*, Antoninus' last poem as a monk, strives to assimilate and terminate another love-relationship with a woman by subsuming its graphic sexual details in an "Epilogue" which experiences Incarnation not as idealized humanity but as animistic totem:

> Dark God of Eros, Christ of the buried brood,
> Stone-channelled beast of ecstasy and fire,
> The angelic wisdom in the serpentine desire,
> Fang hidden in the flesh's velvet hood
> Riddling with delight its visionary good.

After the first public reading of this poem in December, 1969, Brother Antoninus stripped off his religious habit and announced to his shocked audience that he was leaving the Dominican Order. Shortly thereafter he married, first outside the Church and later in the Church, Susanna Rickson, to whom *Tendril* is dedicated. They live near Santa Cruz, where Everson teaches at the University of California.

* * *

The precipitate departure indicates how much as a thunderclap it came, even to himself; and the poems of *Man-Fate* (1974) are the words of a man caught in a psychic cross-fire: Antoninus become Everson again. During the years as Brother Antoninus, nature had remained a strong religious presence for him. The elegy for Jeffers, *The Poet Is Dead*, works almost completely through images of the California coast, and poems like "The South Coast," "A Canticle to the Waterbirds," and "In All These Acts" project pantheism into Christian mystery. Now Everson withdrew again to nature to validate his break with Antoninus, but with a consciousness heightened and complicated by all that Antoninus had come to realize and value, and by the monastery life that Everson found it excruciating to leave behind. In the opacities of the elemental matrix he would be healed or torn apart.

That venture into the primeval is enacted in a sequence of dreams and archetypal fantasies which comprise the climax of the volume. In "The Narrows of Birth" on Christmas night, twenty-one years after his conversion experience, he dreams of joining the clan gathered around the Great Mother of Nature. He bows before her for absolution, but instead sees her followers begin the castration of a young man, whose body is "slumped in its unmistakably erotic swoon." The dreamer finds the Great Mother betraying him to join in the castration. The dream in "The Black Hills" shows Everson fighting his way back in psychic as well as historical time to recover the Indians in all their splendid strength, and to seek the blessing of his dark, dead Father, whom he loves and whom civilization taught him to dread and kill. All but overwhelmed in the furious rush of the braves, he cannot wring a word of recognition from the chief. In the aftermath of the dream he rises briefly to conscious acquiescence in the natural round, which the red men honored and the white men violated: "All Indian at last,/ I lift up my arms and pray"; but even that moment is broken off anti-climactically.

The nightmares tell what Antoninus already knew: that one cannot give over to the *shadow;* abandonment to the powers of darkness without a guide will end in dissolution, chaos, death. For the man, the *anima* can be such a mediator. She is grounded in the shadow-area so strongly that at times she seems merely his vassal and instrument: the feminine as temptation or threat. But in coping with the shadow the man also engages *her.* And if trusted and loved, she can free him from enslavement to the shadow, mediating the unconscious and the passions, drawing them from blind automation into activity and actualization in masculine consciousness, and thus opening the way gradually to selfhood: the apocalypse of the polarized personality into androgynous, undivided identity. The self is the psychological equivalent of the beatific vision, glimpsed in our supreme moments, but mostly striven for through the polar rhythms of living. For in selfhood the individual attains not just what is uniquely himself, but thereby attains participation in the Godhead in which we shall all find ourselves at last.

Under the onslaught of the shadow in *Man-Fate* Everson's response is instinctive and right: he turns to touch his wife. She is the objective verification of the anima: a somnolent but locating presence, waiting for his return from lonely contention with the shadow. For after the powerful consolidation of the anima in *The Rose* and the subsequent poems, now no longer alien and suspect but tallied in his marriage, she lies ready to wake again from drowsy abeyance to spring him into the next thrust towards selfhood. The last words of the book are:

> I have made a long run.
> I have swum dark waters.
>
> I have followed you through hanging traps.
> I have risked it all.
>
> O cut my thongs!
>
> At the fork of your flesh
> Our two trails come together.
>
> At your body's bench
> I take meat.

Expressed in the archetypal terms of the human psyche, the Incarnation is God entering into, permeating and operating through the feminine, just as the Annunciation proclaims. The concluding image above, physical yet suggestive of the sacramental act, constitutes, more immediately and elementally than with the Rose, the personalizing of the regenerative, redemptive mystery in the witness of the wife to the power of the anima. Mother and wife and priestess in one, she administers him nourishment needed now for the way ahead.

Lawrence Ferlinghetti's Fourth Person Singular and the Theory of Relativity

by L.A. Ianni

Lawrence Ferlinghetti's novel *Her*, as well as a number of his poems and plays, is permeated by one dominant precept: that love is the prime value that gives meaning to human existence. The paramount concern for the central character of *Her* is the recognition and the attainment of love. He fails in both endeavors and, consequently, in finding any meaning in life. His beliefs prevent him from reconciling the experience of love with his expectations. No reconciliation of experience and expectation is possible for Andy Raffine because his views are not derived from experience but are anticipations of experience; they are absolute rather than relative in the sense that he chooses to adhere to them even though experience consistently negates them. The novel could be called a tragedy of absolute values in a relativistic world. The tragic potential of modern life in this respect engrosses Ferlinghetti in much of his other work, making his work in general a view of life based on the philosophical implications of the theory of relativity.

The most apparent philosophical implication of the relativity principle is epistemological. In science, the principle of relativity has changed man's notions of his knowledge about physical reality. It demonstrates that for certain measureable quantities in the real world, no preferred set of values exists independently of the relations inherent in individual measurements. For example, Martin Gardner summarizes his discussion of some manifestations of the principle in this way:

> The fact that these bewildering changes in length and time are called "apparent" does not mean that there is a "true" length or time which merely "appears" different to different observers. Length and time are relative concepts. They have no meaning apart from the relation of an object to an observer. There is no question of one set of measures being "true," another set "false." Each is true relative to the observer making the measurements; relative to his frame of reference. *There is no way that measurements can be any truer.* In no sense are they optical illusions to be explained by a psychologist. They can be recorded on instruments. They do not require a living observer.[1]

Such a view of the natue of man's knowledge about external reality must inevitably alter man's attitude toward his world as he knows it. As philosophy, the scientific theory does not suggest what the meaning of existence must be, but it reveals something about the circumstances under which values are formulated. The theory of relativity points out that there is no other way of knowing than relationally. Meaning or meaninglessness is a product of a relation between the object being observed and the observer.

It should immediately be pointed out that the term "relativity" as used here is not the equivalent of the philosophical term "subjectivity." The principle of relativity does not re-introduce the traditional philosophical duality between relative or subjective ontology and absolute or objective ontology. Adolf Grünbaum provides a very emphatic statement on this point:

> it is not the mere failure of measurement to disclose them [relations of absolute simultaneity] that constitutes their nonexistence as much as that failure is *evidence* of their nonexistence. Only a philosophical obfuscation of this state of affairs can make plausible the view that the relativity of simultaneity (or for that matter, any of the other philosophical innovations of relativity theory) lends support to the subjectivism of homocentric operationalism or of phenomenalistic positivism.... I do not think that the theory of relativity can be validly adduced in support of this homocentric form of operationalism. Einstein's theory asks us to conceive the topology and metric of space-time as systems of relations between physical events and things. But both these things and their relations are independent of man's presence in the cosmos. Our operations of measurement merely discover or ascertain the structure of space-time but they do not generate it.[2]

As a philosophic view of nature, then, the theory of relativity is objective as well as relational. One must note that even those physicists who are inclined to the "subjectivism" that disturbs Professor Grünbaum (for example, the Copenhagen School) are not subjectivists in the traditionally philosophical sense. This statement by Heisenberg makes that abundantly clear:

> Of course the introduction of the observer must not be misunderstood to imply that some kind of subjective features are to be brought into the description of nature. The observer has, rather, only the function of registering decisions, i.e., processes in space and time, and it does not matter whether the observer is an apparatus or a human being.[3]

What Heisenberg has said about the role of man in the discovery of reality certainly would not be contested by those who disagree on other philosophical implications of the theory of relativity. His statement points out something about the process by which we come to our beliefs. For this reason the principle of relativity presents the possibility of reconciling certain dualties of value. Instead of certain values being alternative, irreconcilable possibilities, their exclusiveness disappears before the recognition of the relational conditions of viewing.

This necessity of recognizing the observer as a component in the process of "registering decisions" is that philosophical implication of the theory of relativity that is so much a part of Ferlinghetti's literary exploration of the meaning of life. Because man is the instrument for evaluating reality, he must have an awareness of his presence and his orientation so that he can function accurately as an evaluator. He must be aware that his evaluations are made relationally; therefore he must know his frame of reference. In *Her*, Ferlinghetti has Andy Raffine wrestle with the identification of his frame of reference for making decisions about life. Raffine views life through an outlook he calls *the fourth person singular*. Actually, his interior monologue conveys that there are two fourth person singulars to him, one called *the true fourth person singular* and one called simple *the fourth person singular*. Ferlinghetti has provided some insight into the meaning of the term *fourth person singular* in a poem entitled "He." It is a scathing portrait of a poet who is preoccupied with death. This poet's point of view is called in the poem "the mad eye of the fourth person singular."[4] It is a distorted vision through which the poet "sees and is mad/ and is mad and sees." This, too, is the condition of Andy Raffine in the novel.

Viewing through the eye of the fourth person singular results in a number of problems in evaluating love as an experience. The conflict in the central character of *Her* is based on the dilemma of reconciling observation with expectation. Andy literally and psychologically pursues an ideal love which contains the essence of purity and sensuality. Such a view of woman is the dream of the naive romantic. The woman is proprietously aloof and chaste until a man wins her and then she fulfills his warmest expectations of sensuality. Ferlinghetti ridicules the concept in a poem about literary romances. The poem describes the heroine of such a tale as sexlessly chaste until:

> ... one day
> she who has always been so timid
> offs with her glove and says
> (though not in so many big words)
> Let's lie down somewheres
> baby[5]

The diction certainly signals the speaker's doubts about the validity of such expectation. But such doubts do not exist for the hero of the novel. The "Her" of the title, whom Andy Raffine imagines and experiences variously in the novel as a girl in a dirndl dress, a sculptress with whom he is fascinated from afar, and a subdued, aesthetically-inclined girl he attains physically, is a concept of taintless womanhood that he could love unreservedly and thus give meaning to his life. His failure to reconcile himself to the unattainability of love according to his ideal ends in his suicidal leap from the Cathedral of Notre Dame.

The chief device used in *Her* to achieve the effect of the fourth person singular is a certain pattern of images that recur in the interior monologue of the main character. For example, Andy periodically imagines life as a movie in which it is unclear to him just what his role is, if, indeed, he is in the movie or is just a viewer of it. The movie, which is as much a recapitulation of human experience to Andy as it is his own story, progresses in an invariable way although the sequence of action may be taken up at any point. Andy's seeing the movie so clearly but being unsure of his relationship to it is an excellent device to dramatize the concept of the fourth person singular. His inability to see himself as a component in the viewing process is well embodied through this illusion since it reflects his inability to recognize his frame of reference and to define his observational position. His view of life is illusive because he cannot separate himself from it although, ironically, he constantly feels isolated from people. Andy has no clear sense of viewing life through a recognized concept of self. At one point, he refers to his viewpoint as:

> ... the seeing-eye of the fourth person singular that saw everything and understood nothing, yet still saw, the eye that saw and understood everything but myself, not able to see that in which it was itself imbedded....[6]

We note even in this brief passage the confusion about the external world that results from a failure to identify one's self in a way that helps to clarify the relation between oneself and external reality. Even the set of objects connected with Andy's search for the ideal of perfect womanhood are affected by this situation of the undifferentiated observer. From the image of a girl in dirndl to the women he experiences, Raffine relates them all to his mother and eventually to the Mother of All, from whose cathedral he leaps to his death. He cannot experience women as separate from the sources of his own life.

The fourth person singular, as Andy Raffine's observational point of view, molds his philosophical position. Andy believes in a set of first principles that take precedence over any conclusions drawn from experience as a basis for registering decisions about life. His adamance in the adhering to such a philosophical position is expressed in this section of the interior monologue which occurs at a decisive point in his search for a love to give purpose and meaning to his life.

> ... perhaps you will all excuse me now if I run along after life and live, for the first thing God made was love though the second thing he made was blood, although perhaps you will not admit that, for it is at best a rude surmise that essence really preceded being, and the third hip thing that God made was the long journey that I, not to mention everybody else, is on, yes I am on the way to myself through what I hope is love or through what at least I would take for love yes I am on my way to myself through the illusions of sense through the illusions of happiness and beauty to find that innermost swinger beyond the self [pp. 59-60].

Clearly, from this passage we see that, for Andy, experience is not essential reality. The fourth person singular, that name that Andy gives to his observational position, is supposed to see through experience (that is, "blood" in the preceding passage) to essence ("love").

Andy's quest to discover himself through love does not succeed, however. It fails because he cannot recognize love. He cannot do so because to him it is synonymous with essence, not experience. Ferlinghetti suggests, on the contrary, in one of his poems that love is not a transcendent thing but a quality belonging to the world of experience. In "Flying Out of It"[7] the speaker in the poem is in literal, mechanical flight which suggests to him the possibility of figurative, spiritual flight beyond the limitations of the real world. After contemplating the sin and prejudice of the world, the speaker entertains a faint hope of escaping from it into eternity. However, the poem concludes, there is no room for love in that eternity. Consequently the poem sugggests that eternity is an escape of dubious value by calling it a "Pied Piper's cave." The implication is that earth is the best place there is for love. Andy's attempt to use it as a means of escape, therefore, cannot succeed.

Not all of Ferlinghetti's poems suggest that a plane of life that transcends sensory experience is a Pied Piper's Cave. One poem in which Ferlinghetti flirts with the notion that essence precedes being is a lengthy piece entitled "Hidden Door."[8] Throughout most of the poem it is asserted that the mysterious quality of life is both universal and appalling. The format is to juxtapose a number of images culled from reality with the term "hidden door." Reality, it is proposed, is obscured rather than revealed by the world as one sees it.

> Hidden door pathetic fallacy
> of the evidence of the senses
> as to the nature of reality

Tangible reality is a hindrance to real insight, the speaker states as he muses during a river journey toward the Inca ruins at Machu Picchu.

> ... hidden door made of mirrors
> on the waters of this river
> on the waters of this river
> in which I cannot see beyond myself
> because my body's in the way

At the end of the poem some degree of understanding comes by transcending the limitations imposed by the body as an aspect of tangible reality. The poet suggests a kind of intuitive truth gained by surrendering the physical self.

> Hidden door at last I see through

> beyond dear dead body bag of bones
>   which I leave naked on a rock
> Hidden door I wigless climb to
>   beyond that river
> Hidden door at last I fall through

This poem, however, is not satisfying in respect to what insight is gained that constitutes a deeper truth about reality. It ends with only a brief statement that the speaker has arrived at the Inca ruins. The reader cannot avoid the feeling that the grasp of things has eluded the seeker. If this is the grasping of essence, the search seems as much a failure as it was for the central character of Ferlinghetti's novel.

Because of his belief in the pre-eminence of essences, Andy sees meaning or significance as a quality of creation of which man is a recipient. For him, the perfection of feminine love and purity is not a version of what exists but a vision of what has from creation presumably existed. Dedication to this view leads him to the ultimate disaster. As repeatedly as he tries, he finds it impossible to accept his real experiences as the limits of possibility. He confronts the resulting dilemma once when he encounters a sensitive and tender woman who gives herself to him.

> And instead of beginning in dream and voyaging off into the actual world and then returning afterward to dream, I would this time begin with the real and stick to it, voyage nowhere out of it. Here was a tall thin girl whose 'reality' was strange enough without shadows, standing in front of the tiny fire, clutching her elbows as if still trying to get warm ... [p. 113].

The pattern of dream, reality, and dream is the recurring pattern of behavior for Andy induced by his beliefs. He has expectation; he experiences and is disillusioned; and he retreats to his expectations again. His concept of the essence of love always makes his experiences disappointing. What Andy calls the fourth person singular is his fixation upon that concept of essence which colors all his experiences.

The anguish of Andy Raffine stems from his awareness that he may well be foolish in his pursuit of idealized love, which is for him an ultimate value from which he cannot deviate. His Paris address, for example, is Rue du Cherche Midi, a shortening of the phrase "chercher midi à quatorze heures," meaning "to create difficulties where there are none." The flesh and blood women of his experience do not create the sort of ecstasy or transport from reality that fulfills his expectations. The kind of perplexity felt by Andy is suggested in one of Ferlinghetti's poems in which he recollects a summer scene full of vibrant life. Yet of that scene he writes:

> And in the poet's plangent dream I saw
> no Lorelei upon the Rhone

> nor angels debarked at Marseilles
> but couples going nude into the sad water
> in the profound lasciviousness of
> spring in an algebra of lyricism
> which I am still deciphering [p. 80]

For Andy, the physical love of his experience is "an algebra of lyricism" which he cannot decipher. His romantic expectations demand the unity of the physical and spiritual in love; yet his experiences with physical love negate any possibility of the spiritual. The disillusionment is of the type that Ferlinghetti dramatizes in yet another poem where the speaker's first acquaintance with a woman brings hopes of rising above the mundane plane of life. After an interlude, however:

> Only the next day
> she has bad teeth
> and really hates
> poetry [p. 22]

Only woman in the abstract retains the possibility of realizing Andy Raffine's ideals. During one part of his search for love he falls in love with a sculptress because her work seems to have such an apparent quality to it. However, he finds when he comes to know her that she is an indiscriminate sensualist, quite unlike his expectation of a woman whose body would be subordinate to her mind.

Since the belief of the character in Ferlinghetti's novel fails, we can be sure that in the author's poems the meaning of love is found in the experience of it. In some poems the experience of love is sensual and earthy. One poem describes an encounter with a widow who, in her enjoyment of the sensual, seems very reminiscent of Chaucer's wife of Bath (p. 38). It is a love poem rather than just a sex poem since it suggests that sexual love is the expression of the widow's soul. There is no expression of guilt in the contact between the lovers, rather there is a clear statement of satisfaction with the intensity of the interlude. Other poems make clear, on the other hand, that exclusive sensuality is not the only aspect of love. One poem portrays a young woman full of spiritual love whose dreams of the physical aspect of love are frighteningly vulgar (p. 36). She is plagued by an image of "drunken sailors ... scattering semen/ over the virgin landscape." Eventually, the woman of the poem surrenders her hopes for love on a spiritual plane and turns to God, presumably by becoming a nun. That this is a surrender rather than an attainment of the love she sought is suggested by the metaphor of her heart as a vessel which "puts about/ searching the lost shores." Like the Andy Raffine, the character in this poem clings to an ideal. She differs from him in confronting experience in a way that makes life tenable.

The poem just discussed implies that the girl had a notion which she hoped subsequent experience would fulfill. Ferlinghetti embodies in another poem the implication that the development of such expectations about love are unrealistic (p. 35). The speaker in the poem is a very young adolescent who is in a candy store when a rather mature and attractive girl runs in to escape a sudden shower. The youth's attraction to her is the initial awakening in him of the sensual possibilities of life. But she is unattainable for him. Speaking of the situation in retrospect, the speaker refers to it as "where I first/ fell in love/ with unreality." We can infer that dreams of love will be companions of the boy hereafter despite the falling leaves of that afternoon whipering to him "Too soon! Too soon!" This poem is faintly reminiscent of the dream image of Andy Raffine. He too had become enamored of the possibility of love, his own falling in love with unreality.

The alternative to the unreal quality lent to life by the viewpoint of the fourth person singular is a world view that appears in Andy Raffine's stream-of-consciousness as the true fourth person singular. The true fourth person singular is a position for viewing life objectively, without the "soul bridge" associations that invest the real world with the meanings that man has projected into them. Andy refers to life seen through this true fourth singular as "the *table rase* or true new Big Table of perception." (pp. 91-92) This is life swept clean of preconceptions, like Andy's own ideal of love that colors his view of reality. The true fourth singular, however, is ultimately not a viewpoint that Andy Raffine can attain, fixated as he is on a set of values that derive from an earlier philosophical tradition of essences. He meditates anguishedly on his inability to adopt the position:

> but I keep slipping off the new-wiped table because I and no one has the true fourth sight to see without the old associational turning eye that turns all it sees into its own, and it is this fourth singular voice of which nobody speaks but which still exists unvoiced that will speak in tomorrow's seeing man and which will see truly how there is no rapport of any kind between himself and natural objects except a rapport of strangeness ... [p. 93].

The position described here constitutes a relative perspective of viewing, where the separateness yet relatedness of viewer and viewed is accounted for in the observation process. It is a non-scientific philosophical recognition of the conditions of viewing inherent in the scientific theory of relativity. It is not, as earlier emphasized, subjectivism, but relationalism. Truth is not the desire to validate expectation but a decision registered from experience. The character of Ferlinghetti's novel cannot define love as a decision registered from experience. His awareness of the possibility of "another way of seeing" makes him consider breaking away from the impasse of the world view he calls simply the fourth person singular, that way of seeing that "saw and understood everything but myself." In this outlook, the observer is not recognized as a component in the act of observation. It is antithetical to a relative concept of viewing, which implies that one must know what and where one is if one is to know accurately what he has seen. The distinctive feature of relative viewing is to recognize that the nature of the observer is inseparable from the viewing.

The impasse that confronts Andy is not mandated by the nature of life. Ferlinghetti suggests in one poem that life only seems inpenetrable from certain approaches (p. 31). The poem begins with an imaginative description of Kafka's castle as a metaphor for the unapproachability of the meaning of life. Yet, as the conclusion of the poem makes clear, the unattainability of the heights is not an intrinsic feature of the situation but a product of the approach we have taken. The ending of the piece has general as well as specific implication. The Kafkian impasse, like other barriers of belief, is avoidable by a change of position.

> We ogle the unobtainable
>   imagined mystery
> Yet away around on the far side
>   like the stage door of a circus tent
> is a wide vent in the battlements
>   where even elephants
>   waltz thru

The delineation that Andy makes between the fourth singular and the true fourth singular is a difference in position that removes the mystery from existence and permits one to go to the summit of it. The attainment of love is impossible in Andy's world because his approach to it, rather than the absence of it, makes it unobtainable. Andy always approaches love on the basis of a preconception of purity, which is symbolized in his mental visions by a piece of white thread. Before long, the string is soiled or falls into the mud. This inevitably happens because his faulty preconception mandates that the love of his experience cannot be anything but impure.

Ferlinghetti has dramatized the problem of the pervasive influence of assumptions in two of his plays entitled "The Three Thousand Red Ants" and "The Victims of Amnesia."[9] In the first of these, there is no dramatic action to speak of. The lone scene consists of a dialogue between a man and a woman in bed. They discuss the drowning of three thousand Chinese soldiers in terms that suggest that they find it impossible to consider these men as human beings. The whole thing is quite heavy-handed, perhaps most so at its conclusion wherein the male character scans the sea, which they can see from their bed, with binoculars that have a crack in the lens. This prompts them to meditate on the distorted effect of looking at the world through cracked glasses. The brief play is admittedly strident, but the point is nonetheless relevant here. That the couple are rooted to their bed suggests the fixedness of their view on life. Their lack of sympathy is a product of their slanted values, as is their distorted vision of the world outside their room.

In the play "The Victims of Amnesia," the results of preconceptions go far beyond distorted vision to become total intellectual blindness. In this considerably more dramatic play than the other, the situation is that a pregnant woman named Mazda, the name here being an apparent suggestion for light in the sense of knowledge, registers for a hotel room and makes a request of the desk clerk. Reporting that she will probably forget her room number, she asks that the clerk inform her of it if she should stop at his desk and give her name. The clerk, who is a spokesman for the accepted pattern of human social conventions (he repeatedly throughout the play refers to the hotel as "this establishment" in a way that suggests that he means the Establishment of society), promises to do so. Subsequently, the woman Mazda reappears at the desk in several altered forms and requests her room number. First she reappears as a handsome but no longer pregnant woman. Her bedraggled condition suggests the buffeting that truth takes in the world. Then she returns as a twelve-year old girl and finally as an infant in a carriage.

What the sequence suggests is that the social Establishment is presented with increasingly less developed forms of knowledge or the truth, but it is only more confused and infuriated with each confrontation. The responses of the clerk, the representative for social authority, are larded with the clichés of popular wisdom. His concluding tirade is a compendium of the rebuttals and threats authority is prone to make to dispensers of uncomfortable truths. Yet the clerk cannot be credited with reaction to a truth which he denies; he cannot recognize the truth when he sees it. The tragedy of the situation, Ferlinghetti seems to be suggesting, is that the closed minds of those in authority make them blind to the realities of life.

Ferlinghetti suggests through the central character of *Her*, who is anything but a member of the Establishment of society, that intellectual fixations are not the exclusive problem of people in authority. Andy Raffine's faulty preconceptions about love prove fatal to him; and so it is with man in general, Ferlinghetti suggests in another poem (p. 39). In the poem, love is envisioned as a vast, deep ocean which man plays around and even sails upon but is unwilling to immerse himself in. Our excursions and activities around the edge of love are base and unlovely compared to the possibilities; yet we are hesitant to explore the depths of possibility. But love ultimately proves irresistible and we must get deeply into it. However, since it is not our element as a result of our denial of its richer possibilities, we cannot survive immersion in it. Such is the situation with Andy. His fourth person singular viewpoint is his playing around the ocean of love. His view does not permit him to accept love totally, which

in terms of the diction of the poem is immersion in the sea of "salt sex."
Andy's unwillingness is evident in the novel by his viewing physical love as
the soiling of virginity.

The erroneous rejection of the physical aspect of love in pursuit of
the spiritual aspect of it serves as the basis of Ferlinghetti's play "The
Soldiers of No Country."[10] The setting is a cave where a few remnants of
humanity have taken refuge against a universal holocaust. There are
three principle characters. One is an old though still vigorous man who
represents selfish, animalistic sensualism. Another is a repressed middle-
aged virgin, who stands for a devotion to purity which is a paradoxical
rejection of human life. The third is a youth who is full of idealistic zeal
but who is sexually impotent. During the course of the play the young
man fails in his attempt to love the woman. His impotence suggests the
sterility of spirituality divorced from sensuality. This situation leaves the
control of the sources of man's endurance in the hands of the cynical
hypocrite. This character, who is literally presented as a psychiatrist
masquerading as a priest, seduces the woman. This seduction suggests the
perpetuation of human life by the source least amenable to the wholesome
development of it. This is emphasized by the conclusion of the play in
which the woman rushes into the arid, radiated world outside the cave
rather than face the prospect of bearing the child of the animalistic sensualist. The point is that he won the woman by default. The impotent
failure of the young man who represents higher human aspirations leaves
the way open for him. It is interesting to note that certain ingredients of
the play are a repetition of the mental imagery of *Her* and help underscore the relatedness of the two pieces. The sensualist as priest symbolizes
his authority over the inhabitants of the cave by a statue of the Virgin.
The woman has a recurrent dream about a white string which belongs to
her. The sensualist as psychiatrist interprets the string for her as a symbol
of her innocence. The woman's feelings toward the young man are con-
fusedly maternal rather than sensual. Her surrender to the sensualist is an
act of futility, like Andy Raffine's physical experiences with the women he
loves. Generally, the effect of the play is to register the disastrous effect of
misplaced feelings about human affection. The two appropriate lovers are
unapproachable to one another as a result of their inappropriate attitudes
toward physical love.

Although many of Ferlinghetti's works define love as a physically
passionate experience, he does not assert that love is "really" sensual
passion rather than a spiritual-intellectual affection. These two
definitions of love are not incompatible with one another. The poet embodies this point in a brief poem that describes what is surely a complete
woman (p. 85). She is sensitive, sensual and intellectual. She appeals to
the speaker in the poem because of both her mental and physical passion.
He says of her:

                    ... she could quote Cocteau
            'I feel there is an angel in me' she'd say
                    'whom I am constantly shocking'
            Then she would smile and look away
                    light a cigarette for me
                        sigh and rise
            and stretch her sweet anatomy
                    let fall a stocking

Love as this woman embodies it unites those facets that seem irreconcilable alternatives to Andy Raffine—that is, to the observer through the
fourth person singular point of view. For Andy, sensuality subverts all
possibility of love in the spiritual-intellectual sense. Ferlinghetti suggests
in one poem that just the reverse constitutes the universal pattern of
human experience in love (pp. 44-46). That is, passionate sensual love is
not only irrepressible but it is an impetus to man's most spiritual in-
clinations.

            And that's the way it always is and that's the way
            it always ends and the fire and the rose are one
            and always the same scene and always the same
            subject right from the beginning ...

If sensuality (fire) and the spiritual-intellectual (the rose) are one, why do
they seem incompatible from the view of essences called the fourth person
singular? Because to take this view mandates that love should
simultaneously manifest itself as a sensual and intellectual experience.
This is not the case, the poem suggests. Love has a cyclic pattern:

            ... everything always ends when that hunting
            cock of flesh at last cries out and has his glory
            moment God and then comes tumbling down the sound
            of axes in the woods and trees falling....

Those activities, like the clearing and building suggested above, in which
man expresses his spiritual-intellectual aspirations are seen to be non-
simultaneous with man's sensual passion; yet they are of that passion and
flow out of it. The being of love is that they are both part of it. This is
recognizable through the observational view of the true fourth singular,
as Andy Raffine called it. Neither of the non-simultaneous manifestations
of love is any truer than the other. They are simply recognizable as part of
the totality of it when viewed through the "rapport of strangeness." The
disparate data of experience is thus unified, and human life, as sustained
by love in the way that Andy Raffine hoped it would be, seems whole and
consistent.
    The key to this wholeness and consistency is that position of

relational viewing which is embodied in the philosophical implications of the theory of relativity. Ferlinghetti's work dramatizes those implications by showing the disastrous consequences of ignoring them and the significance of recognizing them. He has addressed himself to the unique artistic concerns of a world grown to a new level of self-consciousness through the pervasive impact of scientific theory.

[1] Martin Gardner, *Relativity for the Million*, paperbound ed. (New York, 1965), p. 51.

[2] Adolf Grünbaum, "Logical and Philosophical Foundations of the Special Theory of Relativity," *Philosophy of Science*, Meridian Books (Cleveland, 1960), pp. 412 and 425.

[3] Werner Heisenberg, *Physics and Philosophy*, Harper Torchbook ed. (New York, 1958), p. 137.

[4] Lawrence Ferlinghetti, "He," *Starting from San Francisco* (New York, 1958), pp. 36-41.

[5] Lawrence Ferlinghetti, *Coney Island of the Mind* (New York, 1958), p. 86. Poems in this volume are untitled; therefore only page references will be given in parentheses.

[6] Lawrence Ferlinghetti, *Her* (New York, 1960), p. 134. Hereafter references in parentheses will refer to this edition.

[7] *San Francisco*, pp. 26-30.

[8] *San Francisco*, pp. 31-35.

[9] In *Unfair Arguments with Existence* (New York, 1962), pp. 29-46 and pp. 65-84 respectively.

[10] *Unfair Arguments*, pp. 1-28.

Allen Ginsberg: The Origins of *Howl* and *Kaddish*

by James Breslin

Most literary people have probably first become aware of Allen Ginsberg through the media, in his self-elected and controversial role as public figure and prophet of a new age. Ginsberg's public personality has changed over the years — from the defiant and histrionic angry young man of the fifties to the bearded and benign patriarch and political activist of the sixties and seventies — but the personality has remained one that most literary people find hard to take seriously. Compare Ginsberg's reception with that of Norman Mailer, another writer who is also a public figure and one who, like Ginsberg, wants to replace rational with magical thinking as the mode of public discourse. Mailer's public appearances and his confessional writings characteristically begin by humiliating but end by promoting himself, and they have been enormously successful: Mailer's talents have been widely exaggerated, especially by academic critics, who already have produced several studies of his work. Mailer has succeeded because his theorizing on all matters from the digestive to the political system, no matter how bizarre or brutal the content, are developed by a kind of intellectualizing most literary people respect, even when it is adopted (as in Mailer) half in the spirit of the put-on. Ginsberg is at least as intelligent, a lot less brutal, and often a lot more self-aware, but the man who took off his clothes at a Los Angeles poetry reading, who chanted "Om" during the gassings in Grant Park at the 1968 Democratic Convention in Chicago, and who has experimented with a wide variety of drugs, strikes those manning the literary armchairs as at best a figure of fun or, more likely, a threat to western civilization. Ginsberg's role as a public figure has been part of his attempt to reassert the romantic role of the poet as prophet; but one result of it has been that his genuine literary talents and more admirable personal qualities have been obscured.

It is true that, so far, the quality of Ginsberg's writing has been too inconsistent for him to rank as a major poet. Ginsberg writes often, quickly, and, as his career has advanced, apparently without too much revision; his cult of spontaneity results in unevenness, but it also generates some of the real strengths of his writing. A poet like Eliot, carefully turning a lifetime's experience into a single volume of highly finished work, helped to create the myth (dominant when Ginsberg began to write) of the modern artist who, a literary revolutionary in spite of himself, remained a hard-working, disciplined craftsman. Like many contemporary poets, Ginsberg, an avowed revolutionary, seems much more willing to risk imperfection, even failure; what he hopes to gain is an honesty and immediacy of feeling, rather than the finish of a well-wrought work of art. When he is least successful, Ginsberg has drifted into the solipsism of purely private associations, as he does in the drug poems in *Kaddish* and *Reality Sandwiches*, or he has fallen into the predictable patterns of thought and feeling characteristic of a polemicist, as he does in much of his political poetry. But the really exciting moments in reading Ginsberg come when he breaks through to new orders in the poem and in self-understanding. "Howl" (1956), "Kaddish" (1959), "The Change: Kyoto-Tokyo Express" (1963), and "Wales Visitation" (1967) — all poems of some length, all evolving from the pressures of some personal crisis — these poems seem to me to be the main such moments in Ginsberg's career.

Of these the most powerful — and influential — appear to be "Howl" and "Kaddish." Several poets have testified to the importance of Ginsberg's early poetry in establishing an alternative to the well-made symbolist poem that was fashionable in the fifties, and his early work does fuse two modes — the confessional and the visionary — that were to become important in the sixties.[1] Not that a case for Ginsberg can only be made on historical grounds; both poems, given the intense and concentrated energy of their surrealistic language, their vivid creation of a world of primitive terrors and hallucinatory brilliance, their striking shifts of voice and mood, have genuine literary merit. For a long time, their explosive *poetic* energy has been missed, partly because of the distractions of a "shocking" language and matter (drugs, madness, suicide, homosexuality, incest), but mainly because many readers, still not sympathetic to the *kind* of form found in these poems, have accused them of an *absence* of form. Moreover, while they achieve literary form and attain a public impact, these poems derive from deep, long-standing private conflicts in Ginsberg — conflicts that ultimately stem from his ambivalent attachment to his mother, his difficulties in asserting a separate, independent personality. While there is a progression of self-awareness from "Howl" (1956) to "Kaddish" (1959), both works seem to me to expose rather than to resolve these conflicts, though they make valiant efforts at such resolution. Nevertheless, it is Ginsberg's ability to probe these areas of conflict that largely explains their innovative energy and powerful appeal.

* * *

Allen Ginsberg is a mystical and messianic poet with intense suicidal wishes and persistent self-doubts, a would-be spontaneous artist whose most spontaneous thoughts characteristically turn toward feelings of being stifled and inhibited — walled and bounded in — and thus toward longings for some painful, apocalyptic deliverance — ultimately death itself. To read the notebooks and journals that Ginsberg has kept from adolescence onwards is to encounter a man with grandiose hopes for himself, but one who relentlessly flagelates himself for his failures and who tends to assume that all his undertakings will end, just as they have ended, in disaster.[2] Just the published *Indian Journals* (kept during 1962-63) amply reveal how this outwardly serene bard is intrigued with failure and death, spending too much of his time contemplating the *ghats* where the Indian dead are cremated. Of the Ginsberg of the late fifties and early sixties, Lawrence Ferlinghetti remembers, "he is the flippy flesh made word/ and he speaks the word he hears in his flesh/ and the word is *Death*."[3] To say all this is not to say that Ginsberg's public manner is false but that, on the contrary, it has been hard-won. And poems like "Howl" and "Kaddish" have a key place in the evolution of his personality, developing out of a time in his life when his creative impulses came into something like a balance with his propensities for self-destruction. As Ginsberg himself tells it — a version of his life we should approach skeptically — the story of his literary career and in a way the real story of his life begin with his removal from New York to San Francisco in 1953.

"Howl" is not — contrary to popular impression — the work of an angry *young* man. When he wrote the poem, Ginsberg was 30; in 1953, when he left family, friends and the established literary culture behind him in the East, he was 27 — being, like his friend Jack Kerouac, a romantic wanderer who found it difficult to sever family ties. Ginsberg himself sees the 1953 journey west as a crucial and symbolic kind of act: "It was like a big prophecy, taking off to California. Like I had passed one season of my life and it was time to start all over again."[4] It was not quite this easy and final, as we shall see; but moving west was a dramatic attempt to loosen the parental grip — to free himself from pressures created by his mother's long history of psychotic illness as well as his frequently acrimonious relation with his father. Going west was, in short, a turn away from the threatening images of failure, disintegration, suffocation he associated with home — a gesture toward the future, toward life, an attempt to start all over again as *his own man*. Yet it is also true that Ginsberg made this journey half looking back over his shoulder — just as in "Howl" he would return to the experience and emotions of his life in New York in the late forties and in Part III of the poem ("Carl Solomon, I'm with you in Rockland.") deny that he had ever left. It is certainly mistaken to imagine a recreated Ginsberg floating into San Francisco on a magic carpet, dressed in long robes, with flowing hair, hand cymbals and a "San Francisco Poetry Renaissance" banner. The Ginsberg that emerged in "Howl" — Ginsberg the rancorous and somewhat gloomy mystic seer — must in some sense have been there, but he was apparently hidden at first beneath a deferential and conventional exterior. In fact, it would be more accurate to imagine him arriving in a three-button suit, striped tie, and an attaché case. Soon after his arrival in San Francisco, Ginsberg was looking for a job in market research, and he quickly found one. There was no reason he shouldn't — since this was precisely the kind of work he had been doing back in New York.

Not long after he secured the job, Ginsberg became involved with a woman, with whom he eventually moved into an apartment in San Francisco's posh Nob Hill district. Life went along in this style for several months in the fall of 1953 — until Ginsberg began seeing a therapist at Langley-Porter Institute, a Dr. Phillip Hicks, to find out why neither the job nor the woman seemed to satisfy him. According to Ginsberg, at one point in his treatment, the doctor asked,

> "What would you like to do? What is your desire, really?" I said, "Doctor, I don't think you're going to find this very healthy and clear, but I really would like to stop working forever — never work again, never do anything like the kind of work I'm doing now — and do nothing but write poetry and have leisure to spend the day outdoors and go to museums and see friends. And I'd like to keep living with someone — maybe even a man — and explore relationships that way. And cultivate my perceptions, cultivate the visionary thing in me. Just a literary and quiet city-hermit existence." Then, *he* said, "Well, why don't you?"[5]

In several interviews Ginsberg discusses this encounter, mythologizing it into The Great Breakthrough that allowed him to start a new life. As Ginsberg tells it, the doctor's tolerant acceptance of Ginsberg's unconventional desires encouraged self-acceptance and the end of his misguided attempts to please his father — both of which, in turn, generated "Howl." So, the story goes, Ginsberg wrote a report showing how his firm could replace him with a computer; they fired him and he went on unemployment, free to enjoy a "quiet city-hermit existence." By this time he had already met Peter Orlofsky, then a student living with the painter Robert Lavigne in North Beach, and Ginsberg's increasing involvement with Orlofsky disturbed the woman he was living with. The eventual result — again not following too long after the episode with Dr. Hicks — was that Ginsberg left affluent Nob Hill for downtown, Montgomery Street, to live with Orlofsky. And soon after these dramatic shifts in his life he began writing "Howl."

Yet Ginsberg's account of these events sounds suspiciously like a fantasy of a magical cure, and a reading of the journals he kept at the time reveals that even chronology has been transformed a bit to promote the myth of the Breakthrough.[6] Actually, Ginsberg continued to work at his market research job for three or four months *after* he moved in with

Orlofsky and in so far as his journals reveal his mood at the time, they suggest he felt depressed, not liberated, when he lost his job. Moreover, while Ginsberg strongly implies that his therapy (and even the need for it) ended with his doctor's laying on of hands, the journals indicate that he continued in treatment, perhaps for as long as several months, including the time in which "Howl" was written. Moreover, the lengthy and almost daily entries from late 1954, when he first met Orlofsky, show that Ginsberg entered into this relationship with the same expectations of salvation and the same premonitions of disaster with which he then launched all his activities. An entry for April 20, 1955 — written four months after he had started living with Orlofsky — vividly conveys his mood at the time, and it was not one of emancipated self-acceptance:

> Not writing enough what can I say — rapid exchange of events, jobloss, peterloss, — isolation, no one I love loves me no contact, the isolation — facing loss of Jack [Kerouac] and Bill [Burroughs] as previous loss of contact with L — the myths held for the decade to fill time.[7]

"Howl" does affirm its author's capacity to survive an agonizing ordeal; yet the poem is charged with equally strong feelings of personal and literary failure, isolation and, most powerfully, loss, the feelings of this journal entry and many others like it. In fact, both "Howl" and "Kaddish" react to loss in precisely the way suggested in the journal — not by acceptance and working through the loss, but by idealizing, mythologizing, the lost object ("the myths held for the decade to fill time").

In addition, a more careful look at what Ginsberg tells of the transaction with his psychiatrist suggests a different interpretation from the one supplied by Ginsberg himself. In this encounter, he has clearly transferred onto the doctor, speaking to him as if he were speaking to his father, confessing his intimate feelings about work, about homosexuality, about "visionary" or hallucinatory experiences that he (like his mother) had experienced. He knows his father disapproves of all this, and he disapproves himself of these impulses, but projects such criticism onto the doctor: "I don't think you're going to find this very healthy and clear." He expects to be denounced, but what he hears is what he always wanted to hear from his father — permission. Permission is not, however, the only possible interpretation of the doctor's "Well, why don't you?" — a remark that could have led Ginsberg to examine his inhibitions and, ultimately, the origins of his wishes, all yearnings that, as we shall see, align him with the mother, against the father. The doctor, Ginsberg revealingly comments, gave him "the authority, so to speak, to be myself" — as if this authority were external to him.[8] In *Young Man Luther*, Erik Erickson points out that young men in a state of "identity diffusion," as Ginsberg clearly was at this time, often transform their therapy into "something like Jacob's struggle with the angel, a wrestling for a benediction which is to lead to the patient's conviction that he is an alive person, and, as such,

has a life before him."[9] Ginsberg, seemingly satisfied with a "benediction" rather than a fuller exploration of his wishes and fears,
temporarily wrestles himself "free" from guilt—but remains dependent
upon the authority of the forgiving father for permission to be himself. In
this exchange we can see some of the motives for Ginsberg's own later
adoption of the role of the tolerant, benign patriarch toward younger
people—while he himself continually turns toward older men (from Martin Buber to Swami Shivananada) in search for reassurance that he does
indeed have the authority to be himself, a right to a life of his own.

It should come as no surprise that by virtue of moving across the
country and acquiring an idealized father figure in his doctor, Ginsberg
had accomplished a less than complete break with his past. Both the
removal to a "safe" distance and the supportive context of therapy
probably helped him more to explore, rather than shed, the past, and it
was the very insistence of his private life as *the* material for his poetry that
pushed Ginsberg away from the predominant idea of the poem as impersonal artifact and toward a sense of the poem as confessional outpouring.
In reality, the Ginsberg of the late fifties manifests a powerful wish to
strike out on his own, along with an equally powerful fear of freedom. A
poem like "Howl" angrily asserts the "real" self of its author, the "angel-
headed hipster" persecuted by social and paternal authority, and the
poem does so with a kind of tormented exhilaration that suggests the
release of long-repressed feelings. More a cry of pain than of anger, "Kaddish," an elegy for Ginsberg's mother, also seeks to affirm a new and
separate life for the poet. Yet for all of the rebelliousness of "Howl" and all
the protestations of accepted loss in "Kaddish," both poems view independent life (in the language of the journal) as "isolation" and "loss."
Independence and submission, struggling toward the future and being
drawn back into the past: such are the conflicts that inform the best of
Ginsberg's poetry—in ways that we can see even more clearly by
examining the dynamics of his attachments to both his parents.

Anyone who has met Louis Ginsberg or heard him read his poems
at one of the joint readings he's given with his son will have encountered
a short, sturdy man well into his seventies, with large inquiring eyes and
a slightly frowning, rather oppressed expression. At first glance he seems,
in his poems as well as his person, a modest and mild man, a very likely
candidate for just that kindly, forgiving father that Ginsberg wished for,
a man whose weakness might be a reluctance to assert his authority rather
than in withholding his sympathy. Yet the attitude of mutual respect
which the two men now display toward each other has the quality of an
uneasy truce which, if unlikely to break into open hostilities is still filled
with critical sniping from both sides. At least this is the impression created
by Jane Kramer in her *Allen Ginsberg in America*, especially in her report
of a Sunday morning conversation in Paterson, prior to one of their

father/son reading performances. Louis inquires if Allen has "some good clothes for the reading tonight," twits his son for not being home enough, scolds him for not writing enough when away, denounces the lack of discipline in Allen's life and poetry, and alludes uneasily to his son's greater fame. Allen himself, showing perhaps more discipline than his father credits him for, responds with gentle tolerance, even when the issues become a little more charged. At one point, after Allen's friend Maretta announces that her *sadhana* is hashish, Mr. Ginsberg asks,

> "What's with this Maretta? Why can't you bring home a nice Jewish girl?"
>
> Ginsberg, laughing, threw up his hands, "For the love of God, Louis," he said, "here for years you've been saying, 'Please, just bring home a *girl* for a change,' and now that I do, you want a *Jewish* one?"
>
> "You're such an *experimenter*, Allen," Mr. Ginsberg said. "Tibetan Buddhist girl friends. Swamis, Drugs. All this talk from you about pot — 'It's so elevating, Louis. So ecstatic. My soul is outside my body. I see ultimate reality.' " Mr. Ginsberg frowned. "You know what I say? I say, 'Allen, take it easy.' "[10]

With Louis in his seventies and Allen nearing 40, the father still does not accept the son's style of independence, while the son's experimental style itself seems arrived at as a direct challenge to the father's authority and a test of his love. In this exchange the most sensitive and persistent issues between the two are touched on — family loyalty, drugs, homosexuality, visions of ultimate reality — in a manner that suggests a mollifying (here through humor) of conflicts that were earlier expressed with much more acrimony. In John Clellon Holmes' novel of the Beat Generation, *Go* — a book he says he tried to make as factually accurate as possible — the conversations between David Stofsky (Ginsberg) and his father seem to represent the original clashes, ritualistically repeated on a much later Sunday morning in Paterson.

> When [Stofsky] got home, he announced to his father that he had "visions," and when this brought forth little more than a pseudo-literary reaction, he appended, reckoning on its effect, that he was afraid he was going mad. His father rewarded him with the same sort of hysterical outburst that had seized him when, after several weeks of hesitant feelers, Stofsky had confessed his homosexuality. The two had an uneasy relationship anyway, at the bottom of which was mutual distrust, and when they were together they invariably squabbled over philosophical matters or Stofsky's "evil companions of the city" (as his father called them).[11]

The Allen Ginsberg Archives at Columbia contain an incomplete but still quite extensive correspondence between the father and son, dating from Allen's days at Columbia in the mid 1940s down to the early seventies. Much of the correspondence is given over to intricate and often heated political, moral, and literary debates. At a time when his son, still an undergraduate, was self-consciously identifying himself as a decadent and ardently reading such advanced modern thinkers as Gide, Spengler, Rimbaud, and Baudelaire, Louis advised: "A little of the Greek ideal of

moderation would do you no harm, m'lad";[12] and the father's perspective
can be briefly characterized as a deliberate cultivation of a moderate,
well-balanced, practical approach to life, though with a decided tilt
toward the cautionary in his dealings with his son. Once in a while, the
father explodes. As late as 1955, with Allen nearing 30, Louis wrote: "All
your vehement, vaporous, vituperations of rebellion move me not one jot.
Your attitude is irresponsible — and it stinks."[13] In a much earlier letter,
probably written during Ginsberg's second year at Columbia, the father
proposes the safety of accommodation and warns against precisely those
"deviant" routes his son was to take up.

> Even if normal values are rationalizations as well as abnormal ones, the
> latter, as normal values *qua* normal ones, result in a better and safer ad-
> justment to society and a greater integration of the person. According to
> your blanket statement, you would bracket the rationalizations of a
> homosexual or an insane person as satisfactory for society and for the per-
> son. The homosexual and the insane person is a menace to himself and to
> society. Danger and disaster lie that way! Your clever verbal solutions are
> incongruous with [the] reality of life. You are developed intellectually;
> but, emotionally, you lag.[14]

In his letters, as in his poetry, Louis Ginsberg's manner is characteristically sententious; but his timeless truths are often avowedly based
either on the authority of his greater experience in the world or appeals to
the "safety" of his position rather than its intrinsic value. The letters show
a genuine concern for a troublesome son, but it is also easy to see how his
son might get the impression that the father holds that truth can be
arrived at by carefully examining both sides of every question, then
coming down resoundingly in favor of the status quo. The trouble with
Allen's undergraduate literary hero Rimbaud, his father tells him, is that
the French poet sought "*absolute* moral values" rather than "*adequate*
moral values."[15] At about the same time, just after reading Karl Shapiro's
Essay on Rime, Louis asserted that, of course, modern poets reject the
"superstitions in religious faith" and they detect the hypocrisies beneath
the surface mores of contemporary society, BUT they should not leap to
pessimistic conclusions: they must remain "clear-headed" enough (unlike
Allen) to reject "decadence" as well and opt for "pragmatic values."
"Concluding, I say, Allen, suspend your judgment; walk balanced between the seen world and the unseen one; and take care of your health!"[16]
In fact, in the letter warning against Rimbaud, Louis had pronounced
that one "must resign himself to pragmatic values or commit suicide."[17]

But the son, who later was to solve the problem of values by adopting a "religious faith," not only refused to suspend his judgment; he asserted radical views, declaring, for instance, all modern civilization corrupt
and disintegrating. Such views the father dismisses, in a key term, as "off-
balance."[18] It is clear that each, questioning the other's love, questions the
other's sense of reality and demands that the other "see things as I do." A

visionary poem sent to Louis in 1958 is judged as "brilliantly myopic."[19]
In their long cold war political debate beginning in the late fifties, Allen is
accused of distorted *vision*, which makes him too harsh on the United
States and too easy on Soviet Russia. And in their ongoing literary arguments, attitudes of parental caution again clash with adolescent egotism
and rebellion. The older man conceives of poetry as a practical craft,
generated by emotion and shaped by individual vision but designed to effect immediate communication with a fairly wide audience and hence
comfortably drawing on traditional resources of technique and language.
Louis Ginsberg, a steadfast traditionalist after 40 years of modernist experiment, likes verse "neat,/ Exact,/ Compact—/ To file/ My style/ And
pare/ It bare";[20] but the son who, as we shall see, feels he can only really
identify himself in acts that shatter established boundaries (of self, of
literary form), insists on poetic means that are more ample, more
free—and more grandiose. In a follow-up letter on the Shapiro poem,
Louis attacks modernist verse as "willfully obscure," unnecessarily
creating a "gulf between the poet and the intelligent reader."[21] In his
view, "the ideal of a poem is that it give a general meaning to the many
and a deeper and more complex experience to the few," an ideal enacted
in his own practice.[22] Moreover, the letters frequently offer comments on
exchanged poems: Allen's earliest verses are often praised, but just as often criticized as too "knotty," "impacted," "inchoate"—in a word, obscure.[23] Again the message is that the son should quit his pretentious inaccessibility, his literary decadence, and accommodate himself to his
audience. "Not bad advice," anyone who has read these poems might conclude, but it no doubt struck the young poet as philistine old fogeyism.
Allen's poems are faulted, however, on deeper than stylistic grounds; their
"false assumptions" about life are questioned as well.[24] A key instance is
Louis Ginsberg's reaction to "Howl," a poem in which his son publicly
admitted to the very hallucinations, drug use, and homosexuality his
father had warned him against. Significantly, Ginsberg sent a copy of the
poem to his father not too long after its completion, as if the poem, far
from being simply a pure and naked confession of Ginsberg's inmost soul,
made some kind of hostile reference, and perhaps an appeal, to the father,
who responded with a characteristically balanced assessment. " 'Howl,' "
he wrote "is a wild, volcanic, troubled, extravagant, turbulent,
boisterous, unbridled outpouring, intermingling gems and flashes of pic-
turesque insight with slag and debris of scoriac matter. It has violence; it
has life; it has *vitality*. In my opinion, it is a one-sided neurotic view of
life; it has not enough glad, Whitmanian affirmations."[25] The poem does
have emotional force, vitality, BUT its vision of life is, again, off-balance,
sick—"one-sided" and "neurotic" in its angry disillusionment.

　　In view of the deep, persistent, and often acrimonious conflicts between the two men, it is tempting to read "Moloch," the wrathful child-

devouring deity of "Howl," as an angry representation of the father. But to derive from the poem a picture of the author as the essentially innocent victim of sadistic, persecutory authorities is to derive exactly the picture the author would like us to carry from the poem. "Howl" may be an honest confession of Ginsberg's conscious feelings at the time he wrote it, but many of the poem's rebellious attitudes actually serve as a defense against feelings that he is less able or willing to admit. It is true that Louis Ginsberg became the focus for many of his son's resentments, and while many of these grievances really derived from other sources, the anger also had some genuine basis in reality, as did his criticisms of the social system. Even their correspondence, where conflicts might be more in abeyance than in personal encounters, reveals paternal vituperation and ultimatums — e.g., a letter sent to Allen in the summer of 1948 which consisted simply of the sentence "Exorcise Neal," a reference to Ginsberg's erotic attachment to Neal Cassady at the time[26] — and the father seems to have insisted upon the son's successful completion of college and his becoming, as Allen put it, "a fine upstanding completely virile son."[27] Moreover, the father often questions not just his son's judgments but his very mental balance, a sensitive issue given his mother's history of psychotic illness.

Yet as Allen feared his father as a severe judge and angry persecutor, it is also clear that he felt a deep attachment and admiration for Louis Ginsberg, the origin of the recurrent image of the idealized, tender father in his poetry. It was his father, after all, who introduced Ginsberg to poetry and literature, an area in which Louis himself seemed to display real mastery and which his son was to make his own life's work. Moreover, Naomi Ginsberg was a mother who was often emotionally or even physically absent — or frighteningly present. As Louis Ginsberg remembers in a memoir called "My Son the Poet,"

> In the early years of my marriage, a shadow of sorrow fell on our family. My wife, Naomi, somehow developed a neurosis, which, as the years went on, thickened into a psychosis. She would spend two or three years in a sanitarium, then I'd take her out for half a year or a year. After that, ominous hints of her worsening condition made me take her back.

Once, when he had decided to take her back to the hospital, she threatened, then attempted suicide, slashing her wrists in the bathroom.

> She opened [the door] and came out with blood oozing at both wrists. They were surface cuts, so I bandaged them and got her to bed. The boys stood there, shivering in their night clothes, panic in their eyes. What traumas, I thought, might sink into them and burrow into their psyches.[28]

In view of Naomi Ginsberg's illness, apt to make her rigid in her expectations of her son's behavior and unpredictable in her own, it is likely that her son turned to his father as a refuge, hoping to find both a point of stability in the family and a benign protector. And it is in such yearnings for (and memories of) a tender attachment with a tolerant older male that we find the beginnings of Ginsberg's later search for a kind of maternal father, of the sort he felt he'd found in Dr. Hicks in San Francisco and in such literary mentors as Whitman and Blake. "The Father is merciful," Ginsberg ecstatically proclaims in "Transcription of Organ Music"; what he continually seeks is some mild, accepting, Christ-like saviour, who will protect him from the terrifying aspects of the mother and offer the tender acceptance that she does not. Seeking salvation from the father (rather than reconciliation with him) inevitably led to disappointment, but even during the bristly period of his adolescence, Ginsberg clearly courted the older man's love and approval by striving to perform "good works." If Allen could condemn his father's assessment of one of his short stories as "a symptom of the smug normalcy of the bourgeois intellectual attitude," he assured his father in the same letter that he was no longer cutting classes, indeed was dressing decorously (even wearing a conservative black tie) and had "started to really get an education, making the most of the College by returning unread to the library" all his volumes of Gide and Baudelaire.[29] Similarly, when he wrote a few years later that he was post-poning his final term at Columbia, he explained that he was doing so in order to save enough money to start psychoanalysis, a course earlier suggested by the father himself. "Don't worry about me becoming a per-manent wastrel just because I'm trying to 'save my soul' as scientifically as possible," he wrote.[30]

Such yearnings to yield to the father (or his surrogate, the psychiatrist) also threaten Ginsberg, however real his attachment and his desire to please. For Ginsberg's basic image of the father, during adolescence and early manhood, is neither that of the powerful foe nor that of the benign protector, but that of a timid, rather withdrawn man, one who, with his cult of practicality and normality, has himself surren-dered to external pressures and is thus finally feared not because he is too powerful, but because he is not strong and certain enough to save his son. The picture of Louis Ginsberg we get in "Kaddish" is that of an intro-verted, neglectful man, frightened, worried, and humiliated by his wife's paranoid hallucinations but whose attention, it seems, can only be caught by such apocalyptic means. In this view, mother and son are linked as vic-tims of the father's weakness and neglect; the final impression of the father is one of ineffectuality, inconsequence: Naomi Ginsberg, the psychotic mother rather than the poet-father, is celebrated as her son's muse. Moreover, Louis Ginsberg was a literary intellectual and writer who taught English in the high schools of Paterson and who published poems in places like the editorial pages of the *New York Times* and the *Herald-Tribune*. What may have seemed like impressive accomplishments to a very young boy must have come with the increasing sophistication (and grandiosity) of adolescence, to signify a singular lack of daring and ambition. It is not too surprising, therefore, to find in the introduction that Ginsberg wrote to the father's collection, *Morning in Spring* (1968), that beneath the affectionate respect with which the now world-famous son writes of his father, we should hear persistent hints of disappointment. "Living a generation with lyrics wrought by my father, some stanzas settle in the memory as perfected," Ginsberg opens.[31] This (uncharacteristically) deliberate, well-formed sentence carefully defines an attitude of respectful but hardly enthusiastic admiration, a striking contrast to Ginsberg's frequently effusive praise of such of his contemporaries, like Jack Kerouac, who share his own ultimate assumptions. The son, remembering "some stanzas" but apparently no whole poems, is clearly not going out on any critical limbs for the old man, whose well-balanced views are now turned back on him. As soon as Louis Ginsberg is introduced, he is pitted (in a losing battle) against W.C. Williams. " 'In this mode perfection is basic,' W.C. Williams wrote, excusing himself for rejecting my own idealised iambic rhymes sent him for inspection" (p. 11). Imitating Louis' idealized verses, Ginsberg went astray — until he was saved by a bolder, and more successful guide. In fact, in the first three pages of the introduction, Ginsberg mentions Williams and Pound four times each, every time making an invidious comparison between their boldness and his father's timidity. Says Ginsberg of his father's kind of poetry:

> I have resisted this mode as an anachronism in my own time — the anachronism of my own father writing the outworn verse of previous century voices, reechoing the jaded music and faded effect or sentiment of that music in a dream-life of his own sidestreet under dying phantom elms of Paterson, New Jersey — at the very time that Paterson itself was (having been articulated to its very rock-strata foundations and aboriginal waterfall voice in W.C. Williams' epic) degenerating into a XX Century Mafia-Police-Bureaucracy-Race-War-Nightmare-TV-Squawk suburb [p. 14].

While Williams dauntlessly combines primitive solidity with an awareness of contemporary social reality, Louis Ginsberg *neglects* the present, timidly withdrawing into the "dream-life" of his peaceful suburban street. It is not just that this establishes him as an irrelevant "anachronism," an unreliable guide for a young man entering a bewildering world; the cost of such withdrawal is finally the loss of real autonomy and even life. The father's guiding voice is hollow, a mere echo, not *his own* voice: Daddy is nobody. All the language associated with Louis Ginsberg in this passage — "anachronism," "outworn," "jaded," "faded," "dying phantom elms" — suggests death, as if the life had been sapped out of him. The son may take a certain satisfaction in such diminishing thoughts of that parental authority whose judgments he feared. Yet disappointment with the defeated actual father generates the "Pater Omnipotens Aeterna Deus" of "Howl," the "Lord" of such poems as "Kaddish," "Laughing Gas" and "Magic Psalm" — all fantasies of an all-

powerful father whose strength *can* heal and direct the writer. So, during
the early phase of Ginsberg's career, the earthly father, whose "failure"
the son anxiously seeks to avoid for himself, becomes a negative model,
ironic source for the bardic grandiosity, literary experimentation and
daring self-exposures that characterize his son's poetry starting with
"Howl." In fact, what Ginsberg appears to have done in 1955 was to take
up his father's medium of communication (poetry) and, declaring it
hollow and dead, transformed it by infusing it with the hallucinatory
visions and human vulnerability of his mother.

* * *

> "You still haven't finished with your mother."
>   Elise Cowen to Allen Ginsberg, after typing
>   the manuscript to "Kaddish."[32]
>   "If only you knew
>   How your poet son, Allen
>   Raves over the world,
>   Crazed for love of you!"
>   Louis Ginsberg, "To a Mother Buried."[33]

One reason for Ginsberg's disenchantment with his father is that
he often looked at the older man through the terrified — and rancorous — eyes of his mother. In examining the kind of grip Naomi Ginsberg had on her son's feelings the key document is "Kaddish," a con-
fessional/visionary/elegiac poem in five parts in which Ginsberg (like
Sylvia Plath in "Daddy") attempts to transform literature into therapeutic
magic: to exorcise the ghost of a parental influence. Neither of the two
poems, for all their literary brilliance, succeeds in delivering the poet
from the agonizing conflicts that generate the work in the first place,
although Ginsberg comes closer. "Daddy" may heighten hatred into a
form of hard eloquence, but the poem is pure anger and destruction, with
the renounced father simply transformed from a god-like to a satanic
figure: Plath, whose father died when she was just nine, was never able to
make the crucial step of perceiving him as a human rather than a
mythical figure. In "Kaddish" Ginsberg confronts his anger at his mother's
abstraction from life, her abandonment of him in madness, his disgust
with her careless physical habits, his fascination with her sexually seductive manner with him, his guilt about his treatment of her during her
breakdowns — "Kaddish" lays bare all these feelings and then proceeds to
a declaration of love for Naomi Ginsberg. In the poem there is, as Ginsberg announces at the start of Part II, a "release of particulars," and
Naomi Ginsberg is encountered with elaborate and moving specificity, as
a complex human figure.[34] Yet it is also true that by the end Ginsberg has
not resolved his divided feelings about his "fatal Mama" (p. 27) as much as

he claims; the poem tempts us to think, like certain forms of therapy, that to get feelings out is to resolve them. But in fact the poem, far from moving toward idealization of the mother, culminates with an apotheosis of death (as release from the agonizing conflicts of life) and a yearning for fusion with this lost parent.

Naomi Ginsberg, a member of the Communist Party from the time of her youth, believed her life was in danger from political authorities such as Hitler, Roosevelt, and the F.B.I. as well as family figures, notably her mother and her husband. Her fears characteristically concerned an invasion of her self by some external, invisible, and malevolent agency that could subtly creep inside and possess her: poison gas filtering its way under the door, the manipulation of her thoughts by means of three bars inserted in her back and wired to her brain by the F.BI. during one of her stays in the hospital. In "Kaddish" Ginsberg seems to understand these fantasies of political persecution as extensions of sexual fears and, though Ginsberg himself never says so, it would be natural for a young boy to equate these fears of violation with some assault by the father. In any case, Naomi Ginsberg's paranoia was the dark side of what her son calls her "mad idealism" (p.24), her intense yearning for the Pure, the Beautiful, the Ideal evident in her nostalgia for the innocence of her girlhood, her political utopianism (which inspired her to write Communist fairy tales — p. 16), her alternately dreamy and paranoid paintings ("Humans sitting on the grass in some Camp No-Worry summers yore — saints with droopy faces and long-ill-fitting pants" — p.25), her romantic songs played on the mandoline ("Last night the nightingale woke me/ Last night when all was still/ it sang in the golden moonlight/ from the wintry hill"). As a boy Ginsberg must have admired her intensity, been awed by the loftiness of her idealism, and shared her fears of the father's "assaults."

Yet both the fears and the longings of Naomi Ginsberg dissociated her from immediate emotional realities; what made her admirable also made her distant, bewildering, even terrifying — and made her son angry. She, too, neglected Allen. "I will think nothing but beautiful thoughts," says Naomi in "Kaddish," and she tells her son of seeing God the day before: "I cooked supper for him. I made him a nice supper — lentil soup, vegetables, bread & butter — miltz...." At that very moment she is serving Allen "a plate of cold fish — chopped raw cabbage dript with tapwater — smelly tomatoes — week-old health food ... I can't eat it for nausea sometimes" (p. 2). "Kaddish" frequently refers to such nausea-inspiring meals. Naomi was not providing Allen with true sustenance: a son cannot live on beautiful thoughts alone. Moreover, not only did his mother fail to take care of him, Ginsberg was forced at crucial points in her illness to take care of *her*. In Allen's version at least, his father and older brother evaded the reality and responsibilities of Naomi's madness, thus leaving the youngest son with the excrutiating practical problems of dealing with her illness. Both times she was hospitalized during Ginsberg's lifetime, he was the one who had to take her to a rest home or, worse, call the police for help. The first of these two episodes took place when Ginsberg was just 12. At exactly that delicate point of transition between boyhood and manhood, between home and the world, independence and responsibility were thrust on him, leaving him frightened, resentful, uncertain, and tormented with guilt. At that time, when his mother started hallucinating "a mystical assassin from Newark" (p. 13), Ginsberg, who had stayed home from school because she seemed so nervous and distraught, called a doctor, who recommended a rest home. After a long, humiliating bus ride, after being thrown out of one rest home (because Naomi hid in the closet and demanded a blood transfusion), Allen finally left her alone in an attic room, got on the next bus home and "lay my head in the last seat, depressed — the worst yet to come? — abandoning her, rode in torpor — I was only 12."

> 12 riding the bus at nite thru New Jersey, have left Naomi to Parcae in Lakewood's haunted house — left to my own fate — sunk in a seat — all violins broken — my heart sore in my ribs — mind was empty — Would she were safe in her coffin — [p. 15]

The sequence of feeling here — from guilt at abandoning her, to pity for his own isolated fate, to exhaustion and apathy and finally to the wish that she would die — reveals Ginsberg's desire to be relieved of his mother and the conflicts she triggers in him. And the worst *was* yet to come; that night,

> the telephone rang at 2AM — Emergency — she'd gone mad — Naomi hiding under the bed screaming bugs of Mussolini — Help! Louis! Buba! Fascists! Death! — the landlady frightened — old fag attendent screaming back at her [p. 17].

Ginsberg, who had already been criticized by his father for leaving her there, asks himself, "my fault, delivering her to solitude?" It's a possible question: Ginsberg nowhere says exactly why he left her, it was not something he *had* to do, he describes himself sitting on her bed "waiting to escape," and has wished her dead. The situation, filled with painful stresses even for an adult, must have seemed unbearably complex for a boy of 12.

Later, visiting her in the hospital, Ginsberg was confronted with Naomi "begging my 13-year-old boy mercy," saying

> 'Take me home' — I went alone sometimes looking for the lost Naomi, taking Shock — and I'd say, "No, you're crazy Mama, — Trust the Drs." — [p. 19],

and still later, just before her last hospitalization in the late forties, as Naomi imagines herself hounded by Louis and her own mother,

> ' — No wires in the room!' — I'm yelling at her — last ditch, Eugene listening on the bed — what can he do to escape that fatal Mama — 'You've been

away from Louis for years already — Grandma's too old to walk — '
We're all alive at once then — even me & Gene & Naomi in one mythological Cousinesque room — screaming at each other in the Forever — I in
Columbia jacket, she half undressed.
    I banging against her head which saw Radios, Sticks, Hitlers — the
gamut of Hallucinations — for real — her own universe — no road that goes
elsewhere — to my own — No America, not even a world — [pp. 26-27]

Even at this point much later in adolescence, Ginsberg emphasizes the
way his mother's madness removed her into a private, hallucinatory
world ("her own universe") where, beyond all hysterical screaming, she
remained inaccessible ("no road that goes nowhere"). In her madness
Naomi triumphantly transcended reality, but abandoned her son, who,
similarly deserted by his father and brother, was left in the position of
asserting reality, angrily denying the validity of her visions and delivering
her over to those very anxieties — doctors and police — she most feared. In
a situation filled with exhausting stresses Ginsberg reacted with
remarkable strength. In "Kaddish" he asks, "Louis what happened to your
heart then?" — when he was confronted with his terrified wife shrieking
that he had called out the "poison cops":[11] Have you been killed by Naomi's
ecstacy?" Allen was not but he suspected a certain hardness in his
strength, this intensifying the guilt already latent in the situation; "It's my
fault," he must have felt, "if I had loved my mother more, this wouldn't
have happened to her — and to me." As an adolescent, Ginsberg was left
alone, searching for that "lost Naomi" who nurtured him as a young boy,
fearing those ecstatic hallucinations of the "fatal Mama" that seemed to
kill all feeling between them, and yet longing to join her in the dramatic
intensity and transcendence of her madness.
    From the retrospective point of view of the adult poet, the ideal
way to handle this excruciating situation would be to accept a certain
amount of anger and vindictiveness as natural, to emphasize the positive
strength and tenderness that Ginsberg did show and so to view a certain
amount of "hardness" as a prerequisite for self-survival; but this is by no
means what we find in "Kaddish," where unresolved feelings of guilt
prompt the poet to exorcise her spirit and be rid of her at last — a
maneuver that breaks down, however, in view of his even stronger desire
to return and fuse with her in death. The deepest sources of this longing
we can see in a crucial passage of "Kaddish":

One time I thought she was trying to make me come lay her — flirting to
herself at sink — lay back on huge bed that filled most of the room, dress
up round her hips, big slash of hair, scars of operations, pancreas, belly
wounds, abortions, appendix, stitching of incisions pulling down in the
fat like hideous thick zippers — ragged long lips between her legs — What,
even, smell of asshole? I was cold — later revolted a little, not
much — seemed perhaps a good idea to try — know the Monster of the
Beginning Womb — Perhaps — that way. Would she care? She needs a
lover [p. 24].

At first glance this passage seems a daring revelation of an incest wish and a shockingly realistic description of the mother's body. But what we really see here is how one post-Freudian writer, pretending to be open and at ease with incestuous desire, affects sophisticated awareness as a defense against longings and anxieties. The lines are charged with feelings that the poet, far from "confessing out," appears eager to deny. Ginsberg's tone of voice is noticeably more defensive than frank: he assumes an attitude of detached superiority toward the scene — idealizing the act into a mythical/ psychological experiment ("know the Monster of the Beginning Womb") performed more for his mother's emotional gratification than his: "She needs a lover." All of the sexual initiative is attributed to Naomi, allowing her son, innocent in his sophistication, to view himself as a superior, liberated, and compassionate individual, beyond conventional moral restraints and thus willing and able to give a little help to one of his friends. Holding himself above this emotionally charged situation, Ginsberg seeks to deny both the powerful attraction he feels toward his mother — as well as the fears he experiences as soon as he imagines the possibility of acting on it. The persistent emphasis on scars, particularly on wounds made by cutting, suggests an association between the female body and mutilation, an association frequent among male homosexuals who, perceiving the woman's body as the castrated body of a man and frightened at the prospect of a similar fate for themselves, are more comfortable with sexual partners who also have penises. Immediately following the passage I have quoted, Ginsberg dramatically shifts the subject, inserting first the Hebrew words of the "Kaddish" (a mourning ritual) and then turning to the story of his father. It is as if the very thought of incestuous wishes immediately provoked thoughts of death and the presence of the father, who might administer just that punishment his son most fears. In fact, in Part I of "Kaddish" Naomi is lamented as a victim who "fought the knife — lost/ Cut down" by a heartless father wielding a "sharp icicle" (pp. 10-11). Yet in his recollection of incestuous yearnings, Ginsberg's deepest fears seem inspired less by Louis than by Naomi herself. When he does turn to his father in the succeeding lines, he presents his most poignant picture of Louis: "hurt with 20 years Naomi's mad idealism" — father and son linked as victims of the all-powerful mother (p. 24). Moreover, Naomi's womb is imagined as "monster" and images throughout the poem reenforce our suspicion that it is a *devouring* monster. In Part IV Ginsberg speaks of his mother's pubic hair as a "beard" (a trite image of which he is inordinately fond) — as if her vagina were a mouth (p. 34); and in Part II, on his later visit to his mother in the hospital, he imagines the door as a "crotch," on the other side of which lies death. The quotation of the Hebrew words of the "Kaddish" suggest, on the deepest level, Ginsberg's association of incest with death. It is as if, were he to get too close to his mother, she would swallow him up — though he can't finally separate himself from her either. In "Kaddish," as in all of Ginsberg's earlier poetry, the conflict is one of separation versus unity. Separation is never independence but always an absolute, sterile, and frustrating isolation, as in the passage where all members of the family are hysterically screaming at each other yet with each of them locked in a private world of his or her own, incommunicado. The separation is so radical that it cannot be resolved by mere verbal or emotional communication ("her own universe — no road that goes elsewhere"); so Ginsberg longs to be delivered from this agonizing isolation by a kind of self-annihilating fusion with the mother. From this point of view we can understand his incestuous desires as expressing Ginsberg's wish to get inside his mother and see things as she does. The progression of Ginsberg's early career, in fact, is toward a closer and closer identification with her paranoid politics, her hallucinatory visions, even her physical sloppiness and sexual "looseness."

In "Kaddish" — as in "Howl" — absolute isolation alternates with absolute fusion, each poem seeking "resolution" in spiritual transcendence, apocalyptic vision, a total fusion that could only be realized in the static perfection of death. As "Kaddish" proceeds, it comes less and less to accept the loss of Naomi, more and more to yearn for union with her in death or, while life remains, to incorporate her vision as the poet's own. "Die/ If thou woulds't be with that which thou dost seek," says Shelley in the lines from "Adonais" that Ginsberg significantly chose for his epigraph. The poem not only celebrates death as deliverance from the frightening and frustrating separateness of human life; it also identifies Naomi as the source of that vision of death. In this rich sense Naomi is Allen's inspiration, his "muse."

> O glorious muse that bore me from the womb, gave suck first
> mystic life & taught me talk and music, from whose pained
> head I first took Vision —
> Tortured and beaten in the skull — What mad hallucinations
> of the damned that drive me out of my own skull to seek
> Eternity till I find Peace for Thee, O Poetry — and for all
> humankind call on the Origin
> Death which is the mother of the universe! [pp. 29-30]

In just these few lines, Ginsberg characteristically moves from a celebration of his mother as "glorious muse" to thoughts of her suffocating hold on him, so that in the end she is conflated with death, at once feared and sought. At first Ginsberg asserts that the *real* Naomi was not the overweight, scarred, lonely woman locked in a room of a lunatic asylum — but the mother of his earliest memories who fed him physically and spiritually: "gave suck first mystic life & taught me talk and music" — creating an intimacy so complete that he seemed to see with her eyes. Yet such union of mother and son has its threatening aspect; her vision of things is "pained," and her life suggests to her son that the only way out of suffering is through a kind of immolation in it—by being pained into "Vision." Such destructive-redemptive gestures are repeated throughout Ginsberg's poetry, and they derive not just from a self-punishing masochism, but from the need to find experiences extreme enough, painful enough, to shatter the boundaries of the separate self. In this passage the modifying phrase "tortured and beaten in the skull" floats free of any precise referent, allowing it to refer to both Naomi and Allen, joined in suffering, in those moments when they "lose their head." Her suffering, it appears, is his. Yet as such union is hard to bear, so is separation: the curious phrase, "bore me from the womb," makes it sound as if he were *cast out* from her unwillingly at birth. And this kind of resistance to a life of his own is yet another reason why Ginsberg himself is "tortured and beaten in the skull"—i.e., tortured and defeated when locked in the skull of private consciousness. Here, a sentence that began as an apostrophe to Naomi as "glorious muse" and which we expect to continue as some form of prayer to her breaks off to frame a question ("What mad hallucinations," etc.), a question that in turn is never completed as it turns into an agonized and helpless cry: what *drives* him to be like her, to lose his head in "mad hallucinations" like her own! The answer is that both her presence and her absence drive him out of his skull: when near, she absorbs him into her vision; but once separated, he is driven to return, and the only way he can return is by sharing her vision—by fusing with her. Either route ends in a kind of death for the separate personality, but Death itself (now his muse) is affirmed as a release from the frustrating boundaries of the self, and as allowing a peaceful and final merge with the mother.

During his mother's seizures the adolescent Ginsberg had tried to break through to her by asserting a realistic point of view (" 'No wires in the room!'—I'm yelling at her"), a line of approach that ended in rage, frustration, hysteria. But Ginsberg closes the long autobiographical Part II of "Kaddish" by recollecting a moment of communication with Naomi, one that came, "mystically," just after her death. While living in a cottage in Berkeley in 1957, having (he hoped) left familial strifes behind him in the East, Ginsberg dreamed of his mother's spirit—"that, thru life, in what form it stood in that body, ashen or manic, gone beyond joy—/ near its death—with eyes—was my own love in its form, the Naomi, my mother on earth still" and wrote a "long letter" declaring this love "& wrote hymns to the mad." A few days later he received a telegram from his brother, informing him of his mother's death; and two days after *that*, he got a letter from his mother, the first he'd had from her in several years—a prophecy (seemingly) from beyond the grave. The letter wonderfully mixes conventional maternal advice with cryptic visionary utterances:

> "The key is in the window, the key is in the sunlight at the window — I
> have the key — Get married Allen don't take drugs — the key is in the bars,
> in the sunlight in the window.'

The key, according to the mother, is conventionality: "Get married Allen
don't take drugs." But in Part III of the poem Ginsberg picks up on the letter's visionary metaphors, the image of the flash of light that frees the self
from the locked room, the pained head — the prison of solitary consciousness.

> 'The key is in the sunlight at the window in the bars the key is
>   in the sunlight,'
> only to have come to that dark night on iron bed by stroke when
>   the sun gone down on Long Island
> and the vast Atlantic roars outside the great call of Being to its
>   own
> to come back out of the Nightmare — divided creation — with her head
>   lain on a pillow of the hospital to die
> — in one last glimpse — all Earth one everlasting Light in the familiar
>   blackout — no tears for this vision —
> But that the key should be left behind — at the window — the key in the sun-
>   light — to the living — that can take
> that slice of light in hand — and turn the door — and look back see
> Creation glistening backwards to the same grave, size of universe,
> size of the tick of the hospital's clock on the archway over the white door —
> [p. 33]

Naomi Ginsberg, inmate of asylums for many years now, victim of shock
treatments and strokes, locked alone in her room, further isolated by her
madness, lies in a "dark night" on an "iron bed" like a prisoner, a kind of
prisoner of life. As Ginsberg makes clear, it is not just the harrowing experiences of her life that make it nightmarish, it is the very condition of
living in a bounded, physical being — *"divided* creation" — that creates the
"Nightmare." In the midst of all this, Naomi *is* pained into vision, has her
glimpse of "everlasting Light," finds the key to the locked shelf. Yet the
key, as Ginsberg interprets it, is to see physical life, its ordeals, as unreal,
a dream — as brief and insignificant as the tick of the hospital clock. The
vision does not open, as in a Whitman or a Blake, a harmonizing of
physical and spiritual; rather it opts for the apocalyptic, the purely transcendent. The moment of vision, here, is the moment of death; and death
is the key, releasing us from the nighmare of a fleshy (and thus divided)
existence.

In "Kaddish" 's last two sections, Ginsberg shifts from detailed
narrative in long "broken paragraphs" to shorter, more intense liturgical
chants which attempt to let go of the memory of Naomi and accept her
loss.[35] Yet the very means by which Ginsberg comes to terms with her
death is by identifying as his own that very vision of life *as death* which

she had imposed on him from his earliest years. Section IV utters "farewell" to Naomi Ginsberg by cataloguing parts of her body, aspects of her life, that are expressive of her ordeal — as if her life were passing before his mind in final review. As the list proceeds, Ginsberg focuses on her eyes: "with your eyes of shock/ with your eyes of lobotomy/ with your eyes of divorce/ with your eyes of stroke/ with your eyes alone/ with your eyes/ with your eyes" (p. 35). Her eyes convey a kind of mute, helpless suffering and to look into them is to become transfixed, paralyzed *by her vision;* in fact, the emotional force of this section is not toward a "farewell," but to show the poet mesmerized by the Medusa-like glance of his mother. The poem's final section, likewise liturgical in manner, similarly depicts Ginsberg as helplessly transfixed by the memory of his mother. Section V begins as a visit to Naomi's grave and proceeds by alternating the cries of crows in the cemetery ("caw caw caw") with a religious chant ("Lord Lord Lord"). The crows evoke decomposition, the inevitable fate of life in the flesh, while the "Lord" is intended to define an eternal perspective within which such cruel realities can be accepted. But the poem's final line — "Lord Lord Lord caw caw caw Lord Lord Lord caw caw caw Lord" (p. 36) — conflates crow and Lord, temporal and eternal, as devourers, and the effect of the line, which Ginsberg once described as "pure emotive sound," is that of a cry, or a "howl," of a suffering victim.[36] Life, with its impersonal physical processes, its movement through a divided and often indifferent world — that world into which Ginsberg was unwillingly cast — is intolerable. Hence, the only way it can be borne is by seeing it through Naomi's eyes — as a "vision":

> caw caw all year my birth a dream caw caw New York the bus the broken shoe the vast highschool caw caw *all Visions of the Lord* [p. 36, my italics].

Whatever its agonies, life is merely a dream in the mind of an omnipotent Lord — a thought that, it seems, offers safety, if not childhood. Yet it is the threatening qualities of this divinity which are stressed ("great Eye that stares on All," "Grinder of giant Beyonds" — p. 36) and it is clear that this "Lord," with his powerful glance and his threat to devour, is ominous in precisely those ways Naomi is. In fact, all the poem's deific figures — the glorious muse, omnipotent Lord — dissolve into a single figure, "the Naomi," who is the "Origin/Death" — the "Fatal Mama."

A key result of the psychic conflict in the poem is a kind of formal tension. In seeking to link confessional and visionary modes, Ginsberg was advancing a poetic project that had begun with "Howl" and that would prove to be a generative one for contemporary poetry. Yet autobiographical and mystical motives are at odds with each other in "Kaddish." If Part II confronts us with a relentless "release of particulars" into powerful narrative, all remaining sections of the poem strive to chant those particulars into dream, Vision — a strategy that fails on at least two counts. In the first place, the need of the poet to get 'out of his head' in many respects signals a *surrender to*, rather than coming to terms with, the memories of Part II. In addition, most readers will, I think, leave the work more impressed with the psychic conflicts of II than the sought resolutions of the closing sections. Moreover, Ginsberg's account of the poem's composition in "How *Kaddish* Happened" implies the centrality of the second part and reveals that Ginsberg felt that he was in some sense "defeated" by the poem — i.e., by Naomi.[37] While individual sections of "Kaddish" were written spontaneously, some of them in drug-induced moments of "mad hallucination," long intervals separated the writing of these sections, the whole poem taking more than two years. Significantly, the order of composition went: first, part IV (the evocation of Naomi's mesmerizing stare), then a year later I and II, then some indefinite period after this, V; no mention is made of III. Most emphasis is given in the essay to the writing of II, which Ginsberg approached slowly, resistingly, yet felt he *had to* approach; Part II was written in 20 straight hours of effort after a night of no sleep, some mescaline and speed, listening to Ray Charles records and chanting aloud passages from Shelley's "Adonais" and the Hebrew "Kaddish": Afterward,

> I walked out in early blue dawn on to 7th Avenue & across town to my Lower East Side apartment — New York before sunrise has its own celebrated hallucinatory unreality. In the country getting up with the cows birds hath Blakean charm, in the megalopolis the same nature's hour is a science-fiction hell vision, even if you're a milkman. Phantom factories, unpopulated streets out of Poe, familiar nightclubs bookstores groceries dead.[38]

The essay's title, "How 'Kaddish' Happened," implies that the poem *happened to* Ginsberg, surfacing from the depths of his buried self — a familiar claim of romantic poets but one that here carries the added suggestion that the poem was *thrust upon* a somewhat resistant poet. At the same time Ginsberg's account of the writing of the poem depicts the poet — via exhaustion, drugs, and careful selection of urban setting and suitably elegiac literary texts — deliberately flagelating himself into vision, into communing with his dead mother. Both versions, of course, are true — true to his divided fear of and longing for the woman who gave him "mystic life." What Ginsberg sees when he wanders down 7th Avenue at dawn is the city seen through Naomi Ginsberg's terrified eyes; and it is also a landscape of loss — what life looks like to him without her: a hell vision of unbearable isolation in a cold, threatening environment.

After finally getting down a draft of the entire poem, Ginsberg tells us, he waited another year before even typing the manuscript, much less seeking publication. The poem seemed, he recalls, too massive, too messy and too private to reach an audience, suggesting that on an unconscious level the writing of the poem may have been an act of private communication between the poet and his "muse," like the letter he had received from her just after her death. In any case, "Kaddish," all too successfully recreating the overwhelming size, disorder, and inaccessibility of its subject, seemed to have "defeated" its author.

In these self-doubts we can hear the internalized voice of Louis Ginsberg, the side of Ginsberg that feared that identification with his mother's way of seeing things would leave him, like her, trapped in a private vision, with "no road that goes elsewhere." At this point, Ginsberg, showing that he may have derived more strength from the father than he liked to admit, sat down to the "patient scholar's task" of making the poem "shapely."[39] If he began by trying to bring the father's "dead" medium back to life by infusing it with the visions of his mother, it was his commitment to poetry that turned Ginsberg back toward the world, opened a road that did span the gap between private vision and external reality.

Of course, what Ginsberg himself stresses in his account of the composition of "Kaddish" is the need to go "all the way out" in order to capture a "continuous impulse," an emotional and creative thrust that would be stifled in a more orderly work.[40] In his view, poetic (and human) energy can only be generated by going out of one's skull — beyond the "dead form" of reality and back to the Origin, the mother, who turns out to be Death. On a human level such regressive longings mark a kind of defeat, at least the defeat of the quest for independence, for a life, of one's own. Yet "defeat like that is good for poetry," Ginsberg states.

> — you go so far out you don't know what you're doing, you lose touch with what's been done before by anyone, you wind up creating a new poetry-universe. "Make It New," saith Pound, "Invention," said W.C. Williams. That's the "Tradition" — a complete fuck-up so you're on your own.[41]

Such defeat does not guarantee good poetry; but in the literary atmosphere of the late 1950s — dominated by poetry that was self-consciously impersonal and traditionalistic — Ginsberg's breaking of established boundaries released a new life into contemporary American poetry.

For help in writing this essay I am indebted to Dr. Felix Ocko and Margaret Darby, both of Berkeley, California.

Notes

[1] Robert Creeley cites the new sense of form in "Howl" in his "Introduction to *The New Writing in the USA*," *A Quick Graph* (San Francisco, 1970), pp. 44-45 as do Galway Kinnell in "The Poetics of the Physical World," *Iowa Review*, II (Summer 1971), 115-16, and Adrienne Rich, "Talking with Adrienne Rich," *The Ohio Review*, XIII (Fall 1971), 28-46.

[2] All of these journals are part of the Allen Ginsberg Archives at Columbia University. Quotations from material in the collection are made with the kind permission of Allen Ginsberg and Columbia University.

[3] *Starting from San Francisco* (New York, 1967), p. 27.

[4] Jane Kramer, *Allen Ginsberg in America* (New York, 1970), pp. 39-40.

[5] Ibid., p. 42.

[6] See "Notebook, 1953-56" in the Allen Ginsberg Archives for information on this period in Ginsberg's life.

[7] Entry for April 20, 1955 in "Notebook 1953-56."

[8] *Allen Ginsberg in America*, p. 42.

[9] *Young Man Luther* (New York, 1958), p. 103.

[10] *Allen Ginsberg in America*, pp. 150-51.

[11] *Go* (New York, 1952), p. 108. The statement about accuracy is made in Holmes' *Nothing More to Declare* (New York, 1967), p. 56.

[12] Louis Ginsberg to Allen Ginsberg, August 8, 1945, in the Allen Ginsberg Archives. All subsequent correspondence cited is also from the Archives.

[13] Louis Ginsberg to Allen Ginsberg, December 12, 1955.

[14] Louis Ginsberg to Allen Ginsberg, n.d.

[15] Louis Ginsberg to Allen Ginsberg, November 2, 1945.

[16] Louis Ginsberg to Allen Ginsberg, October 29, 1945.

[17] Louis Ginsberg to Allen Ginsberg, November 2, 1945.

[18] Ibid.

[19] Louis Ginsberg to Allen Ginsberg, March 10, 1958.

[20] "Terse," in *Morning in Spring and Other Poems* (New York, 1970), p. 119.

[21] Louis Ginsberg to Allen Ginsberg, November 2, 1945.

[22] Louis Ginsberg to Allen Ginsberg, n.d. (but probably sometime in 1948).

[23] Ibid.

[24] Louis Ginsberg to Allen Ginsberg, March 10, 1958.

[25] Louis Ginsberg to Allen Ginsberg, May 27, 1956.

[26] Louis Ginsberg to Allen Ginsberg, July 11, 1948.

[27] Allen Ginsberg to Louis Ginsberg, September 3, 1947.

[28] Paterson *News*, Monday, June 2, 1969, p. 4.

[29] Allen Ginsberg to Louis Ginsberg, n.d. (but probably sometime in 1948).

[30] Allen Ginsberg to Louis Ginsberg, September 3, 1947.

[31] "Confrontation with Louis Ginsberg's Poems," in *Morning in Spring*, p. 11. Subsequent references are made in the text.

[32] "How 'Kaddish' Happened," in *The Poetics of the New American Poetry*, ed. Donald Allen and Warren Tallman (New York, 1973), p. 347.

[33] *Morning in Spring and Other Poems*, p. 93.

[34] *Kaddish and Other Poems*, (San Francisco, 1961), p. 13. Subsequent references are made in the text.

[35] "How 'Kaddish' Happened," p. 345.

[36] Ibid., p. 346.

[37] Ibid.

[38] Ibid., p. 345.

[39] Ibid., p. 346.

[40] Ibid.

[41] Ibid.

Allen Ginsberg's
Reality Sandwiches

by Thomas S. Merrill

I *The Menu*

Ginsberg's poem "On Burroughs' Work" concludes with the stanza:

> A naked lunch is natural to us.
> we eat reality sandwiches.
> But allegories are so much lettuce.
> Don't hide the madness [*Reality Sandwiches* 40].

The title of this fourth volume of collected poems thus pays homage to two of his most influential friends: Jack Kerouac, who suggested "Naked Lunch" as an appropriate title for Burroughs' novel, and, of course, Burroughs himself. Burroughs contends that "[*Naked Lunch*] means exactly what the words say: NAKED Lunch — a frozen moment when everyone sees what is on the end of every fork."[1] *Reality Sandwiches* presumes to exhibit twenty-nine such "frozen moments" that span a full seven years of Ginsberg's development (1953-60).

Both Ginsberg's and Burroughs' titles promise the reader a taste of pure reality and demand that he savor its sweetness and bitterness with a vital palate. Both writers presume to serve an Existential feast devoid of hypocritical condiments which might disguise "the madness." In either case, the program is ambitious and suggests the radical, synesthetic entreaty that Ginsberg once made to Peter Orlovsky when he dedicated *Kaddish and Other Poems* to him: "Taste my mouth in your ear."

The reader gets a good taste of Ginsberg's mouth in his ear in this collection, which, as usual, is uninhibitedly and often flamboyantly honest. As a poetic method, unadulterated honesty is hardly a new departure for Ginsberg. The limits to which honesty have led him are marked by jail sentences, obscenity trials, and a "second-rate creep image that was interpreted to the public via mass media."[2] Honesty has also led him to the lonely regions of isolation where death and self struggle to negotiate a viable program of being. There is much discussion in these poems of what Heidegger would have called the "authentic" versus the "inauthentic" life as well as some further jousting with the problem of Death. The menu is varied and the service is erratic; but, true to his word, Ginsberg is sparing with the lettuce in his sandwiches and the taste of madness is strong.

II *Illuminations*

The initial poem, "My Alba" (7), is an experiment within traditional forms which bears, as do so many of Ginsberg's early verses, a strong affinity to the style of William Carlos Williams. The subject is wasted time, and the method is the catalogue. Williams' poem, "*Le Médecin malgré Lui,*" might easily stand as the model; but Ginsberg thrusts beyond the structural ennui of "*Le Médecin*" to arrive at a description of a human being poised for a spring into authentic existence. It is a morning song that anticipates an awakening. The poet seems to be undergoing the shock of discovering that his life has been non-being; his metaphor is the paraphernalia of the business office. His life is not measured in coffee spoons, but worse: "Sliderule and number/ machine on a desk/ autographed triplicate/ synopsis and taxes...." This catalogue documents a wasted "five years in Manhattan/ life decaying/ talent a blank."

One successful technique is the sense of boredom that has been created by the incessant run-on lines and by the complete avoidance of punctuation of any kind. The result of the lack of punctuation is an abundance of suggestive liaisons which occur between thought patterns: "...Manhattan/ life decaying ... blank/ talking disconnected/ patient ... mental/ sliderule...." The feeling that Ginsberg creates and sustains by the use and the strucure of language in the body of the poem is decisive in making possible the structural tension that the title lends to the entire poem. The juxtaposition of the awakening, implicit in the title "My Alba," with the ostentatiously banal poem which follows is an example of Ginsberg's borrowing of Williams' typical method of creating significance from structure.

As reinforcement to the structural significance of the poem, Ginsberg also adds a final note of Existential urgency: "I am damned to Hell what/ alarmclock is ringing." By this time, the reader realizes that the preceding stanzas have attempted to chart the precincts of Hell and that the ringing of the alarm clock is the sudden awareness of a crisis. The "autographed triplicate/ synopsis" is a carbon-copy existence; it is inauthentic, and it is time to awaken to a naked breakfast.

The penultimate stage of illumination that this poem suggests reminds the reader of traditional experiences of religious regeneration in

which one is "reborn" to a new understanding of existence. The second
selection in this volume, a Zen poem called "Sakyamuni Coming Out
from the Mountain," deals with the difficulty of being twice-born: "how
painful to be born again/ wearing a fine beard,/ reentering the world"
(10).

The form of this poem seems to be once again derivative from the
experiments of William Carlos Williams with the three-step, variable foot
line in *Paterson, The Desert Music and Other Poems,* and *Journey to
Love.* A single specimen from *Paterson II* suffices to illustrate the
similarity:

> The descent beckons
>   as the ascent beckoned
>   Memory is a kind
> of accomplishment
>   a sort of renewal
>   even
> an initiation...[3]

The obvious characteristics of this style are that each of the three steps is
intended to be equal and that, after each step down, there is a caesural
pause. The effect is rather like syncopation; the lines come, as John Ciardi
has suggested, just "off the beat" of iambic pentameter, and they follow
the general rhythmic patterns of modern jazz.[4] For Williams, the method
was "a way of escaping the formlessness of free verse,"[5] and the intention
was also presumably Ginsberg's. At the same time, however, the Oriental
flavor of the poem was an additional concern for Ginsberg, and one could
easily make a case for the form's congeniality with *haiku.*

Liang-k'ai was a painter of the Sung dynasty (959-1279), and his
work represents a relationship between man and nature which ignores
priorities. In other words, his landscapes depict "a world to which man
belongs but which he does not dominate."[6] This attitude does much to explain the final declaration of Ginsberg's poem: "humility is beatness/
before the absolute World," which in turn provides a nexus to Heidegger's
thesis that the predicament of man is that he has been "thrown" into a
world with which he must come to terms. Hence, the poem is rich in
philosophical possibilities which emerge from a matrix of Taoism, Zen,
Beatness, and Existentialism.

The theme of the aimless life, so characteristic of Zen thought, is
presented in the opening description of Arhat who "drags his bare feet/
out of a cave ... wearing a fine beard,/ unhappy hands/ clasped to his
naked breast ... faltering/ into the bushes by a stream" (9). The issue of
priority between man and nature is then introduced: "all things
inanimate/ but his intelligence." The function of the intelligence within
the context of the Zen attitude is not to separate man from nature but to

perform as a receptor of momentary glimpses — glimpses, perhaps, into authentic Being which testify to man's oneness with the world. Humility (Beatness) begins to emerge in the reader's mind as a state whereby a man realizes that he is nothing special in the face of "the absolute World." This recognition seems to be the denouement that the narrative poem offers.

Arhat has been seeking Heaven "under a mountain of stone," and in typical Zen fashion he has "sat thinking" (not imposing his thoughts upon nature, but passively awaiting an understanding) until an awakening occurs. He realizes that "the land of blessedness exists/ in the imagination." This realization is analogous to the ringing of an alarm clock, and Arhat is reborn; his "inauthentic" existence is authenticized and he is made humble:

> he knows nothing
>   like a god:
>   shaken
>   meek wretch — [10]

In essence, Ginsberg's poem supplies an answer to one of the fundamental questions that Existentialism poses:

> ... are we disclosed to ourselves as existents who are always already in a world — a world with which we are concerned and involved in all kinds of ways — so that it is out of this total situation that we must seek after whatever understanding of Being may be possible for us; or are we, as the traditional Western philosophy has been inclined to regard us, primarily thinking subjects, before whom there is spread out for our inspection a world, and this world is to be understood in a genuine way only along the lines of detached theoretical inquiry?[7]

Clearly, "beatness" or "humility" understands only the first option.

"Over Kansas" (42) is another poem which describes a similar illumination, but a contemporary American backdrop replaces the misty forests and lonely rocks of the Sung landscape painters. The situation of the poem is an airplane journey across the United States, one that becomes, in the poet's consciousness, a subjective journey that takes him from ego-less non-being, through a vision of Kansas at night, to a form of self-realization. Two implicit themes seem to embrace in the consummation of this poem: death and nakedness. Death haunts the stanzas in the several references to "death insurance by machine" and the hypothetical poet below in Kansas who is "Someone who should collect/ my insurance!" More profoundly, however, death enters the meditations of the traveler as he ponders the fact that he is "Travelling thru the dark void/ over Kansas yet moving nowhere/ in the dark void of the soul." Death is also present in his mind when he muses that "Not even the human/ imagination satisfied/ the endless emptiness of the soul."

Clearly, this latter appreciation of death is more than biological: it is a death bred of a man's forgetfulness of what it means to be. Hence, the poem takes an Existential turn which recognizes that anxiety over death brings a new seriousness to life which awakens one to an authentic life. The poet moves from the airport waiting room crowded with businessmen to the dark, isolated sky above "imaginary plains/ I never made afoot." He finds himself in "the dark void" above the ground where men actually live, breathe, make love, and "collect the streets and mountain tops/ for storage in ... [their] memory." The illumination comes "in a sudden glimpse" by the poet of his own non-being in the airplane ("me being no one in the air/ nothing but clouds in the moonlight..."), while underneath him living creatures copulate.

The solution to the dilemma of being versus non-being is summed up in Ginsberg's ubiquitous metaphor: nakedness. All of his poetry is about nakedness, he is always ready to assert; but precisely what "nakedness" means is rarely explained. In this poem, for example, he says, "Nakedness must come again — not sex,/ but some naked isolation." This statement seems to suggest an unqualified openness to being, but the sexual suggestiveness of the term is certainly overt in such expressions as "that football boy/ in sunny yellow lovesuit...." The reader is also told that "the starry world below [Hollywood]" also expresses nakedness:

> that craving, that glory
> that applause — leisure, mind,
> appetite for dreams, bodies,
> travels: appetite for the real,
> created by the mind
> and kissed in coitus —
> that craving, that melting!

But this is merely an expression of nakedness, imaginary because it is "created by the mind." It is only an appetite for nakedness rather than the real thing, and the reader is immediately informed that "Not even the imagination satisfies/ the endless emptiness of the soul."

Then comes the official illumination over Hutchinson, Kansas, where the poet peers beyond his own reflection in the window ("bald businessman with hornrims") and sees a "spectral skeleton of electricity"

> illuminated nervous system
> floating on the void out
> of central brainplant powerhouse
> running into heavens' starlight
> overhead.

The vision is an emblem, presumably. The lights of Hutchinson emanating out of a "central brainplant powerhouse" (the human mind) "floating on the void." Because this "illuminated nervous system" is seen by the poet to be "running into heavens' starlight/ overhead," it seems apparent that "the vision" reveals the potentiality of the human imagination to connect the heavens and this world—in a word, mysticism.

What the reader is up against, then, is the familiar credo of the Angel "hipster." "It'd be a lot easier if you just were crazy," Ginsberg has said, "... but on the other hand what if it's all true and you're *born* into this great cosmic universe in which you're a spirit angel....?"[8] After the illumination, the poet is in Chicago between flights and decides that this city is "another project for the heart,"

> six months for here someday
> to make Chicago natural,
> pick up a few strange images.

This spirit angel is on the lookout for missionary work, and it begins to come clear that "nakedness" is merely the unaccommodated man finding in his misery that all are brothers under the skin, that all are angels. In Ginsberg's world, unauthenticated angels rarely fly; their feet trod the dusty earth where life takes place:

> Better I make
> a thornful pilgrimage on theory
> feet to suffer the total
> isolation of the bum,
> than this hipster
> business family journey
> —crossing U.S. at night—

There are so many complex constituents to Ginsberg's illuminations that it is often difficult to analyze or even comprehend precisely the response that is expected. The fact that Ginsberg himself often confesses that he is usually not aware of exactly what he means at the time of writing lends little comfort.[9] Nevertheless, even when exegesis fails, communication of a sort often breaks through. Graffiti collectors are reported to have uncovered this interesting specimen in a men's lavatory: "Ginsberg revises!" If the legend were true, perhaps the task of the explicator would be simplified. For good or for bad, Ginsberg does not write for expositors but for angels; and one must be alert to Wordsworth's counsel that "We murder to dissect."

"Sather Gate Illumination" (54-58) may not present as many problems as "Over Kansas," but the honest lyricism of its celebration of a moment in space and in time manages to avoid the straining for effect that many of the poems in *Reality Sandwiches* exhibit. The poem is Whitman-inspired through and through from the gracious "Dear Walter, thanks-for-the-message" tribute in the beginning to the illumination proper at the end: "Seeing in people the visible evidence of inner self thought by their treatment of me: who loves himself loves me who love myself." Almost any line picked at random from "Song of Myself" serves to explicate the general theme of Ginsberg's piece:

> I CELEBRATE myself, and sing myself,
> And what I assume you shall assume,
> For every atom belonging to me as good belongs to you.

or

> There was never any more inception than there is now,
> Nor any more youth or age than there is now,
> And will never be any more perfection than there is now,
> Nor any more heaven or hell than there is now.

Even more informative are the lines: "Clear and sweet is my soul, and clear and sweet is all that is not my soul/ Lack one lacks both, and the unseen is proved by the seen,/ Till that becomes unseen and receives proof in its turn."[10]

"Dear Walter's" message is no stopgap communiqué for Ginsberg, but a program of positive perception as well as a healthy dose of self-vindication. It reaffirms the brotherhood of angels: "Why do I deny manna to another?/ Because I deny it to myself" (54). The key to the illumination is the acceptance of self which the poem affirms from the start: "Now I believe you are lovely, my soul, soul of Allen, Allen — / and you so beloved, so sweetened, so recalled to your true loveliness,/ your original nude breathing Allen/ will you ever deny another again?"

There is precious little that is new so far as content is concerned in this poem, and its effect probably rests on the fact that the poet's mind has been liberated for mere observation. There is a dazzling array of commonplace scenes and incidents raised to significance by the slender support of Whitman's insight and buttressed by poetic sensitivity. There is also moral tension structurally built into the poem by the leitmotif of the "Roar again of airplanes in the sky" whose pilots "are sweating and nervous at the controls in the hot cabins" (54). These bombers with their "loveless bombs" perform as a mobile umbrella shadowing both the giggling girls, "all pretty/ every-whichway," and the crippled lady, who "explains French grammar with a loud sweet voice:/ Regarder is to look."

Looking is the genius of this poem, and it is not only the "scatological insight"[11] that Ginsberg's eye exploits as he observes the "pelvic energy" of the crippled girl's bouncing body, but it is the deeper vision of the "unseen" being "proved by the seen." Professor Hart, "enlightened by the years," walks "through the doorway and arcade he built (in his mind)/ and knows — he too saw the ruins of Yucatan once —" (56). The unseen which the poet reveals through his perception surely is the sense of community that binds all mankind together: "... we all look up," Ginsberg observes, "silence moves, huge changes upon the ground, and in the air thoughts fly all over filling space" (58).

The salutary moment is both spiritual and poetic. "My grief at Peter's not loving me was grief at not loving myself," the poet concludes. Minds that are broken in "beautiful bodies [are] unable to receive love because not knowing the self as lovely." The illumination is no less poignant because it derives from Whitman. Indeed, from Whitman the poetic impulse behind the creation becomes much clearer; for, in the words of the "True American," Walt Whitman, Ginsberg's literary foundation can be seen: "I know I am solid and sound/ To me the converging objects of the universe perpetually flow,/ All are written to me, and I must get what the writing means."[12]

III *Love and Nakedness*

The doctrine of "nakedness" that Ginsberg continually preaches is implicit in "Sather Gate Illumination"; and it, too, owes much to Whitman. "Undrape! you are not guilty to me, nor stale nor discard," one reads in "Song of Myself": "I see through the broadcloth and gingham whether or no,/ And am around, tenacious, acquisitive, tireless, and cannot/ be shaken away."[13] Clothes are not only a hindrance to lovemaking; they are the garments of illusion with which men shamefully hide their humanity. Mind, too often, is the grim tailor, which appears to be one of the underlying themes of "Love Poem on Theme by Whitman" (41). In this poem, the poet shares the nuptial bed of "the bridegroom and the bride" of humanity whose "bodies fallen from heaven stretched out waiting naked and restless" are open to his physical visitation. As he buries his face "in their shoulders and breasts, breathing their skin ... bodies locked shuddering naked, hot lips and buttocks screwed into each other," he hears the "bride cry for forgiveness" and the groom "covered with tears of passion and compassion." What is described so sensually is an orgasm of community — a nude coming together of primal human hearts from which the poet rises "up from the bed replenished with last intimate gestures and kisses of farewell."

The graphic extremity to which the erotic description takes one is an all-out blitzkrieg against shame. The bed is a possible world of contracted time and space — the identical bed threatened by the "busy old fool, unruly Sunne" that John Donne so beautifully has celebrated.[14] In Ginsberg's poem, however, it is not the "Sunne" which is the intruding landlady of this secret tryst but the mind. Once again, the "cold touch of philosophy" withers primordial love. The conclusion of Ginsberg's poem drops an ironic veil between love and life as it is lived. Shameless physical love occurs

all before the mind awakes, behind shades and closed
doors in a darkened house where inhabitants roam
unsatisfied in the night, nude ghosts seeking each
other out in the silence.

Some of the pathos of Ginsberg's personal attempts to revive "nude
ghosts" can be appreciated in his mock-heroic epic, "The Green
Automobile" (11-16), a visionary, yet autobiographical excursion with
Neal Cassidy to Denver, where the two latter-day cavaliers seek to

... be the angels of the world's desire
and take the world to bed with us before
     we die.

Sleeping alone, or with companion,
     girl or fairy sheep or dream,
I'll fail of lacklove, you, satiety:
     all men fall, our fathers fell before ... [15].

Love is the prize, the holy grail, of these deprived wanderers, and the
urgent necessity of drinking from this universal cup erases hetero- and
homosexual boundaries. "*Malest Cornifici Tuo Catullo*" (47) is just one of
Ginsberg's several poetic, homosexual confessions; and few can deny the
poignancy of its brief, candid apology:

Ah don't think I'm sickening.
You're angry at me. For all of my lovers?
It's hard to eat shit, without having visions;
when they have eyes for it's like Heaven.

IV *The* Ubi Sunt

One of the universals of poetic expression is the mood which
remembrance of things past evokes. The modern "*Ubi sunt*" sometimes
arouses a poignancy that rivals even the most powerful of the Old English
lyrics. The subject is the same: alienation; the mood, however, is more
personal because the bygone times are less distant and the feelings are
closer to man's sense of how rapidly the ravages of time close in upon him.
"The Wanderer" and "The Seafarer" give a taste of the loneliness of the
unaccommodated *scop*, bereft of his mead hall and the comfort of his
protecting thane. Modern mead halls lack the magnificence of Heorot;
"matter is water" (72) the twentieth-century singer must confess. And so
the heavy nostalgia of an Anglo-Saxon heritage must be translated into
faster tempos and tawdrier, less localized scenes. The universal feeling has
not changed, but the props are demythologized. The result is a poem such
as "Back on Times Square Dreaming of Times Square" (70-71).

The conflict of this poem is measured by the collision of actuality with memory. The medium is place — Times Square — and the kinetic throwoff of the poem is the sad contrast of what *is* with what *was*. Times Square, a "memorial of ten years," is now emotionally neutralized by the imposing facticity of "the green & grooking McGraw/Hill offices" (70). A "sad trumpeter" is petitioned to "stand on the empty streets at dawn/ and blow a silver chorus to the buildings of Times Square"; but obviously the time for silver choruses is long past — ten years past — and what music now exists belongs to a solitary cop walking by who is "invisible with his music."

Surprisingly, the contrast is not traditional; that is, present loneliness versus past joy. The contrast is between two distinct types of loneliness which superimpose one quality of alienation with a deeper tint of the same. The polar symbols are the McGraw-Hill offices of the present moment and the "Globe Hotel" of memory. Both poles share a grimness which the fine discrimination of the poet separates with the subtle reminiscence. "I was lonely," he confesses, just as he implicitly avows his present loneliness. The modern mead hall ("The Globe Hotel") boasted little of the comfort and solace of its historical antecedents, for it was a place where "Garver lay in

> grey beds there and hunched his
> back and cleaned his needles —
> where I lay many nights on the nod
> from his leftover bloody cottons
> and dreamed of Blake's voice talking ... [70].

Returning to this place is acknowledging the quickened pace of mutability: "Garver's dead in Mexico two years, hotel's vanished into a parking lot/ And I'm back here — sitting on the streets/ again" (70).

The *"Ubi Sunt"* lament which speaks through this poem is the forlorn query: Where are the not-so-good old days before mass media raped man's special mission? It is a lament to the stolen Beat Generation — an attitude that was popularized to extinction:

> The movies took our language, the
> great red signs
> A DOUBLE BILL OF GASSERS
> Teen Age Nightmare
> Hooligans of the Moon [70].

Underlying the lament is the apologetic protest of misrepresentation:

> But we were never nightmare
> hooligans but seekers of
> the blond nose for Truth [71].

The theme, then, of this poem is missionary martyrdom. From the ashes of an apparently defeated memory arises the poet's conviction about the prophetic validity of what had once occurred. "We are legend," he concedes, "invisible but legendary, as prophecied" (71).

The next poem, "My Sad Self" (72), is less protestant, less prophetic. It is difficult to defend much of this poem from the charge of "crude sentimentality" which the *Times Literary Supplement* insists "is of a piece with the equally crude rhetoric, the hamfisted philosophizing, and the wholesale misuse of imagist and neosurrealist techniques" which pervade *Reality Sandwiches*.[15] This poem is a sentimental one, but it is somewhat superior to "Tears" (63) which is indeed an example of Ginsberg's apparent "belief that an emotion stated is an emotion conveyed."[16] "My Sad Self" baldly states an emotion: sadness; and this emotion is presented more or less as a premise as the poet gazes at New York from the top of the RCA Building. From this vantage point he catalogues various places, each with its attendant nostalgia ("my history summed up, my absences/ and ecstasies in Harlem"). The universalizing lever in this poem — the device that lifts it from pure nostalgic sentimentality — is the concept of transiency that is suggested in the final lines of the first stanza:

> — sun shining down on all I own
> in one eyeblink to the horizon
> in my last eternity —
> matter is water.

Ginsberg owns all he sees because of his subjective relation to it ("Who digs Los Angeles IS Los Angeles!" [H, 21]). The natural corollary to this stance is the intransigence of things: "matter is water" (72).

The remainder of "My Sad Self" is a meandering journey through New York with the usual Ginsbergian reactions to the things he sees about him. For example, he stares "into all man's/ plateglass, faces,/ questioning after who loves..." (72); and, near the end of the poem, he unleashes his prophetic voice and painfully observes that "this graveyard ... once seen/ never regained or desired/ in the mind to come ... must disappear" (74).

V *Spontaneity and Meditation*

Norman MacCaig, who has admitted that "there's a great head of pressure built up in all that Allen Ginsberg writes," remarks that "the trouble is that often the fabric of the poem can't contain it — it explodes messily in your face, spattering you with gobbets and fragments of what may have been a fine body of experience."[17] This description seems an accurate one of

```
FFFFF  U        U  NN     N
F      U        U  N N    N
FFFFF  U        U  N   N  N
F        U    U    N     N N  NY    DEATH
F         U  U     N      NN
F          UU      N      N
```

"I Beg You Come Back & Be Cheerful," "Aether," and several others. In these poems, "syntax is shot at sight, things are described in a catalogue of gasps, the light is lurid, distances enormous [and] ... the wind blows from hysteria."[18] "Aether," perhaps, contains the justification for these excursions:

> Yet the experiments must continue!
> Every possible combination of Being — all
> the old ones! all the old Hindu
>   Sabahadabadie-pluralic universes
>   ringing in Grandiloquent
>   Bearded Juxtaposition ... [84].

Many of these experiments were accomplished under the influence of various stimulants and drugs, but the literary significance is clear: the method is spontaneous dictation of experience without benefit of afterthought. Perhaps the typical reaction is, again, MacCaig's, whose summary is: "Terribly Romantic, in a diabolical sort of way. And tediously self-regarding.... It's the continuous pumping-up that I distrust."[19]

"Siesta in Xbalba," the best poem of *Reality Sandwiches*, is not "pumped up" at all; but, as James Scully feels, it "recalls ... the quieter vision of Henry Vaughan."[20] What is reminiscent of Vaughan is control more than anything else. The reader is not asked to fill his mind with abstract eternities or chaotic meanderings of a turgid mind; instead, he finally has something tangible to deal with. Ginsberg presents in this poem a real, vibrant world to consider; and, at the same time, it is a world pregnant with intimations of immortality.

Like Vaughan's "The World" ("I saw Eternity last night..."), "Siesta in Xbalba" makes the effort for revelation:

> Late sun opening the book,
>   blank page like light,
> invisible words unscrawled,
>   impossible syntax
> of apocalypse — [21]

The poem even programs a method: "let the mind fall down" (21). From the very beginning of the poem, therefore, there is a yearning for an apocalyptic vision — a setting almost assured of producing the proper mystic mood — and, finally, a yielding up of the rational discipline so that the poet becomes almost pure receptor. What occurs in the poem from this point on is what George Poulet might describe as the "infinite receptivity" which is the genius of Walt Whitman's thought. Ginsberg obviously enjoys the stance. He is in a hammock, suspended, so to speak, above the world and yet still of it, while white doves copulate underneath him (21) and monkeys bark. The reader is told that the poet has "succumbed to this temptation" of "doing nothing but lying in a hammock" (21); and he is prepared for observation and apocalyptic musing.

The musing initially takes place in the form of a dream flashback — "an eternal kodachrome" (22), Ginsberg calls it — where his friends at a party are frozen in his mind. Clearly, the idea is to present an *inauthentic* contrast to the *authentic* situation the poet is in at Xbalba because the people are described as "posed together," with "stylized gestures" and "familiar visages." They are all, he concludes, "posturing in one frame,/ superficially gay/ or tragic as may be,/ illumed with the fatal/ character and intelligent/ actions of their lives" (23).

Immediately following this dream flashback is a description of the poet's own pretentiously stark surroundings: "And I in a concrete room/ above the abandoned/ labyrinth of Palenque/ measuring my fate,/ wandering solitary in the wild/ — blinking singleminded/ at a bleak idea —" (23). Clearly, there is a note of superiority here. Friends are trivial, but "I" am serious is the note Ginsberg seems to strike; there is, of course, the usual cosmic trump card to be played: the oncoming mystic vision. Fatigued from gazing at the bleak idea, the poet awaits the moment when

> my soul might shatter
> at one primal moment's
> sensation of the vast
> movement of divinity [23].

There is obviously an inchoate quest operating in the debris of the mind that has fallen down, and it seems to be directed toward the usual eternity which so often is the misty goal of Ginsberg's poems. The reason is probably the same as Whitman's: "Eternity gives similitude to all periods and locations and processes, and animate and inanimate forms, and ... is the bond of time." Such a valuable commodity as this bond is certainly worthy of the highest poetry, and it helps once again to explain Ginsberg's views concerning drugs. If eternity is the "bond of time" — the thing which glues everything together into community and permits everyone to be an angel — then it is reasonable that any access to this state would be well worth the price. Even without drugs the search for Eternity can be salutary:

As I leaned against a tree
        inside the forest
expiring of self-begotten love,
I looked up at the stars absently,
        as if looking for
something else in the blue night
        through the boughs,
and for a moment saw myself
        leaning against a tree ... [23].

Time and eternity, as the glue that binds all things together, is developed as a concept later in the poem when Ginsberg meditates upon a death's-head. Part of his fascination with the death's-head is its relevance to the principle of prophecy. He is impressed by the fact that it "thinks its way/ through centuries the thought of the same night in which I sit/ in skully meditation" (26). Here is an instance of eternity indeed obliterating time but in the fashion of biblical prophecy. The anterior artisan, the maker of the death's-head, sculpted his artifact until it fully represented his idea; but now, Ginsberg muses, the death's head communicates that idea across time:

but now his fine thought's vaguer
        than my dream of him:
and only the crude skull figurement's
        gaunt insensible glare is left.... (26)

The philosophical substratum of this small passage of the poem would seem to be the idea that truth (even history) is entirely subjective. Works of art, be they poems or death's-heads, have the capability of triggering or exciting thoughts in future individuals. The sense of oneness that eternity brings with it acts as a sort of guarantee of this phenomenon and presents the possibility of bridges across time. Real history, then, does not operate chronologically, logically, or rationally. History is apocalypse, so that Ginsberg can say:

I alone know the great crystal door
        to the House of Night,
a legend of centuries
        — I and a few indians [29].

Any other access to history — any other solution to the "impossible syntax" of the hieroglyphics — cannot possibly yield what the death's-head potentially can surrender subjectively to the eternalized viewer. Unless the mind is allowed to "fall down," the rational apparatus will filter out the past:

Time's slow wall overtopping

all that firmament of mind,
as if a shining waterfall of leaves and rain
were built down solid from the endless sky
   through which no thought can pass [28].

The first part of the poem ends with a rejection and a tentative affirmation: "There is a god/ dying in America" (33) which is the institutionalized religious impulse. At the same time, there is also "an inner/
anterior image/ of divinity/ beckoning me out/ to pilgrimage" (33).

Part Two of this poem, "Return to the United States" (33), pos-
sesses a stark, generally crisp descriptive style and only one real intrusion
of Ginsbergian metaphysics. The reader is told, finally, that "The problem is isolation" (36), a statement later followed by the lament: "What
solitude I've finally inherited" (37). What these lines appear to mean is
that Ginsberg has failed in a way. If what he hoped to retain from his
night in Xbalba was a vision of Whitman's "vast similitude [which] inter-
locks all,/ All spheres grown, ungrown, small, large, suns, moons,
planets,/ All distances of place however wide,/ All distances of time...,"[23]
what he actually returned with was less ambitious: a few Traditions,/
metrical, mystical, manly/ ... and certain characteristic flaws" (38). The
isolation, it would seem, is not entirely his own; it's the isolation of the
whole universe. The temptation for social criticism becomes too strong in
the final lines, and the *real* loneliness and the *real* isolation are finally
diagnosed as natural consequences of "The nation over the border [Amer-
ica]" which "grinds its arms and dreams of war" (39).

Intellectual sentimentality appears to be Ginsberg's Achilles' heel,
and one reason for the success of "Siesta in Xbalba" is the fact that the
thundering onslaughts upon God, upon eternity, upon the cosmos, and so
on, are kept unusually under control. There is more attention to things in
this poem than in most of the others, which anchors it to a refreshing empirical plane too often missing in the later work. An Oriental clarity in
some places in the poem even brings metaphysics nearer to the reader's
grasp, much in the way suggested in "Cézanne's Ports," for example. One
such instance is the simple description of the night in the midst of the rain
forest:

         I can see the moon
moving over the edge of the night forest
         and follow its destination
through the clear dimensions of the sky
            from end to end of the dark
      circular horizon [25].

If nothing else, the idea in this short excerpt is *rendered* rather than gar-
rulously bellowed. It is structural, not strident; and the quiet control of

"Siesta in Xbalba" is a welcome reminder that the best poems are most often made rather than notated.

VI *Assessment*

It is very difficult to assess *Reality Sandwiches* as a whole because the book, which spans seven years of poetic development, modestly claims to be merely "scribbled secret notebooks, and wild typewritten pages, for yr [*sic*] own joy." It would be silly to pretend that many of the poems are not simply amateurish, pretentious, clumsy, and, at times, even downright dull. One bittersweet reviewer of the *Times Literary Supplement* has conceded that "in among this amateurish material ... there are moments of real excitement, and poems which are firmly restrained and delicately balanced. There are not many, but there are enough to give one hope for Mr. Ginsberg's future development."[24] The assessment is probably true, but what the reviewer hopefully regards as signs of "future development" are perhaps more accurately carry-overs from Ginsberg's less flamboyant earlier versifying. Ginsberg is not working *toward* what would be considered traditional control; he is fleeing from it as rapidly as possible.

One is left, then, with the kind of response to which James Scully invariably resorts when he reviews Ginsberg's work: Scully finds Ginsberg's worth in his "sense of humanity." The phrase is ambiguous and slippery, and even Scully's attempt to clarify does no more than suggest the type of power that he finds in the poems. Nevertheless, according to Scully this sense of humanity is Ginsberg's attempt "to uncover a community";[25] and such attempts have perfectly respectable credentials. Walt Whitman, for example, was doing the very same thing when he wrote:

> Divine am I inside and out, and I make holy whatever I touch
> or am touched from,
> The scent of these arm-pits aroma finer than prayer,
> This head more than churches, bibles, and all creeds.[26]

In a way, Whitman's liturgy of the divine, human self appears to be the one constant, yet elusive, goal toward which Ginsberg has been striving throughout most of his career.

Notes

1. William Burroughs, *Evergreen Review*, IV (January, 1960), 15.

2. Letter from Allen Ginsberg to this author, November 22, 1966.

3. William Carlos Williams, *Paterson II* (New York, 1948).

4. John Ciardi, "How Free Is Verse?" *Saturday Review* (October 11, 1958), 38.

5. William Carlos Williams, *I Wanted to Write a Poem*, ed. Edith Heal (Boston, 1958), p. 92.

6. Alan W. Watts, *The Way of Zen* (New York, 1959), p. 173.

7. John MacQuarrie, *Studies in Christian Existentialism* (Philadelphia, c. 1965), pp. 48-49.

8. "The Art of Poetry VIII," *Paris Review*, XXXVII (Spring, 1966), 40.

9. See *Ibid.*, 22.

10. *Song of Myself*, XX, 403-405.

11. James Scully [review of *Reality Sandwiches*], *Nation*, CXCVII (November 16, 1963), 330.

12. Walt Whitman, *Song of Myself*, XX, 403-405.

13. *Ibid.*, VII, 145-47.

14. "The Sunne Rising."

15. *Times Literary Supplement*, CCXII (September 20, 1963), 706.

16. *Ibid.*

17. Norman MacCaig, "Poemburgers" [review of *Reality Sandwiches*], *New Statesman*, LXVI (July 5, 1963), 20.

18. *Ibid.*

19. *Ibid.*

20. James Scully [review of *Reality Sandwiches*], *op. cit.*, 330.

21. George Poulet, *Studies in Human Time* (New York, 1959), p. 342.

22. Walt Whitman, *The Complete Poetry and Prose*, ed. M. Cowley (New York, 1948), II, 92.

23. *Ibid.*, I, 249.

24. *Times Literary Supplement* [review of *Reality Sandwiches*], *op. cit.*, 706.

25. Scully [review of *Reality Sandwiches*] *Nation*, CXCVII (November 16, 1963), 330.

26. *Song of Myself*, XXIV, 524-26.

Whatever Happened
to Bob Kaufman

by Barbara Christian

My students respond to the name of Allen Ginsberg, howling Jewish-incantation style, to the name of Ted Joans, bopping in Black rhythms, to the name of Jack Kerouac, forever on the road. But Bob Kaufman — who is he? A hurt mutter rushes to my brain — the same damn thing again. Movements that change literature and language, and hence the world they're a part of, but some of the real movers are forgotten, their sacrifices, work erased. But not forever. "Bob Kaufman," I begin, "is one of the poets who helped shape the Beat movement in American poetry, and, as usual when somebody Black makes something new in America, he's the one who's apt to be forgotten."

The situation just described constantly occurs, even as we rediscover our Black creators. It is with the somber awareness that our knowledge of our wise men is always in danger that I write this tribute to Bob Kaufman, a Black poet who is still alive and who need not be praised after his body is gone and only his poetry remains.

Little has been written about Kaufman's life; I know little of the facts that are invariably used to describe a life. What I know I have found in his two published volumes of poetry: *Solitudes Crowded with Loneliness* (1959) and *The Golden Sardine* (1960). These two books project the philosophy of the Beat poet, of the man who challenged middle-class American values in the Fifties, when many Black and white intellectuals were yet to see the connection between the incredible blandness of American life and the destruction America as a government and as a propagandist idea symbolized.

Like Ginsberg, Joans and Kerouac, Kaufman's poetry began to take hold on the Lower East Side — the fringe of New York City, of America — where artists, poor people and exiles from the mainstream gathered. Along with these and other poets, Kaufman was a part of that outlandish, rebellious element of American life which emerged in the midst of Eisenhowerian conformity and mediocrity. The potpourri of people on the Lower East Side, who had nothing to lose but a hard life, created a life-style different from that of the mainstream, a life-style which became the basis for the Beat Movement. The lie that was America stuck out there, could not be successfully disguised by slick TV commercials or glamorous billboards. At home and abroad, America was racist, money-crazy and destructive. The Lower East Side with its newly-arrived exiles, Bowery drunks, disenfranchized citizens, crazy niggers, bore witness to the lie of America. The Lower East Side exploded with color; life refused neat categorization into linear pigeon holes*:

> Angry, fire-eyed children clutch transient winds
> Singing Gypsy songs, love me now, love me now.
>
> The echoes return, riding the voice of the river,
> As time cries out, on the skin of an African drum.
>   "East Fifth St. (N.Y.)" [p. 18]

The Lower East Side is a haven for the dreamer, who cannot, even if he tries, conform to already prescribed models and images, for he must create his own:

> Remember, poet, while gallavanting across the sky
> Skylarking, shouting, calling names ... walk softly.
>
> Your footprints in rain clouds are visible to naked eyes.
> Lamps barnacled to your feet refract the mirrored air.
>
> Exotic scents of your hidden vision fly in the face of time.
>   "Forget To Not" [p. 55]

The Lower East Side is the no-man's land from which the mainland can be cursed and criticized:

> The cold land breathes death rattles, trembling
> The dark sky casts shadows across the wounds
> Beneath the bright clothing of well-fed machines
> The hungry heart inside the hungry hearts
> Beats silently, beats softly, beats, beats.
>   "TeeVee People" [p. 50]

Much of Kaufman's poetry is inherently critical of America, protesting its scurrilous ways, calling attention to its blood-thirsty appetite. Passionately, Kaufman reviews its past, illuminates its present, projects its future while he measures the reality of America against the myth it broadcasts. "Benediction," a poem which was performed by Vinie Burrows at the 1969 Algerian Festival, is one of the most damning poems written about America, damning not because it uses invective, but because it uses well-placed irony so effectively:

*Page numbers from Solitudes.

Your ancester had beautiful thoughts in his brain.
His descendants are experts in real estate.
Your generals have mushrooming visions.
Everyday your people get more and more
Cars, television, sickness death dreams.
You must have been great
Alive.
          "Benediction" [p. 9]

The poem concentrates on both racism and imperialism, on America not
only as a threat to the American Black and the American poor, but to the
entire world as well. Written in the early Fifties, Kaufman's poem could
be read at the Festival in 1969. More than 10 years after Kaufman wrote
it, Blacks had just begun to appreciate how far-reaching was America's
oppressiveness. In fact, Kaufman's poems seldom allude exclusively to the
plight of the Afro-American. His poems always couple domestic racism
with American criminal behavior abroad. He attacks the basic values of
America, seeing the race problem in its midst and its behavior toward the
rest of the world as reflections of the country's internal corrosion.

America's tentacles, which tamper with the world's psyche, are the
various forms of its media — the means through which meta-messages are
subtly imprinted on the mind. Like LeRoi Jones in the Fifties, Kaufman
takes great pains to warn us of the termite eating at our spirit. His media
poems are set against the background of the West, Los Angeles and San
Francisco, for in this wild rootless land, recently taken from the Indians
and Mexicans, medialand constructs its images. The lie of the media is
tucked away in the West, heavily camouflaged by the glitter of the sweet
life. Remember, Kaufman cries, that Hollywood actually represents:

Five square miles of ulta-contemporary nymphomania
Two dozen homos, to every sapiens, at last countdown
Ugly Plymouths swapping exhaust with red convertible Buicks.
Twelve year old mothers suing for child support,
Secondhand radios making it with wide-screen TV sets,
Unhustling junkies shooting mothball fixes, insect junk,
Unemployed pimps living on neon backs of
Unemployed whores.
          "Hollywood" [p. 24]

In this Babylon of the modern world, language becomes lies; grotesque
nightmares are transformed into soft dreams, dreams sent out as am-
bassadors to whet the peasant's desire and compel his respect for an
illusionary America. No wonder Charlton Heston, as head of the Movie
Actors Association, reminded (President) Nixon that movies are America's
greatest and most effective export. Ironically, Hollywood makes its bait

under the name of Art, and in so doing insults the craft of Bob Kaufman. Kaufman retaliates. In ending his poem to Hollywood, he salutes it as "the artistic cancer of the universe": "I want to prove that L.A. is a practical joke played on us by superior beings on a humorous planet."

Kaufman not only attacks Hollywood, he senses that the ambitious movers of medialand are efficient, having capsulized their product into a portable machine. TeeVee, the machine par-excellence of hypnosis, has created a land of drugged people:

> The younger machines occupy miles of dark benches,
> Enjoying self-induced vacations of the mind,
> Eating textbook rinds, spitting culture seeds,
> Dreaming an exotic name to give their defeat,
> Computing the hours on computer minds.

So Hollywood, in essence, is plugged into the homes of America, and is yearned for by the hungry people of the planet as a drug to ease their pain. For Kaufman, Hollywood and TeeVee are manifestations of America's emptiness and decay, just as the Bowery drunks are evidence of her falseness.

As one reads more and more of Kaufman's poetry, this attitude toward America prevails. Her only saving grace comes from those she casts off: for example, from the Black whose music, grace and mores keep her going. "War Memoir" ironically plays on this theme, for in its imagery, the poem juxtaposes the technical stuff America creates for destruction alongside jazz, a music which absorbs everything, even technology, making it into a thing of beauty:

> What one-hundred percent redblooded savage
> Wastes precious time listening to jazz
> With so much important killing to do?
>
> Silence the drums that we may hear the burning
> Of Japanese in atomic colorcinemascope
> And remember the stereophonic screaming.
>   "War Memoir" [p. 52]

Jazz as a protest music permeates Kaufman's being—its modal variety and flexibility adapts itself to every situation. And in the late Forties and early Fifties, Jazz as taken higher by Charlie Parker expressed the alternate route that America's outcasts could take. Kaufman soaks himself in Parker's music, in bop strains of electricity and blood-rhythms. One of his poems, "Walking Parker Home," is studded with those intricately carved word jewels of a genuine poet in communion with a master musician:

In that Jazz corner of life
Wrapped in a midst of sound
His legacy, our Jazz-tinted dawn
Wailing his triumphs of oddly begotten dreams
Inviting the nerveless to feel once more
That fierce dying of humans consumed
In raging fires of Love.

Jazz is the subterranean music, existing as it protests, developing as it rejects, becoming fuller as it strips away the debris of rot.

To continue to maintain an authentic existence in the face of so much falsehood and decay is a long, hard fight. Charlie Parker heroically conquers American decay with his music. Kaufman expresses the psychic loneliness of a man who is plagued by his environment and turns in on himself. His psyche cannot always stand the loneliness imposed upon him:

The whole of me
Is an unfurnished room
Filled with dank breath
Escaping in gasps to nowhere.
Before completely objective mirrors
I have shot myself with my eyes
But death refused my advances.
"Would You Wear My Eyes?" [p. 40]

There is loneliness throughout many of his poems, not just the loneliness that might come from solitude, but an even more devastating psychic loneliness that can come only from knowing so few people who share his perceptions. Such loneliness haunts a man who sees more than the people of his time. Images of dissolution, of being unable to come up from under, burst from these poems as if they, the poems, are the writer's only companion. The absence of any widespread awareness about the visions Kaufman breathed, and the lack of any expansive Black cultural context certainly contributed to Bob Kaufman's loneliness. He was a decade too early — or rather he had to suffer alone so that others in later years could create together.

The extreme objective correlative of this loneliness in our society is the prison. Kaufman's "Jail Poems" protest both America's injustice and succinctly, painfully reveal his own psychic prison — the real prison from which he cannot escape. Surrealist images, dada symbols jet-stream through these poems. And Kaufman is magnificently graphic in rendering this loneliness, for he knows the mind often perceives what it cannot logically express. Certain states are irretrievably beyond logic:

I am sitting in a cell with a view of evil parallels,

> Waiting thunder to splinter me into a thousand me's.
> It is not enough to be in one cage with one self;
> I want to sit opposite every prisoner in every hole.
> Doors roll and bang, every slam a finality bang!

As we discuss the plight of political prisoners today, our minds are now ready for the "Jail Poems" of Kaufman. The prison cell is an appropriate symbol for America's way of life and can trap the man who opposes America more through his life-style, than because of any specific act.

Living with the present, living existentially, lies at the core of the Beat philosophy, and necessarily befuddles, thwarts a life-style based on systemization. Kaufman was well-acquainted with the formal outlines of existentialism, as his "Poem to Camus" indicates, but he felt that existentialism itself had become too codified.

The Abomunist Manifesto picks up where existentialism left off. Like (Richard) Wright in *The Outsider*, Kaufman realizes the limits of all *isms*, the eventual decay of all systems. Kaufman's anti-philosophy, Abomunism, is finally as much a put-down of itself as it is of anything else. The very name makes serious fun of *isms*, manifestos and the like, transforming sense into nonsense, turning reality upside down. Signed "Bomkauf," the manifesto was duly written in legal, political structure. There are "Notes" and "Further Notes," "Craxions," a glossary, an anthem, founding documents, and even a newscast. The Abomunist world frinks, digs its own music, even has its own brand of children. A sample of the Abomnewscast...on the hour...illuminates the method behind Kaufman's "madness:"

> Cubans seize Cuba, outraged U.S. acts quickly,
> cuts off tourist quota, administration intro-
> duces measure to confine all rhumba bands to
> detention camps during emergency ... Both
> sides in Cold War stockpiling atomic missiles
> to preserve peace, end of mankind seen if
> peace is declared. UN sees encouraging sign
> in small war policy, works quietly for wider
> participation among backward nations....

Defined as "a rejectionary philosophy founded by Barabbas and dedicated to the proposition that the essence of existence is reality essential and neither four-sided nor frinky, but not non-frinky," Abomunism derides logic, philosophy, academic and political jargon, and whatever manifestations exist in response to the need to systematize the world. Commercialized religion, as a major form of systemization, is singled out for commentary by the Abomunists. "Further Notes (taken from Abomunism and Religion by Tom Man)" discusses religious props:

Krishnamurti can relax the muscles of your soul,
Free your aching jawbone from the chewinggum habit.
Oupensky can churn your illusions into butter and
Give you circles to carry them in, around your head.
Sabud can lock you in strange rooms with vocal balms
And make your ignorant clothing understand you.
Zen can cause changes in the texture of your hair,
Removing you from the clutches of sexy barbers.
Edgar Cayce can locate your gallstones, other organs,
On the anarchistic rockpiles of Sacramento.
Voodoo Marie can give you Loas, abstract horses.
Snorting guides to tar-baby black masses.
Billy can plug you into the Christ machine. Mail in your
Mind today. Hurry, bargain God Week, lasts one week only.
      [p. 79]

The Abomunist Manifesto creates a world counter to mainstream American life; in effect, it is a blueprint for a revolutionary way of life. It does not purport to know the right way to live; rather, it gives the Abomunist guidelines for avoiding the snares of systematic living, while thwarting the system itself. In some ways, it is the precursor of the hippie and professional revolutionary life-styles. Kaufman saw that in order to live with any kind of freedom, and to be able to fight American mediocrity and destructiveness, a life-style rooted in protest must be invented. In effect, this manifesto is the creation of an alternate community, one in which Kaufman might have been able to function.

Kaufman's poetry, his Abomunist Manifesto, are all the result of a new language, a new mode of perceiving. In striking at the lifeless English language, Kaufman creates a new language, linked to Jazz. His poems, along with those of Ted Joans, use Jazz's concept of improvisation as their stylistic core. Casting aside traditional and even more avant-garde forms and images such as the recent breathline, Kaufman plays with word rhythms and dada images:

Smothered rage covering pyramids of notes spontaneously
    exploding
Cool revelations / shrill hopes / beauty speared into
    greedy ears
Birdland nights on bop mountains, windy saxophone
    revolutions
            "Walking Parker Home" [p. 5]

He uses the same words with different emphases, sticking close to the oral tradition of poetry — sometimes moving to the pitch of a chant, sometimes speaking at a conversational level:

They fear you, Crane … you whispered aloft, pains they
        buried forever …
They hate you, Crane … your sur-real eclipses bloat out
        their muted sun …
They miss you, Crane … your footprints are on their
        rotting teeth …

But where is Bob Kaufman? — the Black poet who challenged the
American life-style with his own, who fought with the pen as passionately
as many do with weapons or rhetoric, who pointed the way to the painful
visions Blacks lived through in the Sixties: political prisons, the need for
an alternate life-style, America's rottenness, the sacredness of jazz. He
wanders the streets of San Francisco, mostly unknown and forgotten, considered mad by many, cared for by few. As his books circulate, the
question of responsibility, the responsibility that Black cultural
organizations have to protect such a man, screams to be heard. If we do
not care to sustain our own wise men who suffered, sacrificed, were attacked and assaulted, then can we really speak of "nation-building"? Who
will look to Bob Kaufman — if we don't?

The Dionysian Vision
of Jack Kerouac

by Lee Bartlett

The work of Jack Kerouac has not fared well with critics. While some early reviewers of *On the Road* compared the book favorably with *The Sun Also Rises*, others seemed to agree with Truman Capote's judgment that Kerouac's novels were "typing, not writing," referring to *On the Road* as "uncouth," "cut-rate Thomas Wolfe," and "the Romantic Novel's last whimper." A few good articles by such sympathetic critics as Warren Tallman, Seymour Krim, George Dardess, and Thomas Parkinson have appeared, but almost thirty years after the publication of Kerouac's first novel we still await the appearance of a satisfactory book-length critical treatment of his work. It is as if most critics still seem reluctant to view the literature of the "Beat Generation" as anything more than cultural phenomena, and reeking of the worst excesses of the French Revolution at that. In his brief essay "Dionysus & the Beat Generation," however, William Everson attempts to bring this work into comprehension by seeing in novels like *On the Road* and *The Subterraneans*, and in poems like "Howl" and "Kaddish," the re-emergence of the Dionysian impulse in American literature.[1] In the frontal attack of the Beats on "precisionist" (here read Symbolist) poets like Eliot and Stevens, novelists like James, and their formalist-critic counterparts, Everson, a Jungian, envisions the re-enactment of the archetypal conflict between the Dionysian impulse towards the primitive, the ecstatic, and the unconscious, and the Apollonian tendency towards culture, education, and the ego. The argument is between symbol and image or metaphor, and in his cultivation of spontaneous prose technique, Kerouac emerges on the side of the former.

1

As Albert Gelpi has argued in his remarkable study of the psyche of the American poet from Taylor to Dickinson, *The Tenth Muse*, American writing has been Janus-faced from the beginning. For Gelpi, this split resides in the dichotomy between *types* and *tropes*. In Biblical exegesis,

115

types are in essence symbols. Jonah prefigures Christ as a *type* of Christ, just as Abraham's legitimate son is a type of the elect, while his illegitimate son is a type of the damned. This typology becomes, Gelpi concludes, "a way of perceiving the eternal plan in the contingencies of time."[2] Conversely, tropes are creations of the human will, products of Coleridgean fancy, analogous to Wallace Stevens' "fictions." They have no transcendental dimension, no registration to the infinite "I Am," but as allegory and metaphor depend for their meanings on the ingenuity and craft of their human maker.

The distinction here is between symbol and sign, *Sinnbild* and *Zeichen*, and it is at the very core of the conflict between Freudian and Jungian aesthetics. According to Jung, Freud recognizes essentially no difference between symbol and sign. The Freudian symbol is equated with the "conscious contents [of the psyche] which give us a clue to the unconscious backgrounds."[3] Symbols are therefore reduced to signs, in that for Freud (and neo-Freudians like Rank and Jones) they are finally knowable. In this view it follows that all symbolic expressions (most especially dreams and artworks) are reducible to a dysfunction in the personal unconscious (the libido). In Freudian analysis, the patient's neurosis is thought to be sourced in an early trauma later repressed; it becomes the task of the therapist to recover the specific trauma and thus clear the path to regeneration of psychic balance for the patient.

While Jung agrees in part with Freud, he argues that the distinction between sign and symbol is a crucial one. "The true symbol differs essentially from [the sign], and should be understood as the expression of an intuitive perception which can as yet neither be apprehended better nor expressed differently."[4] For Jung, then, the symbol may be equated with the type; its referent, if it is to be *perceived* (rather than *created* through personal trauma), is "out-there," and its resident meanings will be a nonspecific complex. While signs may indicate dysfunctions, symbols are apertures into a nonordinary reality. Unlike tropes, they are for Jung "never thought out consciously," but "always produced from the unconscious in the way of so-called revelation or intuition."[5]

In this way symbols have an exceedingly important function for they become the mediating principle between consciousness and what Jung terms the *archetypes of the collective unconscious*. Accepting Freud's notion of a personal unconscious composed of specifiable contents (signs) originating in a particular individual's past, Jung posits a deeper layer of the unconscious which he terms *collective*. The contents of this collective unconscious "do not originate in personal acquisitions but in the inherited possibility of psychic functioning in general, namely, in the inherited brain-structure. These are the mythological associations — these motives and images which can spring anew in every age and clime, without historical tradition or migration."[6] In his *Symbols of Trans-*

formation, Jung details how in conducting dream analysis of an only moderately educated patient, he was faced with symbols which bore a remarkable similarity to other more ancient and distant cultural artifacts. Because his patient could not have had previous conscious knowledge of these artifacts, Jung inferred the existence of a collective unconscious, "an inborn disposition to produce parallel images, or rather identical psychic structures common to all men."[7] These psychic structures Jung calls *archetypes* are a priori transpersonal dominants, which are not specifiable signs, but rather psychic dispositions. Archetypes thus become *ways* of apprehending or intuiting as opposed to specific apprehensions or intuitions.

For Jung, then, one of the central problems in the human experience resides in one's disposition toward the objective world:

> The contents of the collective unconscious are represented in consciousness in the form of pronounced tendencies, or definite ways of looking at things. They are generally regarded by the individual as being determined by the object—incorrectly, at bottom—since they have their source in the unconscious structure of the psyche, and are only released by the operation of the object. These subjective tendencies and ideas are stronger than the objective influence; because their psychic value is higher, they are imposed upon all impressions.[8]

In *Psychological Types*, Jung discusses the problem of "pronounced tendencies" which have an extrapersonal source. He takes as an epigraph for the study a passage from Heine's *Deutschland*, in which the poet contrasts the Aristotelian and the Platonic: "These are not merely two systems, they are types of two distinct human natures, which from time immemorial, under every sort of disguise, stand more or less inimically opposed." In Jung's introduction to that volume, he explains that in his clinical work he discovered Heine's polarity to be apt, that his patients tended toward one of two *attitude types*: the "introverted" and the "extraverted."

"The introverted attitude is characterized," he argues, "by an upholding of the subject with his conscious ends and aims against the claims and pretensions of the object; the extraverted attitude, on the contrary, is distinguished by a subordination of the subject to the claims of the object."[9] This idea of an unconscious disposition which determines perception, the split between the introvert (who has a negative relationship to the object) and the extravert (who has a positive relationship to it), highlights for Jung the primary aesthetic problem, one he deals with in two extended essays, "On the Relation of Analytical Psychology to Poetic Art" and "Psychology and Literature."

There are two modes of artistic creation, Jung argues, the psychological and the visionary, and they can be differentiated according to their subject matters and their methods of creation. The psychological mode (which is tropic) draws its subject matter from the "vast realm of conscious human experience—from the vivid foreground of life."[10] The psychological artist tends to the introverted, however, and sees his role as bringing some sort of meaning and order to this experience. His work may deal with specific political issues, more general social concerns, and even, like James, personal interactions and confrontations which have their resolution on the conscious plane. The mode is *psychological* because it is understandable, knowable. "Even the basic experiences," Jung suggests, "though non-rational, have nothing strange about them; on the contrary, they are that which has been known from the beginning of time."[11] The artist whose disposition is toward the psychological mode sees himself primarily as a craftsman — a weaver of figures in the carpet — and this of course informs his method of creation. Because his work is "an interpretation and illumination of consciousness," his method of composition is a conscious one; that is, in his attempt to bring the objective world into clearer focus (or to create an objective world), he will remain aware of his self-imposed role as shaper and definer (or, in Robert Duncan's words, "constructivist"). In this way, the "material" of his artwork (and art is always for him a work, an arrangement) is only the "material" of his artwork. It is at all times subject to his rational, his tropic, artistic purpose. Moreover, the psychological *poet*, for example, will often use forms and meters as consciously imposed structuring principles, ways of ordering reality. For him a poem's form may well precede its subject, for the two are finally separable.

However, the subject matter of the *visionary* mode is for Jung a little more difficult to define, being "a strange something that derives its existence from the hinterland of man's mind."[12] It is symbolic, in the sense of the German *Sinnbild*, where *Sinn* conveys some form or complex of meaning, *Bild* the thing itself, the image. The product of the symbol becomes, in alchemical terms, a *conjunctio* where the Sinn and the Bild are fused into a perfect *hermaphroditus*. Because for the extraverted artist, the visionary, the phenomenal world is symbolic, his art begins in the concrete, though he assumes a registration somewhere behind the curtain of appearances, a registration with the archaic and the cosmic. Where for the psychological artist consciousness is so important to his role a shaper, a giver-of-meanings, for the visionary artist consciousness is a profound stumbling block, constantly attempting to subvert his descent into the id. It becomes the task of the visionary artist to flee consciousness (and all things connected with consciousness — education and a sense of a "literary" tradition most especially) for the unconscious, flee the trope for the type. His impulse is finally not to bring order or meaning to the world, but rather lead us to the order and meaning which resides there.

William Carlos Williams is at best a problematic figure in this context, yet he is helpful here: "Say it, no ideas but in things." Not no ideas *but* things, rather no ideas but *in* things, and this is crucial. Thus the red wheel barrow upon which all things depend. The extravert believes he cannot shape the phenomenal world, bring his rational sense of what is or should be to it and call an order; nor does he need to. Williams is, at least in spirit if not always in practice, below it all a transcendentalist — which is, for him, the American Grain. There is an order beyond the phenomenal, and the world we experience (with the *I* through the *eye*, in Charles Olson's sense) is in registration with those eternal and perfect forms. It is not the *image* for Williams (and here is, it seems to me, his major split with Pound) that concerns us — not the *made* thing final in itself — nor the metaphoric (and here his split with the Symbolists), whose specific referent outside the trope is again a *made* thing, only here denying the resonance of the concrete. "Say it, no ideas but in things." Again, not *no* ideas, but no ideas abstracted from their source. Hence for Williams the symbolic complex: concrete phenomena — trees, chickens, a white thigh — as things which by their very concreteness are apertures into those transcendental forms, flowering into meaning. We begin with a wheelbarrow, a plum, a paper bag — we end with Whitman's leaf of grass, a notion of God.

2

In response to questions concerning the composition of *The Subterraneans*, Kerouac wrote "Essentials of Spontaneous Prose," his primary statement of his aesthetic position. The language of spontaneous prose, or "sketching," Kerouac envisioned, would flow unchecked from the writer's mind:

> Not *selectivity* of expression but following free deviation (association) of mind into limitless blow-on-subject seas of thought, swimming in sea of English with no disciplines other than rhythms in rhetorical exhalation and expostulated statement...Blow as deep as you want — write as deeply, fish as far down as you want....[13]

In contrast to Flaubert's ideal, the writer of spontaneous prose (Jung's visionary artist) would not seek *le mot juste*, and once the free run of his thought was down on paper there would be no revision save for obvious mistakes and "inserting." The best writing, Kerouac argued, was confessional, songs of the self, "painful personal wrung-out tossed from cradle warm protective mind." Finally, during the act of composition, the writer's state of mind was that of the semi-trance; this would allow the unconscious

> to admit in own uninhibited interesting necessary and so 'modern' language what conscious art would censor, and write excitedly, swiftly, with writing-or-typing cramps, in accordance (as from center to periphery) with laws of orgasm, Reich's 'beclouding of consciousness.'[14]

In a *Paris Review* interview published ten years after the appearance of "Spontaneous Prose," Kerouac expanded on these ideas. He had spent his apprenticeship in *The Town and the City* as a writer with an almost deadly sense of craft, writing and revising so carefully that sometimes he would only produce one sentence a day, and a sentence, he said, without "feeling" at that. In reading the "first person, fast, mad, confessional" letters of his sidekick Neal Cassady (Dean Moriarty, Cody Pomeray), however, Kerouac hit upon the idea of a spontaneous style. Through this technique a writer could render the workings of a mind in action with the immediacy of the spoken word. When did a man speaking to his friends at a bar "go back to a previous sentence to improve it, to defray its rhythmic thought impact"? As Keats had written 150 years before, the writer must allow himself to exist in an atmosphere of uncertainty and mystery, must put his trust in the play of the unconscious on the chords of experience.

In that same interview Kerouac pointed to Goethe's prophecy that literature in the West would move more and more towards the confessional. For spontaneous writing to be successful, for it to be more than random images transcribed as quickly as a writer could type, it would have to move in one of two directions. Either an author would, like Walter Scott, have to content himself with turning out formula fiction — not dealing in symbol, but cliché — or like Henry Miller he would have to reach into the depths of his own experience. Kerouac took the latter course. All his books are highly autobiographical (he prided himself on his photographic memory), and save for his first novel, all are written in the first person. Like a prize-fighter training for a fight, before the actual writing of a book Kerouac would relate long stories of his adventures to friends, all the time allowing patterns to manifest themselves. Then when time came to "pay the rent," he would sit down and tell the story again on paper as if he were engaged in a fast-paced, late-night, drunken reminiscence, throwing off the super-ego restraints which the psychological novelist cultivated.

In *Psychological Types*, Jung broadens his notion of the split in personality attitudes, adopting the Nietzschean dichotomy between the Apollonian and the Dionysian (though where Nietzsche looks to classical Greece for the origin of the Apollonian-Dionysian duality, Jung sees this duality in terms of archetypal dispositions). For the Greeks, Apollo held reign as "the shining one," god of light and perfection, the "sculptor god." Over against Apollo stood Dionysus, god of wine and frenzy. Dionysiacus, Dionusiakos, Dionysus. The mad god surrounded by his train of ecstatic maenads garbed in animal skins and carrying *thyrsi*. "Oh, thou leader of the choral dance ... appear, sovereign, with the women who attend thee, the Thyiai, who dance the night through in ecstasy for thee...." He does appear. He does possess them. And out of their frenzy, as the light and reason of Apollo slips into darkness, comes the dance.

Ecstasy is thus the central factor in the Dionysian vision, the method through which the visionary artist (from Paleolithic shaman on) has courted the type. As William Everson points out, the Dionysian artist

"represents simply the flow of unconscious life in the whole psyche."
When Kerouac talks about the need to do away with "selecting of expression" and traditional notions of structure, when he speaks of writing
"without consciousness," he is centering himself in the Dionysian stream.
The art of the Apollonian is, according to Nietzsche, "the art of the
shaper"; the art of the Dionysian is "the non-plastic art of music." Hence
the importance of jazz, for Kerouac the most thoroughly Dionysian of all
musical forms (though certainly no more Dionysian than primitive tribal
chants or mid-sixties acid-rock, and here Kerouac's conservatism is
showing).

Music and writing are of course two different modes of expression,
yet Kerouac seems to be arguing for a *likeness in sensibility* between the
jazzman and the Dionysian writer. "Jazz," writes Warren Tallman,
"swings in with the moment."[15] The group gives shape to the piece, a fixed
background, as the soloist then takes off from the pattern into a sort of
frenzy. In *On the Road*

> The behatted tenorman was blowing at the peak of a wonderfully
> satisfactory free idea, a rising and falling riff that went from 'EE-yah!' to
> a crazier 'EE-de-lee-yah!' and blasted along.... Uproars of music and the
> tenorman *had it* and everybody knew he had it. Dean was clutching his
> head in the crowd, and it was a mad crowd. They were all urging that
> tenorman to hold it and keep it with cries and wild eyes ... [pp. 196-7].

There can be no mistake here—the black jazzman has plugged into Dean
Moriarty's "It," sending himself and the audience into a Dionysian frenzy.
Like the jazz musician, Kerouac seems to be saying, the novelist must also
work within an established form—the physical limitations of the book itself. Yet, the writer of spontaneous prose can work freely within this
structure, "blowing" as deeply and as truly as Charlie Parker, not stifled
by the mechanics of Apollonian perfection but rather free to flow with the
ecstasy of the dance.

The notions of spontaneity and ecstasy are sourced also for
Kerouac in the work of Wilhelm Reich. In *Function of the Orgasm*, Reich
argues that the orgasm represents a spontaneous discharge of sexual excitation, that "the involuntary bio-energetic contraction of orgasm and
the complete discharge of excitation are the most important criteria for
orgastic potency."[16] As the point of orgasm is reached in sexual intercourse, a "clouding of consciousness" occurs which errupts into the
ultimate Dionysian transportation out of the ego, into the id. Reich
discovered, however, that both male and female patients suffering from a
variety of neuroses were unable to fully experience this transport, that
they all retained a great degree of lucidity during orgasm. He concluded
that this produced a *sexual stasis* in the individual, a clogging-up of sexual
energy that fueled the neurosis. It was only when "full orgastic
gratification took place in the immediate present," that sexual
equilibrium and mental health could be restored.

According to John Tytell, it was William Burroughs who introduced both Kerouac and Ginsberg to Reich's *The Cancer Biopathy*,[17] and in *On the Road* Old Bull Lee (Burroughs) has one of Reich's "orgone accumulators." Kerouac invokes Reich's theory of orgasm in his discussion of "mental state" in "Essentials of Spontaneous Prose." He draws the analogy between the act of "writing without consciousness" and Reich's "beclouding of consciousness" in orgasm. If the novelist is to pass beyond his equivalent of the sexual stasis, an Apollonian hyperconsciousness manifested by an obsession with precision and the intellect, he must surrender himself to the spontaneity of Dionysian ecstasy. This forces him to work in Reich's "immediate present," relying on his own experiences and language as they rise up from the unconscious in the rush of the moment, trusting in the symbolic nature of the world as meaning.

Kerouac's work is a record of his efforts to realize this Dionysian ideal, and that, it seems to me, is its key. While his first novel took three years to write, and underwent constant and intensive revision, *On the Road* took three weeks, *The Subterraneans* three nights, *The Dharma Bums* ten sittings, *Mexico City Blues* three weeks, *Big Sur* ten nights, *Visions of Gerard* twelve nights, *Doctor Sax* one month. How Kerouac developed his spontaneous prose technique can be traced through his first novels, *The Town and the City*, *On the Road*, and *The Subterraneans*.

The Town and the City, Kerouac's earliest book, was published in 1950. Written "according to what they told [Kerouac] at Columbia University" about fiction, the novel is a traditional work in the manner of Thomas Wolfe, relating the changes that confront a New England family as they move from a rural area to the city. As with the later books, *Town and City* is largely autobiographical. The central character is Peter Martin who, like Kerouac, is thirteen years old when the novel opens in 1935. Like his creator, Martin gets a football scholarship to a large university, his father dies, and at the end of the novel he heads out "on the road." The prose style is rich, Wolfean,

> He was on the road again, traveling the continent westward, going off to further and further years, alone by the waters of life, alone, looking towards the lights of the river's cape, towards tapers burning warmly in the town, looking down along the shore in remembrance of the dearness of his father and all of life ... [pp. 498-9]

though one feels throughout the book a sense of a lyricism highly polished and crafted. Still, in the long breath lines the seeds of spontaneous prose are there. *Town and City* also anticipates the sort of subjects Kerouac will focus on in his later work: sketches of Ginsberg (Levinsky), Burroughs (Dennison), and Huncke (Junkey), Peter's hitch-hiking, Liz Martin's interest in jazz and jazz musicians, and the theme of coming of age. Interestingly enough, *Town and City* is the only one of Kerouac's novels that is not told in the first person. While the novel has some powerful scenes, it is clearly imitative — Kerouac is searching for his voice.

It had taken three years to complete his first novel, and by the end of that time Kerouac had come to the conclusion that the traditional novel form was dead. "I broke loose from all that," he told Ann Charters in 1966, "and write picaresque narratives — that's what my books are."[18] In contrast to the painfully crafted *Town and City*, Kerouac wrote *On the Road* in three weeks in April of 1951 on a roll of paper "100 miles long, then later [he] typed it up double-space on the typewriter with made-up names." Actually, the final draft of the book underwent several revisions, both substantive and accidental, yet here Kerouac had begun to settle into his archetype.

On the Road is written in the first person and is pretty thoroughly autobiographical. The action of the book picks up the year *Town and City* concludes, and centers on a series of cross-country trips Kerouac made between 1946 and 1950. Here again we have sketches of Ginsberg, Burroughs, and Huncke, but the bulk of the novel centers on Dean Moriarty (Neal Cassady), who hovered like a spector over Kerouac's career.

Dean Moriarty, "a young Gene Autry" whose soul "is wrapped up in a fast car, a coast to reach, and a woman at the end of the road," is the archetypal Dionysian. Like the jazzmen he worships, he is caught up in the frenzy of the present, and Sal Paradise (Kerouac) is attracted to him because he is one of the

> mad ones, the ones who are mad to live, mad to talk, and to be saved, desirous of everything at the same time, the ones who never yawn or say a commonplace thing, but burn, burn, burn like fabulous yellow roman candles exploding like spiders across the stars and in the middle you see the blue centerlight pop and everybody goes 'Awww!' [p. 8].

He rushes through the world looking for the ultimate Reichian charge, "IT," and often gets so intensely involved in ecstatic conversation with Sal that he stops mid-sentence, sweating, out of breath, wild-eyed. Dean wants to learn how to write from Sal, yet it is Dean himself who stresses the very problem of stasis with which Sal is coping. "How to even *begin* to get it down," Dean asks, "without modified restraints and all hung-up on like literary inhibitions and grammatical fears..." (7). His one "noble function is to *move.*

In *On the Road* the writing is much flatter than in Kerouac's first novel — Wolfean lyricism has been replaced with a certain terseness, a style much more conducive to surface description than to metaphor. Still, for the most part the narrative reads grammatically straight; leaving aside the question of the extent of the editing Kerouac's publishers insisted upon to bring the manuscript in line with their house style, it would be difficult to reconcile the sentence structure of the text as we have it with the idea of spontaneous prose. It was, however, Neal Cassady's wild letters that gave Kerouac insight into what he wanted to do with his prose, and in the mad rush and manic speech of Dean Moriarty we see the emergence of the Dionysian attitude.

In *The Subterraneans* Moriarty's "modified restraints" disappear as Kerouac's spontaneous prose, the most obvious manifestation of his Dionysian vision, kicks into high-gear. Kerouac wrote the novel in three "full moon nights" on a long roll of paper, while taking benzedrine. Later, in the *Paris Review* interview, he described the frenzy as an athletic feat: "After I was done I was pale as a sheet and had lost fifteen pounds and looked strange in the mirror." Like a crazed desert saint touched by the Holy Ghost, he had been swept up on the archetype and had abandoned himself to it.

Aside from the fact that Kerouac shifts the scene of the action from New York to San Francisco, and that he again creates fictional names for his friends (Ginsberg is Adam Moorad, Burroughs is Frank Carmody, Holmes is Balliol MacJones, Corso becomes Yuri Gligoric), *The Subterraneans* is highly autobiographical. "The book," he wrote in a blurb for the Norwegian edition in 1960, "is modelled after Dostoevsky's *Notes from the Underground*, a full confession of one's most wretched and hidden agonies after an 'affair' of any kind." The novel traces Kerouac's affair with a black woman he calls "Mardou," whom he met in the Village in 1953 at Ginsberg's apartment. A prototype of the media "beatnik," Mardou, like Liz Martin, was interested in jazz; she spent her time in "bohemian mystery, drugs, beards, semi-holiness and ... insurpassable nastiness." In the novel, Leo Percepied (Kerouac) is attracted by Mardou's "fellaheen Darkness," as Sal Paradise was attracted to the brown sensuality of the young Mexican whores in *On the Road*. For Kerouac, as for Hemingway, these brown women are a link to the primitive, and Mardou is a decidedly Dionysian figure. Unfortunately for Leo, however, it is Mardou's sexuality that brings the affair to a close after two months, when she makes love to Yuri Gligoric in a drunken stupor.

Kerouac was proud of *The Subterraneans* and he felt that he had finally broken through the Reichian stasis with a burst of Dionysian spontaneity. In the Norwegian preface he explained that here was "the prose of the future, from both the conscious top and the unconscious bottom of the mind ... UNINTERRUPTED AND UNREVISED." As the writing progressed with no concern for traditional syntax or grammar in an attempt to catch the combination of incident and impression as it sped through Kerouac's memory, it registered with the spontaneity of the jazzman. The book's structure was based, he explained, on

> jazz and bop, in the sense of a, say, tenor man drawing a breath, and blowing a phrase on his saxophone, till he runs out of breath, and when he does, his sentence, his statement's been made ... that's how I therefore separate my sentences, as breath separations of the mind.... Then there's the raciness and freedom and humor of jazz instead of all that dreary analysis.[19]

The sentences are long, constantly shifting between narrative and observation, moving freely from the present to the past then back again. The fourth sentence in the book is an example. It is 313 words long and has, as Warren Tallman points out, seven shifts from the simple narrative line. This is what Kerouac calls "association" in "Essentials of Spontaneous Prose." Joyce, Faulkner, and Woolf all used variations of the same idea, of course, but for each of them the association was simply a literary device, an attempt to portray the psychology of a character's *consciously created* mind. Because Kerouac makes no attempt to separate himself from his narrator, his association becomes truly spontaneous in the Wordsworthian sense, a rushing forth of a mind caught, like the jazzman's, between surface "melody" and archaic resonance, between world as fact and world as meaning.

In an essay called "The Last Word," published in *Escapade* in 1959, and revised in 1967 not long before his death, Kerouac wrote that shame

> seems to be the key to repression in writing as well as in psychological malady. If you don't stick to what you first thought, and the words the thought brought what's the sense of bothering with it anyway, what's the sense of foisting your little lies on others? What I really find 'stupefying in its unreadability' is this laborious and dreary lying called craft and revision.

Can art lie? For the Modernists the question itself was moot, and for postmodernist critics like Susan Sontag the ability to lie has become one of the chief attributes of the artist. As Sontag has recently pointed out in *On Photography*, the artist's obligation to inform us about the nature of the world and man's place in it becomes at best a minor concern, as the art object is stripped of moral function in favor of the primacy of the aesthetic dimension. The artist, for Sontag, works in the world but he never transcends it; rather, he creates imaginative alternatives, second orders of reality, "supreme fictions." And for the introverted artist, the psychological artist, the Apollonian, it is because these orders of reality are not always in registration that art can, in Sontag's sense, "lie."

For Kerouac, however, the artist's obligation to inform becomes the primary and, finally, the only obligation. The artist works in the world, but rather than a creator of imaginative second orders, he is an aperture to the transcendental dimension. "The function of poetry," Robert Graves wrote in *The White Goddess*, "is religious invocation of the Muse," and Kerouac would agree. As an extravert living in a world of meaning he could see the artist's vocation only in its most archaic sense—the vocation of the *fili* and *derwydd*, the vocation of priest and shaman. In *Town and the City*, then, Kerouac felt he had "foisted his little lies of craft and revision" on both himself and his readers. From that point on, however, his books were a record of his attempts to capture the pulse of the jazzman, to move progressively into the realm of the visionary artist, to surrender himself to the womb of the collective unconscious, bodying forth the Dionysian ideal.

[1] William Everson, "Dionysus & the Beat Generation," in *Earth Poetry: Selected Essays and Interviews of William Everson* (Berkeley, 1980).

[2] Albert Gelpi, *The Tenth Muse: The Psyche of the American Poet* (Cambridge, Mass., 1975), pp. 45-6.

[3] C.G. Jung, "On the Relation of Analytical Psychology to Poetic Art," in *Contributions to Analytical Psychology* (New York), p. 231.

[4] "On Psychical Energy," *Ibid.*, p. 56.

[5] *Ibid.*, p. 53.

[6] C.G. Jung, *Psychological Types* (London, 1953), p. 616.

[7] C.G. Jung, *Symbols of Transformation* (London, 1956), p. 157.

[8] *Psychological Types*, p. 467.

[9] See Chapter X, "General Description of the Types," in *Psychological Types* for fuller treatment.

[10] Morris, Philipson, *Outline of Jungian Aesthetics* (Evanston, 1963), pp. 104-05.

[11] *Ibid.*, p. 105.

[12] *Ibid.*, p. 106.

[13] Jack Kerouac, "Essentials of Spontaneous Prose," in *A Casebook on the Beat*, edited by Thomas Parkinson (New York, 1961), p. 66.

[14] *Ibid.*, p. 67.

[15] Warren Tallman, "Kerouac's Sound," in *A Casebook*, p. 218.

[16] Wilhelm Reich, *The Function of the Orgasm* (New York, 1942), p. 85.

[17] John Tytell, *Naked Angels: The Lives and Literatures of the Beat Generation* (New York, 1976), p. 39.

[18] See Ann Charters, *A Bibliography of Works by Jack Kerouac* (New York, 1967).

[19] See Kerouac's interview with Ted Berrigan and Aram Saroyan in the *Paris Review*, 43 (Summer, 1968).

The Delicate Dynamics
of Friendship: A Reconsideration
of Kerouac's *On the Road*

by George Dardess

When Norman Mailer asserted, in *Advertisements for Myself*,[1] that Jack Kerouac "lacks discipline, intelligence, honesty and a sense of the novel," he was giving voice to an opinion so generally accepted that no critic to this day has attempted to refute or even qualify it. Yet Kerouac's books continue to be read, and even his unpublished manuscripts are receiving attention. (*Visions of Cody*, a work written in 1951-1952, was published in January 1973 by McGraw-Hill.) In addition, a full scale biography has recently appeared (Ann Charters, *Kerouac*, Straight Arrow Press, 1973), and another is in progress. Nevertheless, critical reassessment lags. Readers admire hesitatingly, even helplessly, as if they were unsure how to describe a writer for whom few terms, except pejorative ones, have been invented. What is needed to counteract the negative influence of unproved opinions like Mailer's is not, however, a vocabulary of praise but one of careful critical judgment like that recently accorded Mailer himself.[2] Kerouac's work deserves understanding. If, after treating the work fairly, we find condemnation justified, we can pass with good conscience to worthier objects.

A close look at Kerouac's work suggests that his "sense of the novel," though not identical to Mailer's, is carefully and rigorously developed; and his "discipline, intelligence, honesty" are indeed evident, perhaps most clearly so in the novel for which he is best known, *On the Road*. For though many readers of *On the Road* have thought it a modern version of the picaresque,[3] its structure is formidably complex. Here is no loose scribbling of notes whose only organization is geographical and chronological, but a delicately constructed account of the relation between the narrator, Sal Paradise, and his friend, Dean Moriarty — an account built according to a classic dramatic design. *On the Road* is a love story, not a travelog (and certainly not a call to Revolution). It is told with all the "art" — the conscious and unconscious shaping of verbal materials — one expects from the best writing. Kerouac may legitimately

127

be, even on the basis of *On the Road* alone, a great American author—an author the equal of Mailer himself.

A comparison between the opening and closing paragraphs of *On the Road* gives a preliminary idea of the book's structural complexity. Where the book begins cautiously, with careful distinctions made between the narrator's present, his Moriarty past, and his pre-Moriarty past, it ends with a complicated paragraph in which temporal and spatial boundaries are obliterated. A similar change occurs in the emotional associations attributed to each paragraph's treatment of time. Where the book opens with a gleam of happiness ("the part of my life you could call my life on the road"[4]) preceded by darkness (by "the miserably weary split-up" between the narrator and his wife), it ends with a mix of hope and discouragement, of expansiveness and resignation. (In the last paragraph, for instance, the discouraged wisdom of the phrase "nobody, nobody knows what's going to happen to anybody besides the forlorn rags of growing old" is contained within a panoramic gesture embracing the entire American continent.) The book begins with the narrator's construction of distinctions and boundaries; it ends with his discarding them—a discarding which indicates his desire to suspend opposites in a perhaps continuous state of flux. The book moves from hierarchy to openness, from the limitation of possibilities to their expansion.

Such a movement might seem to suggest that *On the Road* becomes incoherent: a book in which the ending does not resolve complexities might seem careless or meaningless. Alan Friedman, in *The Turn of the Novel*,[5] assures us, however, that absence of resolution need not deny fictional closure. It can substitute closure of a different kind, one appropriate to the narrated experience. As for *On the Road*, its narrated experience is such that an open ending is appropriate. The experience consists in the narrator's desire, as shown in the first paragraph of the book, to render events of a happier "part" of his life without, as much as possible, contaminating his feelings about that "part" with his feelings about other parts of his life, including his feelings about the present. The narrated experience also consists, however, in the narrator's final assimilation of the events he is dramatizing with the moment of dramatization itself. In the book's last paragraph the narrator speaks from a present tense ("So in America when the sun goes down and I sit on the old broken-down river pier...") in which all parts of his life, together with the part from which he is now speaking, are included.

Yet the assimilation of times just referred to does not disturb the book's classic dramatic shape. One of Kerouac's accomplishments in *On the Road* is in fact to unify the open ending (in which all points of view in the novel are combined without being resolved) with a time-honored novelistic and dramaturgic structure. The structure is evident in a narration divided into five Parts, the third of which contains what can be called the climax of Sal's and Dean's friendship. Parts One and Two record Sal's gradual development of excited interest in Dean, while Part Four records Sal's development of an apocalyptic fear of him. Accompanying the growing complexity of Sal's relation to Dean is an outfanning geographical movement. Each Part records a circuit of the United States with New York, Denver, and San Francisco serving as the main geographical and cultural axes. In Parts Two and Three, important detours are made from more or less straight lines of progress connecting one axis with another, the first detour by way of New Orleans, the second by way of Chicago. In Part Four, the friends spin off the board altogether towards Mexico City and the "end of the road." In Part Five, Sal and Dean go their separate ways, each friend towards opposite shores of the American continent.

The men's relations are intimately connected to the direction and scope of their geographical movements. As their geographical range increases, so does the range and complexity of their relation. In Part One, for instance, Dean is mostly on the periphery of Sal's experience. Consequently, this is the innocent section of *On the Road*, the one most unqualifiedly romantic. Sal is making his first road trip, alone, across the country, and his feelings are those of boyish delight. Though there are perceptions of *lacrimae rerum* (the "tears of things"), the perceptions do not achieve dramatic coherence. They do not achieve coherence even when Dean enters the center of Sal's life in Part Two, since Sal's attitude towards Dean is at this point too wide-eyed, too bedazzled by admiration. The negative aspects of Dean's conduct are hinted at but never in this Part confronted systematically. Beginning with Part Three, however, Sal begins to confront the consequences of Dean's vulnerability to "IT," to ecstasy, to the promise of being able to reduce time and space to smaller and smaller increments until they disappear altogether as measurements of activity. Where in Parts One and Two "IT" functions as an ultimate mystery to which Dean's relation is priest-like (and Sal's is that of the neophyte), in Part Three Sal takes custodianship not only of Dean but of the "IT" which Dean embodies more consistently and dramatically than anyone else Sal knows. And by taking custody of Dean and "IT," Sal changes from being little more than an admirer caught up in Dean's wake to becoming Dean's father-defender. The change occurs just after Sal arrives at Dean's house and finds that Dean and his wife Camille are at war:

"Why did Camille throw you out? What are you going to do?"

"Eh?" he said, "Eh? Eh?" We racked our brains for where to go and what to do. I realized it was up to me. Poor, poor Dean—the devil himself had never fallen farther; in idiocy, with infected thumb, surrounded by the battered suitcases of his motherless feverish life across America and back numberless times, an undone bird. "Let's walk to New York," he said, "and as we do so let's take stock of everything along the way—yass." I took out my money and counted it; I showed it to him.

"I have here," I said, "the sum of eighty-three dollars and change, and if you come with me let's go to New York." ... "Why yass," said Dean, and then realized I was serious and looked at me out of the corner of his eye for the first time, for I'd never committed myself before with regard to his burdensome existence, and that look was the look of a man weighing his chances at the last moment before the bet. There were triumph and insolence in those eyes, a devilish look, and he never took his eyes off mine for a long time. I looked at him and blushed.

I said, "What's the matter?" I felt wretched when I asked it. He made no answer but continued looking at me with the same wary insolent side-eye.

I tried to remember everything he'd done in his life and if there wasn't something back there to make him suspicious of something now. Resolutely and firmly I repeated what I said— "Come to New York with me; I've got the money." I looked at him; my eyes were watering with embarrassment and tears. Still he stared at me. Now his eyes were blank and looking through me. It was probably the pivotal point of our friendship when he realized I had actually spent some hours thinking about him and his troubles, and he was trying to place that in his tremendously involved and tormented mental categories. (pp. 188-189)

This passage marks the "pivotal point" not only of the friendship but of the book as well. Sal's assuming responsibility for what he now calls Dean's "burdensome existence" — that is, seen *as* "burdensome" in the act of taking responsibility for it — brings out unexpected responses both in himself and his friend. What's more, those responses begin to affect almost immediately the way both of them see the world. The remainder of *On the Road* is concerned with working out the consequences of the new responses dramatically. Later, in Part Three, Sal himself receives possession of "IT" during the friends' journey east; and before they leave San Francisco Sal stands up in defense of Dean before a "jury" composed of Dean's former friends. These would seem, however, more or less predictable consequences of Sal's behavior in the "pivotal" scene. Far trickier psychologically and metaphysically are the consequences of Dean's "devilish look" and Sal's blush.

When Sal says, at the beginning of the passage quoted, that "the devil himself has never fallen farther," we may either dismiss the analogy as hyperbolic or say that the analogy connects Dean not with the devil but with the devil's falling. According to the latter view, Sal would be trying to indicate only the suddenness of Dean's loss of self-control; where "IT" had sustained Dean in Part Two above the world of hurt and family obligation, "IT" abandons him in Part Three. But when Sal assumes the sustaining function of "IT" here, he sees Dean in a new and terrible light. Dean's "weighing his chances at the last moment before the bet" has about it the calculating coldness of the devil himself. Or is Sal the devil? When one adult assumes absolute responsibility for the existence — "Burdensome" or not — of another adult, he does so at what seems a great risk, since both parties sacrifice to each other their independence. Everything one does has direct, immediate, and perhaps mortal effects on the other; there is no escaping the implications of each other's conduct. Later in Part Three, for instance, Sal begins to see Dean in terms of titanic evil: "the Angel of Terror" (p. 233), a "mad Ahab" (p. 234), and finally, at the beginning of Part Four, as "a burning, frightful Angel, palpitating toward me across the road, approaching like a cloud, with enormous speed, pursuing me like the Shrouded Traveler on the plain" (p. 259) — the same "Shrouded Traveler" whom Sal had earlier, in Part Two, identified with Death (p. 124).

These apocalyptic forebodings acquire their greatest significance in Part Four, when Dean, Sal, and another friend make their trip to Mexico City and to what they call the "end of the road" (p. 276). After leaving the United States, the three men suppose that they are entering the land of "basic, primitive, wailing humanity" (p. 280). And in this land they feel close to the source of all understanding, But they feel also — and particularly the narrator, Sal, feels this — a strain between apocalyptic truths and the sensory evidence that ought to support them unequivocally. Mexico City's status as "end of the road" has to be put beside the fact that while there Sal contracts dysentery. And Dean's status as leader has to be put beside his abandoning Sal at the "end of the road." (He does so in order to return to New York with a Mexican divorce from his second wife, Camille, in order then to commit himself to yet a third.) Sal's comment on Dean's shabby act shows a further dimension of the responsibility he took for Dean in Part Three: "When I got better I realized what a rat he was, but then I had to understand the impossible complexity of his life, how he had to leave me there, sick, to get on with his wives and woes. 'Okay, old Dean, I'll say nothing' " (p. 303).

To have responsibility for your friend means not only providing him with companionship or with money, not only defending him before a jury of his peers; it means also — and painfully — maintaining a sense of how your friend sees himself apart from the way you see him. But, perhaps more painfully, it means maintaining a sense of how the friend see *you* apart from the way you see yourself. Maintaining such difficult senses is an act of generosity few people care to perform unless they are in love. And if they are in love, they are people — like Sal Paradise — susceptible to the wild contradictory splendors of human behavior. There certainly is justice in Sal's calling Dean a "rat," though earlier in Part Four Sal claimed, during a particularly strong marijuana "rush," that Dean "looked like God." The one view doesn't cancel out the other; they exist side by side, the sides being defined by the division established throughout the book between those human possibilities which lead to "IT" and those which lead to failure and exhaustion.

But the division is established only to be held in suspension. By choosing one side or the other, by declaring once and for all that Dean *is* a "rat" and nothing else or by declaring that he *is* "God" and nothing else,

Sal could rest on the security of an unambiguous position. Yet what price security? Taking the first option, Sal commits himself to a resigned cynicism; taking the second, to a mindless hero-worship. The third option — to make no choice at all — is described by a writer whom Kerouac strongly resembles, F. Scott Fitzgerald, in *The Crack-Up:* "... the test of a first-rate intelligence is the ability to hold two opposed ideas in the mind at the same time and still retain the ability to function. One should, for example, be able to see that things are hopeless and yet be determined to make them otherwise."[6]

If under the term "function" we can assume that Fitzgerald would include writing (and it is hard to see how we cannot), then *On the Road* is an example of such a test's being taken — and passed, though passing would have to be subjected to the same conditions as those which obtain in the test situation. That "first-rate intelligence" has to see that even a "first-rate intelligence" is, from one point of view, "hopeless." Writing a book about friendship does not allow for tidy endings or unmixed feelings. What takes their place is a fragile, impossible, contradictory structure sustained by the energy of intelligence alone. But such energy is not supplied without cost, and perhaps much of the despair Kerouac (speaking through other narrators) displays in his subsequent writing[7] can be attributed to his awareness of how exorbitant that cost was, though it was a cost he never ceased to pay.

[1] See *Advertisements for Myself* (New York: Berkley Medallion Ed., 1966), p. 428.

[2] Particularly by Richard Poirier in *Mailer*, in the Modern Masters Series, ed. F. Kermode (New York, 1972).

[3] Even someone so close to Kerouac as Allen Ginsberg thinks the book's structure picaresque. See Ginsberg's interview in *Writers at Work; The Paris Review Interviews*, Third Series, ed. George Plimpton (New York, 1967), p. 288.

[4] *On the Road* (New York, 1957), p. 3. The book was written in 1951, six years before it was finally published. All subsequent page references to *On the Road* will refer to this edition and will be found in the text directly after the quoted passages.

[5] Alan Friedman, *The Turn of the Novel* (New York, 1966), esp. pp. 179-188.

[6] F.S. Fitzgerald, *The Crack-Up* (New York, 1956), p. 69.

[7] Especially in *Desolation Angels* (written in 1956 and 1961) and *Big Sur* (written in 1961).

The Poetry of
Gary Snyder

by Thomas Parkinson

I

The poetic pantheon keeps changing for the young. They cannot look on Yeats, Eliot, even Pound as their parents and teachers did — the world before the atomic bomb is as remote to them as Ovid's Rome, and Yeats and Eliot are literature, what is studied in school, artifacts in anthologies, only rarely live books carried into the heart by passion. A new order is established of the living gods, contemporary legends, stars in active influence. The way of the world. Some poets, Allen Ginsberg, Voznesensky, Robert Duncan, Denise Levertov, or Robert Lowell, have the status of such celebrities as Norman Mailer and Stokely Carmichael.

Gary Snyder has not had so much public exposure, having spent most of the past decade in Japan, where he writes and studies. He has become a legend for several reasons: first, he is not merely interested in Buddhism but has studied Japanese and Chinese so thoroughly that he is fluent in conversational Japanese and translates easily from both languages. When he taught freshman English at Berkeley for a year, he was vaguely troubled by the problem of fitting Andrew Marvell's "The Garden" into the history of Chinese poetry. The western world with its dualisms and antinomies he has made alien to himself. His knowledge of Zen Buddhism is not that of a dilettante but, insofar as this is possible for an occidental, of an adept. He is at present completing a study of the history of Zen rituals for the Bollingen Foundation, based on records that have not been available to an occidental nor systematically studied by anyone. Second, he is skilled in the use of his hands. If he were put down in the most remote wilderness with only a pocket knife, he would emerge from it cheerfully within two weeks, full of fresh experience, and with no loss of weight. There is a physical, intellectual, and moral sturdiness to him that is part of each movement he makes and each sentence he phrases. He is gracious, soft-spoken, incisive, and deeply intelligent. Third, he is an extraordinarily skillful poet, and his work develops steadily toward more thorough and profound insight. If there has been a

133

San Francisco renaissance, Snyder is its Renaissance Man: scholar, woods-
man guru, artist, creatively maladjusted, accessible, open, and full of
fun.

This is no way to start a critical essay. I should have a problem, a
critical problem, but these introductory notes are personal and
biographical — perhaps that is the problem. For when one thinks of
Snyder, the personal and biographical obtrude in a way they do not with
Duncan or with Levertov — their work remains intelligible within the
traditions of European poetry; Snyder presents a different set of references and beings. It is necessary to call on different habits of thought, and to
think of the poetry as creating a different set of human possibilities. Nor is
it a simple matter — insofar as such matters are simple — of translating
Eastern into Western nomenclature; Snyder is Western in many direct
and palpable ways. He has effectively done something that for an individual is extremely difficult: he has created a new culture.

The culture was there in potentia for anyone who cared to seize
upon it; to paraphrase Trotsky, Pacific Basin Culture was lying in the
streets and no one knew how to pick it up. The paintings of Mark Tobey
(pre-white paintings) and of Morris Graves and the sculpture of Richard
O'Hanlon prefigured what Snyder would do, and Kenneth Rexroth had
an intuitive grasp. But the peculiar blending of Zen Buddhism with
IWW political attitudes, Amerindian lore, and the mystique of the
wilderness was Snyder's special articulation. He had associates — Phil
Whalen, Lew Welch, Jack Kerouac, Allen Ginsberg — and he has
followers, especially James Koller. Along with Creeley and Lowell, he is a
primary influence on the writing of young people now, though as a
spiritual rather than technical force. His voice is so clear and firm that it is
fatally easy to imitate, so that the Gary Snyder poem that his apprentices
discover and write has a certain mechanical quality — a reference to
Coyote or Bear, a natural (preferably wilderness) setting, erotic over-
tones, plain colloquial language, firm insistence on an objective imagery,
an anecdotal frame, short lines modeled on the Chinese Cantos of Ezra
Pound with much internal rhyme and alliteration, very little dead weight
(the prepositional phrase held in abomination). The sources of the style
are Pound and Rexroth, Pound technically, Rexroth for general political
orientation and stress on beach and high country — the segment of A
Range of Poems called "The Back Country" is dedicated to Rexroth. The
proximity to Pound and Rexroth comes partly from genuine indebtedness
to them but more largely from immersion in the same origins: he started
from the older poets but returned to their sources to see and shape them in
a special form.

II

RIPRAP is Snyder's first book. The title means "a cobble of stone laid on steep slick rock/ to make a trail for horses in the mountain." In a later poem he wrote of "Poetry a riprap on the slick rock of metaphysics," the reality of perceived surface that grants men staying power and a gripping point.

> Lay down these words
> Before your mind like rocks.
>   placed solid, by hands
> In choice of place, set
> Before the body of the mind
>   in space and time:
> Solidity of bark, leaf, or wall
>   riprap of things:
> Cobble of Milky way,
>   straying planets,
> These poems ...

The body of the mind — this is the province of poetry, a riprap on the abstractions of the soul that keeps men in tune with carnal eloquence. The notorious dislike of abstractions in modern poetic theory is here seen in a fresh perspective. Poets are entitled to dislike all abstractions except one, and that is language. For Yvor Winters is entirely right in pointing out that poetry is necessarily abstract because its elements are words. The words may be like rocks, but only in the sense that they are so placed, so composed that the action of placement is carried by the syntax and prosody of the poem. Their gravity depends on their placement, as does their capacity for bearing human weight; Snyder's equation is one of proportion, poetry being to metaphysics as riprap to slick rock. Things and thoughts are not then in opposition but in parallel:

> ... ants and pebbles
> In the thin loam, each rock a word
>   a creek-washed stone
> Granite: ingrained
>   with torment of fire and weight
> Crystal and sediment linked hot
>   all change, in thoughts,
> As well as things.

The final and title poem of *RIPRAP* is programmatic for subsequent work as well, and the program seems to be to deny or transcend or go back of the famous dissociation of sensibility that Eliot identified. The aim is not to achieve harmony with nature but to create an inner human harmony that equals to the natural external harmony. There is not then an allegorical relation between man and natural reality but an analogical one; a man does not identify with a tree nor does he take the tree to be an emblem of his own psychic condition; he establishes within himself a state of being that is equivalent to that of the tree, and there metaphysics

rushes in. Only poetry can take us through such slippery territory, and after *RIPRAP* Snyder tries to find a guide in his *Myths and Texts*. The basic
guide should be style, a style of movement that will account for the
solidity, denseness, and relations of phenomena.

I am not sure that Snyder has, even in his most recent work, found
such a style. He has a personal voice but that is not, except for moments in
printed segments of *Mountains and Rivers without End*, enough; certainly not enough for a poetics that claims, in effect, that poetry is not the
expression of order but the basis. The distrust of metaphysics and of
ethical schemes forces Snyder to that position. The problem is further
complicated by the picaresque structure of the poetry, literally the poetry
of a picaro, the roguishness of the verse being related to the roguish wit of
Zen masters, the tricksterism of Coyote, the travel records of Basho, and
the wanderings of Bindlestiffs: "Down 99, through towns, to San Fran-
cisco/ and Japan." Some of the poetry's pleasure derives from its anecdotal
narrative structures, so that reading a sizable body of the poetry puts the
reader in touch with an amusing cultivated mind, a lovely harsh landscape, and a capricious movement through experience. The result is
rather like reading a good novel. As early as *RIPRAP* these qualities are
evident, in "The Late Snow and Lumber Strike," "Milton by Firelight,"
and the title poem. The crucial poem, "A Stone Garden," shows why
Snyder's style cannot accept the standard line of English poetry, for in
that poem he tries to accept the norm of the five stress lines, and can't hold
to it; can't, not because he doesn't want to but because of the inherent
tendency of that line toward reminiscent meditation. For all its subject
matter it sounds oddly British and New England:

> But with the noble glance I Am Loved
> From Children and from crones, time is destroyed.
> The cities rise and fall and rise again ...
> The glittering ricefields bloom,
> And all that growing up and burning down
> Hangs in the void a little knot of sound.

The entire poem moves from the kind of standard movement seen here to
occasional destruction of the line by the intervention of abstraction that is
not controlled: "Because impermanence and destructiveness of time" is a
mouthful; or toward the kind of ellipse that later marks the poetry distinc-
tively: "The oldest and nakedest women more the sweet." The kind of
trouble that grows from the beat of tradition against his not totally comprehended subject matter upsets the movement of many poems:

> A few light flakes of snow
> Fall in the feeble sun;
> Birds sing in the cold,
> A warbler by the wall ...

All right, up to the point of the last line. Then it becomes, in the pejorative sense, poetic, too much attention to the alliteration and internal rhyme, not enough momentum in the motivation. The poem continues in an almost nineteenth-century form:

> ... The plum
> Buds tight and chill soon bloom.

This is both clumsy and archaic, the inversion not necessary to the style, the heavy closing internal rhyme. The ambiguity of "buds" (verb or noun?) is not controlled and doesn't function, so that the appearance of modernity, the typical Williamsean trick of using line breaks to create functioning syntactic ambiguity, gets held down by the habits of an irrelevant syntax. Often lines move, as they do in Robert Lowell's recent verse, in designs that give and withhold the promise of conventional prosody:

> Beneath the roofs of frosty houses lovers part,
> From tangle warm of gentle bodies under quilt
> And crack the icy water to the face and wake
> And feed the children and grandchildren that they love.

This is hexameter, in my printing, but it is broken hexameter in Snyder's printing:

> ... Beneath the roofs
> Of frosty houses
> Lovers part, from tangle warm
> Of gentle bodies under quilt
> And crack the icy water to the face
> And wake and feed the children
> And grandchildren that they love.

This is not in any sense free verse, nor is it hacked-up prose; it is the product of a mind that moves naturally in traditional meters and then tries to deny the movement. The contention is interesting; the subject matter is compelling; the sensibility is engaged in what it perceives; with RIPRAP alone Snyder's work is an uneasy wedding of European forms with attitudes that threaten and try desperately to break those forms. But it is surprising how many standard lines appear, and at crucial points such as the end of a poem: "... & salvage only from it all a poem." Or the beginning: "Old rusty-belly thing will soon be gone/ Scrap and busted while we're still on earth...." "It started just now with a hummingbird...." Or at a moment of thematic resolution: "The noise of living families fills the air."

III

Myths and Texts is a different matter. Although some of the poems were printed as early as 1952 and Snyder gives its date of completion as 1956, it is a world away from the first book. It has a genuine informing principle and coherence of purposeful movement, and the line has a life that is particular to its subject. The first two sections of the book are on Logging and Hunting, what men do to the earth; the third on Fire, why they do it. In this book appear in complex form the issues that compel the verse at its base. He wants to reach a prehuman reality, the wilderness and the cosmos in which man lives as an animal with animals in a happy ecology. This precivilized reality he finds embodied in Amerindian lore, especially of the Pacific Northwest and of California, and in Buddhist myth. He occupies the uneasy position of understanding this mode of perception and of acting, as logger and hunter, against its grain. This realization is the dramatic core of the book and holds it from sentimentality, granting it a kind of tension and prophetic force (evident in the pro-wobbly poems) that *RIPRAP* and much of his later work lacks. *Myths and Texts* is an elegy of involvement: to have witnessed, it was necessary to be one of the destroyers. His sense of involvement keeps him from invective, except against those exploiters who ordered the destruction of nature and at the same time denied rights to the workers who had the hard nasty labor. The world that Snyder treats is part of his total fabric, and he cannot falsely externalize it. He cannot point with awe to the objects of his experience because they have become attached to him through touch and action. It is not even necessary for him to lament this world which, through his poetry, he has preserved. He moves fluently through this world as a local spirit taking the forms of Coyote and Han-shan and a ghostly logger. In these poems action and contemplation become identical states of being, and both states of secular grace. From this fusion wisdom emerges, and it is not useless but timed to the event. The result is a terrible sanity, a literal clairvoyance, an innate decorum. This poetry does not suffer from cultural thinness. The tools, animals, and processes are all interrelated; they sustain the man; he devours them. But the author of the book and the poet in the book are nourished by a web of being, a culture. To have the support of a culture you have to work in and respect your environs, not as one respects a supermarket (thanks for the grapefruit wrapped in plastic) but as one respects a farm, knowing what labor went into the fruit, what risks were accepted and overcome, what other lives (moles, weasels, foxes, deer) were damaged or slighted in the interests of your own.

One of the touchstone lines for modern poetry is Pound's "Quick eyes gone under earth's lid." It holds its unity partly through the internal rhyme of first and final word, partly through the unstrained conceit of random association between eyelid and coffin lid, and the earth as dead eye and graveyard. Mainly, though, it has no waste, no void spaces, none of the flab that English invites through the prepositional phrase designs of a noninflected language. Solid poetry in English manages compressions that keep up the stress, and relaxations from that motive have their justification in the larger poetic unit of poem or book. The temptation of composition in serial form, the method of *Myths and Texts*, is vindicating the relaxed line in the name of a higher motive, the world view of the poet, the personal relevance. Snyder doesn't fall back on such flimsy supports. Sometimes, straining to maintain the stress he loses control: "... fighting flies fixed phone line ..." This is not only pointlessly elliptical but meaninglessly ambiguous and far too clogged. But in its excesses it demonstrates the basic prosodic motive, full use of consonant and vowel tone as organizing devices, reduction of connective words having merely grammatical function and no gravity.

Snyder himself thinks of this prosody as deriving from classical Chinese forms, and both he and Pound make severe and interesting variations on that line. But variations, and since Pound's Cathay and the Chinese Cantos, people like Snyder are compelled toward Pound's brilliant invention of a line using the Anglo-Saxon alliterative line in conjunction with a line of four and two main centers of stress divided by cesura or by line break.

I talk at such length of prosody because it is the main factor ignored in most recent discussion of poetry. Thanks to Donald Davie and Josephine Miles, attention has very rightly been turned toward poetic syntax, with fine results, and the extension to prosody is inevitable and right. New criticism (old style) placed heavy weight on suggestion and symbolic reference; now as our poetry stresses drama and syntactic movement, vocality, it seems necessary to supplement the notion, and a pernicious one, that poetry functions through symbol mainly. Language functions symbolically and metaphorically, but poetry makes more precise and delimiting use of syntax through its prosodic measure. This is after all what Pound and Williams were agitated about: the dance of language. I don't want to hang everything on syntactic and metric effects and take a plunge into providing new mechanical vocabulary that will deaden poetic study from yet another perspective. What poets like Snyder, Duncan, and Creeley ask is that readers take the poem as indicator of physical weight. Until the day, not far off, when poems are related to taped performances as musical scores now are, the poem on the page is evidence of a voice and the poetic struggle is to note the movement of that voice so that it can be, as is music, followed.

    The groves are down
      cut down

Groves of Ahab, of Cybele
Pine trees, knobbed twigs
   thick cone and seed
   Cybele's tree this, sacred in groves
Pine of Seami, cedar of Haida
Cut down by the prophets of Israel
   the fairies of Athens
   the thugs of Rome
      both ancient and modern;
Cut down to make room for the suburbs
Bulldozed by Luther and Weyerhaeuser
Crosscut and chainsaw
   squareheads and finns
   high-lead and cat-skidding
Trees down
Creeks choked, trout killed, roads.

The procedures of the line here are largely halving and coupling, and the variations are relaxations that reach out semantically to other results:

Crosscut and chainsaw
   squareheads and finns
   high-lead and cat-skidding
Trees down
Creeks choked, trout killed, roads.

The violence of the first four linear divisions creates a tension that is cumulative; the dangers of the catalogue are diminished by the prosody so that it is not a simple matter of adding item to item but of seeing each item as part of design and pattern, a concert of yoked energies. The final line leaves a single word uncoupled, a result, a relaxation into barrenness. The poem is a perversion of religious ceremony, the text of life against the myth of natural sacredness.

This book thus creates and denies one of the greatest of American experiences, that of a wild ecology. But it is not merely American; the human race really is on the way to destroying the planet, if not by some mad outrageous single explosion then by steady careless greedy attrition of all those qualities that have over the centuries kept men as sane as they have been. Curiously, although this has been the overriding historical fact of the past generation, only one extensive book of poetry has tried to tackle this problem as subject and come to some prophetic stance. Yet there is nothing pompous or portentous about *Myths and Texts*; it is genuinely contemplative. It has received no prizes, but over the years it may well become, for those men who care, a sacred text.

Many poems have followed *Myths and Texts* but no book with the unity and impact that Snyder is capable of. The *Six Sections from Mountains and Rivers without End* have the mark of Snyder's style, the same tough placement of words in an order that makes the language articulate. There is in this book a kind of boyishness that is engaging but not up to the best of his possibilities. Simplicity should not seem, as it does in so complex a poet, an affectation. What most tempts Snyder is the anecdotal mode, the candid snapshot, the reduction of perception to objects merely, wondering at the simple. There is an insistence on youthfulness that I find embarrassing — perhaps because of my own great age. In the "Hymn to the Goddess San Francisco in Paradise" he speaks for the Chamber of anti-Commerce with contempt for the tourists because they are too old. Hatred of tourists (did you ever see such a bunch of freaks) is an honorable tradition of all San Franciscans from restaurateurs to bohemians (one of San Francisco's best restaurants does not accept credit cards because, according to the owner, "I don't want a bunch of Texans in here"). But Snyder's "Hymn" is kiddish, a bohemian version of Herb Caen. His attitude toward cities remains that of a young logger from the provinces, as his "This Tokyo" indicates. There is a healthy side to this attitude, that of the Jeremiad; and yes, of all American cities, only New York and San Francisco have managed to work into poetic idiom with any strength. If Gloucester and Paterson become mythical, it will be because of highly individuated local spirits rather than because of any inherent quality. But Snyder seems to be playing on external and sentimental associations, something that poets like Jack Spicer and Ron Loewinsohn have not allowed to happen in their work.

Then there is the hitchhiking poem. Some day a man will write a great novel using the frame of hitchhiking — it is the only way for a current American to do a Don Quixote, Tom Jones, or Pickwick. Consider the varieties of chance associations, mistakes, lures, and wanderings by the way. A modern Chaucer would make his *Canterbury Tales* from such possibilities; a Homer, an *Odyssey*. Snyder's poem is short, as are the presentations of characters met along the way:

Oil-pump broken, motor burning out	*Salem*

Ex-logger selling skidder cable
   wants to get to San Francisco,
   fed and drunk
	Eugene

Guy just back from Alaska — don't like the States, there's too much law	*Sutherlin*
A woman with a kid & two bales of hay.	*Roseburg*

Some of the episodes might cover as much as eight lines, but the characters remain thin: "... a passed-out LA whore/ glove compartment full of booze,/ the driver a rider, nobody cowbody,/ sometime hood...." The places are given brief play:

> Snow on the pines & first around Lake Shasta
> — Chinese scene of winter hills & trees
> us "little travellers" in the bitter cold
>
> six-lane highway slash & DC twelves
> bridge building   squat earth-movers
> — yellow bugs
>
> I speak for hawks.

It's a poem of around four hundred lines, intimate and panoramic, but one thing after another. It lacks conceptual force, and as narrative remains facile drift, with some witty or engaging observation. So the great opportunity of the hitchhiking subject remains sketched, embryonic, waiting its full development.

Other poems from these six sections of what may become a lifework have starker and more concentrated force growing out of Snyder's most passionate apprehension of life. Snyder has spoken often of the importance of the rhythms of various kinds of work for his poetry, and his sense of experience is largely a sense of work, of measured force exerted on the world. When he sees a second-growth forest, he wonders, looking at the stumps, what they did with all the wood; a city evokes in him the tough brutal labor involved, the carpentry and plumbing and simple excavating. His world is a world of energy constantly reformulating itself, and most often a world of human energy, exploited, misdirected, and full of pathos — he can't take it for granted but sees at its base the wilderness and fundamental man, and the products generated through history. This is why "The Market," full of dangers of sentimentality in tone, and mere cataloguing in technique, has an inner vigor that the hitchhiker poem lacks. This is not entirely a matter of mood but of conviction and of consequent drive. Technical considerations aside, poetry like all art comes out of courage, the capacity to keep going when reason breaks down. The equivalences established in "The Market" are equivalences of energy very roughly estimated.

> seventy-five feet hoed rows equals
> one hour explaining power steering
> equals two big crayfish =
>   all the buttermilk you can drink
> = twelve pounds cauliflower
> = five cartons greek olives = hitch-hiking
>   from Ogden Utah to Burns Oregon
> = aspirin, iodine, and bandages
> = a lay in Naples = beef
> = lamb ribs = Patna
>   long grain rice, eight pounds
> equals two kilogram soybeans = a boxwood
>   geisha comb.

equals the whole family at the movies
equals whipping dirty clothes on rocks
   three days, some Indian river
= piecing off beggars two weeks
= bootlace and shoelace
   equals one gross inflatable
   plastic pillows
= a large box of petit-fours, chou-cremes —
   barley-threshing
   mangoes, apples, custard apples, raspberries
= picking three flats strawberries
= a christmas tree = a taxi ride
carrots, daikon, eggplant, greenpeppers,
oregano, white goat cheese
   = a fresh-eyed bonito, live clams
a swordfish
a salmon

And the close of the second section shows the melancholy and weariness that accompanies the breakdown of reason before all this relentless, pointless, back-breaking labor:

    I gave a man seventy paise
    In return for a clay pot
    of curds
    Was it worth it?
    how can I tell

The terrible concluding section leaves us with a vision of a totally human world, a world of monstrosity:

    they eat feces
      in the dark
      on stone floors.
    one legged animals, hopping cows
      limping dogs   blind cats

    crunching garbage in the market
      broken fingers
        cabbage
      head on the ground.

    who has young face.
      open pit eyes
    between the bullock carts and people
      head pivot with the footsteps
          passing by
    dark scrotum spilled on the street
      penis laid by his thigh
        torso
    turns with the sun

> I came to buy
> a few bananas by the ganges
> while waiting for my wife

Contemporaneous with this long-projected series of poems like an enormous Chinese scroll are other poems, more lyric and brief, and many of these have been collected and published this year by New Directions under the title *The Back Country*. Characteristically, the first two sections are called "Far West" and "Far East"; and Snyder's most recent essay is called "Passage to More Than India." The synthesis he is working towards, that obsesses his being, maintains its momentum:

> We were following a long river into the mountains.
> Finally we rounded a bridge and could see deeper in —
> the farther peaks stony and barren, a few alpine
> trees.
> Ko-san and I stood on a point by a cliff, over a
> rock-walled canyon. Ko said, "Now we have come to
> where we die." I asked him, what's that up there,
> then — meaning the further mountains.
> "That's the world after death." I thought it looked
> just like the land we'd been travelling, and couldn't
> see why we should have to die.
> Ko grabbed me and pulled me over the cliff —
> both of us falling. I hit and I was dead. I saw
> my body for a while, then it was gone. Ko was
> there too. We were at the bottom of the gorge.
> We started drifting up the canyon, "This is the
> way to the back country."

IV

Snyder has already written, published, read aloud, and generally made available a large and remarkable body of work. He is distinguished not only as poet but as prose expositor — he has a gift for quiet, untroubled, accurate observation with occasional leaps to genuine eloquence. He has taken to himself a subject matter, complex, vast, and permanently interesting, a subject so compelling that it is not unreasonable to assert that he has become a center for a new set of cultural possibilities. There are two kinds of trouble that readers experience with this impressive accomplishment.

The first is the Gary Snyder poem. I have already described this short, anecdotal, erotic, concrete poem set in the wilderness with Zen masters and Amerindian mythological creatures commenting on each other and on nature. There comes a time when tedium sets in, when the personal style seems to be carrying along for no particular reason except to carry along, keep busy in the act of writing. The poems then exist all at exactly the same level and seem to have interchangeable parts. Objects from one could be moved to another without loss or gain. The prosody retains the same tone. The surfaces are attractive and monotonous. Even though there are variations from high rhetoric to self-deprecating humor, the unanimity of the poems is restrictive. Too much goes along the surface, gliding. And often I get the impression that Snyder doesn't care about the art, that poetry for him is only one of a set of instruments in a spritual quest, that the act of construction is not something that requires its own special resolutions. Like most writers with a coherent world view, he sometimes refuses to let his material be intractable, there is no sense of contention between subject and object, no dramatic struggle toward a new form. Then the poems do not seem *forms* but *shapes*.

I don't think this happens often or that it is a totally crippling defect; otherwise I shouldn't have troubled to write this extended essay. The complaints here registered could have been made against Blake, Whitman, and Lawrence. The second complaint, one that I have heard from students, especially those from large urban areas, is that Snyder does not face the problems of modern life. In this view, the great bulk of Americans live in cities and in an age of anxiety verging on total panic. The wilderness exists only in a mythical past or in the lives of those privileged by money (for pack animals and guides) or skills based on specialized work in areas remote from normal experience. Hence Snyder's poetry doesn't answer to the tensions of modern life and depends on a life no longer accessible or even desirable for men. A mystique of the wilderness based on the humane naturalism of the highly limited Zen Buddhism sect and the primitive insights of American savages can't satisfy the existential *Angst* of modern man. Everything is too simple, too easy, too glib, a boy's book in verse, Huck Finn on the Skagit, Innocents in Japan. The poetry is archaic, not in the sense that all poetry is, but out of tune with life in the 1960s.

It's tempting to reply that only Lyndon Johnson and Barry Goldwater are in tune with life in the 1960s and let it go at that. But the argument that a poet must speak to the problems of the bulk of the people seems to me to support rather than undermine Snyder's work. Properly understood, Snyder's poetry does *speak* to basic current problems, but it does not simply embody them. A usually sensible critic recently praised a poet for writing what he decided was "The poem of the 60's." Now this is a mentality that I understand and abominate. It is the mentality that runs and ruins museums of modern art. Who would think of calling Catullus *the* poet of the sixties (B.C.)? At present commentators and curators seem intent on timely masterpieces, by which they mean representative documents. Qualitative judgments, relevance not to the contemporary limited box but to the continuously human — these do not seem pertinent. Prepackaged history, projected museums, anticipatory anthologies for

survey courses are all silly and pointless enterprises, admired and supported by people who pride themselves on being, of all things, antiacademic.

Snyder's work is not part of that academy. It is rather part of
another academy, an ill-defined and perhaps undefinable group of
people, including historians novelists, poets, artists, various scholars, and
many others, who are seriously seeking some proper answer or at least a
set of questions appropriate to the world in its current stage of history, but
seeing that world against the vast background of all human possibilities.
At present, human power, pure brute controlled energy, threatens the entire planet. Some norms have to be found and diffused that will allow
men to check and qualify their force. Snyder makes this large effort:

> As poet I hold the most archaic values on earth. They go back to the
> late Paleolithic: the fertility of the soil, the magic of animals, the power-
> vision in solitude, the terrifying initiation and re-birth, the love and ec-
> stasy of the dance, the common work of the tribe. I try to hold both
> history and wilderness in mind, that my poems may approach the true
> measure of things and stand against the unbalance and ignorance of our
> times.

He is calling upon the total resources of man's moral and religious being.
There is no point in decrying this as primitivism; it is merely good sense,
for the ability to hold history and wilderness in the mind at once may be
the only way to make valid measures of human conduct. A larger and
more visible vision of man and cosmos is our only hope, and the major
work of any serious person. In that work, Snyder's verse and prose com-
pose a set of new cultural possibilities that only ignorance and unbalance
can ignore.

Clearing the Ground:
Gary Snyder and the
Modernist Imperative

by Robert Kern

Critical claims for the value and significance of Gary Snyder's poetry generally direct attention to the achievements of his perfected ecological style — those poems of his that, most notably in the collection *The Back Country* (1968), successfully present and embody assumptions of unity, balance and interrelationship between man and the natural environment. Snyder emerges from these discussion as the ecological poet *par excellence*, the writer who not only wants to recall us to nature "as the ultimate ground of human affairs"[1] but who has developed a poetic style embodying and promoting a mode of consciousness with which to do it, a mode that eliminates the problem of relationship between man and nature, subject and object, by assuming their unity a priori or supporting it with the evidence of ecology itself. In these terms, Snyder's work can be regarded as a later contribution to the tradition in modern poetry that J. Hillis Miller describes in *Poets of Reality*, the tradition of a poetry of immanence or presence, culminating in the work of Williams, in which the "double bifurcation" between heaven and earth and man and world that characterizes the romantic and idealist traditions of the nineteenth century has been resolved.[2] His poems teach us how to see nature and how to see ourselves in nature, not through discursive or didactic argument but by dramatizing states of mind that pose an alternative to the culture — and ego — driven attitudes by which we normally live. Literally and spiritually, Snyder seems to be providing the poetry of earth that Wallace Stevens asked for.[3]

But helpful and valid as this view of his work is (especially as an answer to dissenting critics who see Snyder as a participant in a "formless project"[4]), it fails to take into account any sense of his development, the fact that the expression of ecological consciousness in his work, while present as a goal from the beginning, is arrived at only gradually in terms of actual poetic achievement. In his early poems, for example, particularly the lyrics of his first published book, *Riprap* (1959), Snyder seems less concerned with the effortless expression of such consciousness than with the dramatization of the problems and difficulties involved in reaching it. He is still one of us at this point, on the near side of his evolution toward the role of spokesman for the natural world. And it is these poems, which tend to be overlooked entirely or dismissed as simply preparatory, that I want to examine.

My argument is not so much that Snyder's development is a neglected issue in need of clarification — in fact it is a complex process, occurring on several levels simultaneously and further complicated by an order of publication that is not strictly chronological — but that his early poetry raises issues and suggests contexts for his work that are surprisingly broad for a poet who is all too often associated exclusively with "nature" and ecological politics. To be sure, an examination of his early work can show where Snyder has come from and how his characteristic style took shape. But the more interesting context for such a discussion, I want to suggest, is the question of what sort of poetics emerges from work necessarily concerned with initiating a career and establishing a poetic identity at a time (the middle and late 1950's) when the literary environment is still dominated by a modernism that is nevertheless in the process, as it now seems to us, of breaking up. Although I am speaking here in terms of literary history and influence, I do not mean to invoke, except in a limited way, the issues that Professors Bate and Bloom have so authoritatively set forth in recent years: the Burden of the Past and the Anxiety of Influence. For one thing, Snyder strikes me as a writer who just might avoid these problems through his commitment to a frame of reference that seems to offer release from typically Western notions of history and psychology; as a poet who has undergone extensive training in Zen, he neither believes in history nor seems threatened by any anxiety. (His work, at least, is clearly designed to give these impressions.) On the other hand, given the question that I do want to raise, that of modernism and the response to it of a writer whose sense of things dictates against total acceptance of its precepts, it seems impossible to avoid some awareness of the past and its enroachments, particularly when that past, designated as "modern," has itself raised complex questions about its relationship with history.

To put it plainly, what stands in the way of simply asserting, with some periodizing critics, that poets like Snyder must be seen as "*post-modern*," their work the outcome of a sharp and total break with the "modernist" past, is the complicating fact (and I am hardly the first to point it out) that it is just such breaks with the past that modernism counsels. Pound's imperative to "Make it new" and Williams' notion of the necessity of "clearing the ground" are both repetitions of Rimbaud's earlier decision to be "absolutely modern." As Paul de Man has observed, such gestures of absolute beginning require constant repetition because they are constantly being absorbed by history.[5] And the issue is only intensified when placed in an American context. Roy Harvey Pearce's remark

that "'The Americanness' of American poetry is, quite simply, its compulsive 'modernism'" points to a kind of permanent impulse toward
renewal, a persistent dream of beginning again in American writing that
is prompted — or ought to be, as Williams sees it — by the newness of the
New World itself.[6] It is Williams' formulation of this dream, in fact, that
is most crucial because it represents a coincidence between the general
modernist demand for originality and the impulse toward it that the New
World has apparently inspired right from the start. What we have in
American literature, then, is a paradoxical history of denials of history, a
tradition of new starts that acknowledge no precedents, so that modernism here is best understood not as an avant-garde, the latest development of a historical trend or tradition, but as a primitivistic ignorance or
deconstructive denial of the past. A book like Snyder's *Riprap* must be
seen as participating in this paradoxical history. Inasmuch as it under-
takes to clear the ground and establish a space for itself in a crowded
literary landscape, it enters into a tradition of such gestures, and to that
extent claims for its post-modernism are deeply qualified. On the other
hand, in appropriating a space cleared of all example and precedent and
thus situating itself in a kind of *pre*historical position, it raises the most
radical questions about its own identity and status as literature, as though
literature were a destiny it could somehow choose to avoid. It will be
necessary, in any case, to be aware of both sides of the paradox in
examining the themes and language of *Riprap*, in seeing how history informs what is nevertheless "new" or at least radically redefined in
Snyder's first published poems.

In a first book the question of what a poet can do can usually be
answered through a consideration of how well he does what others have
done before him, and Snyder is no exception. The presence of Pound,
Williams and, closer to home, Kenneth Rexroth is clear in *Riprap's* objectivity, terse rhythms and plain diction. But the presence is not overwhelming, and these features are common enough in contemporary verse
style to allow Snyder enough scope to work in his own preoccupations. As
soon as the influences are recognized, moreover, one begins to notice differences and qualifications — a prosody and syntax, for example, which, if
they resemble Rexroth's, seem deliberately less smooth, with hardly any
enjambment and much greater concentration on the single line as the
rhythmic unit of speech. This latter feature, as Donald Davie has pointed
out,[7] is Pound's major contribution to modern prosody, part of his war
against traditional rhetorical fluency as the enemy of imagistic clarity;
but in Snyder's hands its effects are even sharper and harder, given the absence in his writing of Pound's visionary lyricism, the mythical or neo-
Platonic dimension of his imagery. One turns, then, to Williams and
stark, objectivist lyrics like "The Red Wheelbarrow." Yet how neatly and
artfully if impersonally composed such poems are in comparison with

Snyder's early lyrics, which are largely narrative or dramatic in structure and more referential than reflexive in effect, clearly flirting, as they do, with the mere description of mimetic copying that Williams disparages in *Spring & All*. Snyder's poems, in fact, are much more literal and metonymic than metaphoric, deriving their structure from the external order of things and events in the world rather than from any internal imaginative order, their concrete referentiality amounting, I would argue, to a far greater acceptance of a mimetic relationship between poem and world than the modernists either wanted or allowed in their work. Of course Williams's poems (particularly those like "The Red Wheelbarrow") are also strongly metonymic, but they are designed to be objects in their own right, what Wallace Stevens referred to as "mobile-like arrangement[s] of lines,"[8] pointing as much to their maker and themselves as to the external world of contiguous things; whereas Snyder aims to minimize and even erase his creative presence in the poem, trying in this way to suggest (as Matthew Arnold remarks of Wordsworth) that nature itself is the poet. A good brief example is the first poem in *Riprap*, "Mid-August at Sourdough Mountain Lookout":

> Down valley a smoke haze
> Three days heat, after five days rain
> Pitch glows on the fir-cones
> Across rocks and meadows
> Swarms of new flies.
>
> I cannot remember things I once read
> A few friends, but they are in cities.
> Drinking cold snow-water from a tin cup
> Looking down for miles
> Through high still air.[9]

Of the two kinds of rhetoric at work in this poem, the dominant one consists of the pure rendering of external objects and events in which the speaker foregoes any acknowledgement of his own subjectivity. The whole first stanza and the latter part of the second are awed, transparent registrations of experience that seem to come through to us whole and unmediated, as though dictated by the sheer pressure or presence of the objects and events themselves. We are given a naming of things without a namer, a deliberately elliptical utterance that suggests the purest kind of attention to the world beyond the self. As Roman Jakobson points out in his pioneering article on metonymy and metaphor, one characteristic of the kind of aphasia ("similarity disorder") that tends toward the exclusively metonymic pole of discourse is the omission of the subject of the sentence, an omission that results in the type of utterance which takes a purely predicative form and whose subjects are thus not defined so much as rendered through their consequences and effects.[10] Snyder's subject most often is the perceiving self, and its suppression in the greater part of this poem is not only expressive of the speaker's suddenly expanded consciousness, a change that is underlined by the momentary lapse into his ordinary self and its more conventional, less elliptical discourse in the first two lines of the second stanza, but is also a characteristic habit of Snyder's style, a sign of his preference for metonymic expression. Another such sign, of course, is the absence of metaphor, which points to an interest in things not in terms of their similarities or potential for taking the place of each other but in terms of the way they manifest themselves through their actions or appearances in the world; and it is these actions and appearances which determine the coherence of the poem as a series of elliptical but predicative responses.

Once it is granted that the literalism, referentiality and metonymic tendencies of Snyder's style bespeak an acceptance of mimesis, however qualified but broadly understood as a hope or faith or conviction that there is an authentic relationship between the words of a poem and what they refer to—along with the necessary corollary of any mimetic theory that the thing represented, the external world, is the primary locus of value, as opposed to the poem itself—then it is possible to begin to see distinctions between Snyder's poetics and that of his modernist predecessors. One major difference clearly lies in their conceptions of the poem, and another in their attitudes toward language. Modernist poetics typically emphasizes the way in which a poem is a separate autonomous object, a primary, independent reality unto itself—MacLeish's "The poem must not mean/ But be," for example, or Stevens' "Not Ideas About the Thing but the Thing Itself." From T.E. Hulme—whose Bergsonian notion of reality as constituted by discontinuous realms of experience leads easily to the idea of the uniqueness of authentic poetic expression— to the New Critics' full-blown contextualism, there is constant stress, implicit and explicit, on the poem's organic unity, its separateness from history and its otherwise privileged nature as a species of language exempt from the inroads of the ordinary temporal world. In its flight toward its own reality, the poem must avoid the discursive and the merely representational. Its major strategy in the twentieth century, as one recent writer puts it, has been "countermimesis,"[11] a relationship with the external world best seen not as imitation but as opposition and even antagonism, so that the poem becomes a critical, almost utopian structure radiating value and meaning in the midst of chaotic flux (provided it can avoid the pitfalls of solipsism and escapism). At its most radical extreme, this idealization of the poem and of poetic language leads to Hart Crane's Mallarméan desire, "using our 'real' world somewhat as a spring-board," to have the poem constitute for the reader "a single, new *word*, never before spoken and impossible to actually enunciate,"[12] referring to nothing in reality but creating a new reality, an extension of experience inaccessible and unrealizable in any other form. But in general the modernist poem is conceived as a formal ordering, a structure that, in its adherence to the values of creative imagination and craftsmanship almost as ends in themselves, is meant to resist the outside pressure (in Steven's terms) of an unordered historical reality.

Just when this post-Symbolist, anti-mimetic bias, with its extreme stress on formalism, begins to wane, it is hard to say, though Charles Olson's essay on "Projective Verse" (1950), Allen Ginsberg's *Howl* (1956) and Robert Lowell's *Life Studies* (1959) would certainly be included among the turning-point events. For a poet like Snyder, at any rate, faced, at the beginning of his career, with several influential examples of making it new and the imperative to do so himself, the poem pretty much ceases to be a self-involved or autotelic verbal activity and the idealization of language turns to distrust, as in his remark that the poet must steer "a course between crystal clouds of utterly incommunicable non-verbal states — and the gleaming daggers and glittering nets of language."[13] He is aware, on the one hand, of a reality that cannot be brought over into language at all and, on the other, of the problem presented by language that is seen as a danger and a trap, albeit an attractive one, to be avoided. This sense of boundaries, as his early work itself suggests, defines the legitimate space of a poetry that is much more in touch with empirical reality, trying not to resist its pressures but to accept them as a determinant of form in harmonious cooperation with the mind, checking the mind's tendencies to impress its own forms and language on the landscape. It is the drama of this acceptance that is one of the main themes of *Riprap*, and it accounts for poems which not only valorize experience over language but which often address themselves directly to the limits of language as a conceptualizing medium — a rather self-limiting activity, one might think, for a poet, but one which is in accord with Snyder's sense of poetry's reduced possibilities.

In a more expansive statement from earlier in his career, Snyder offers a similar conception of the poet's task that throws even greater emphasis on the limits of what poetry can express:

> A poet sort of faces two directions: one is to the world of people and language and society, and the tools by which he communicates his language; and the other is the non-human, non-verbal world, which is world of nature as nature is itself, and the world of human nature — the inner world — as it is itself, before language, before custom, before culture. There's no words in that realm. There aren't any rules that we know and that's the area Buddhism studies, and that's why you can't talk about it: because it's not concerned with anything that you can talk about.[14]

The poet here appears to have left himself with even less space in which to maneuver. If it is his task to mediate between two worlds, one the world of language and society and the other the non-human, non-verbal world, then he has taken on the seemingly paradoxical burden of finding a language for a reality that is prior to language, for an "utterly incommunicable" nature that is non-verbal by definition — a problem somewhat analogous to Milton's task of relating events of the pre-fallen world in a fallen language, in a language that is itself a result of the fall. Such a task can be fulfilled, in Milton's case, only after the poet has been properly "instructed" by the Heavenly muse to serve as a fit vessel for visionary truth. What bridge can there be, however, between a world without words and language whose potential for distortion and excess is unabated? Here too the answer can only be the poet himself, but the poet properly informed by a sense of his own limitations and those of his medium, the awareness that the more he does to call attention to his activity *as* a poet the greater risk that he will ruin his efforts by either trespassing into the zone of the "utterly incommunicable" or falling a prey to language that pursues its own exclusive reality. Given these tight limits, this Scylla and Charybdis situation, craft for Snyder becomes a matter, as he puts it, of steering a course between them, and his major function in the poem is to allow things to speak as much as possible for themselves, in a language stripped of subjective preconception and historical or cultural encrustation, the very process that "Mid-August at Sourdough Mountain Lookout" dramatizes.

It is at this point in his poetics, moreover, that Snyder finds himself on common ground with some of the aims and values of modern poetry in general, particularly with its "objectivist" desire to encounter reality directly and immediately, to see things just as they are, with a perception and response purified, in L.S. Dembo's words, "of conventional reason, sentiment, and even of conception itself...."[15] Charles Olson's version of this desire demands "getting rid of the lyrical interference of the individual as ego,"[16] and in Snyder's early work, in addition to his respect for a reality inaccessible to language and his distrust of language itself, it takes the form of a drive toward reification and demystification, the denial and displacement of the abstract and the systematized by concrete experience, from which the very poems he is writing are not exempt. But here he has already surpassed modernist assumptions about the poem. In his anxiety to clear the ground, Snyder aims to produce a *pre*-literature that can sometimes appear to the reader as an *anti*-literature, a poetry built entirely of sense-impression against myth (in Snyder's own terms) that seems to be on the way, in its appreciation of the universe as "infinitely blank" (R, 33), to complete aphasia or silence. In accord with these aims but unlike the modernists, he foregoes any claim that poetic language or the poetic context provides a unique access to knowledge of essential reality. Such knowledge for Snyder is apprehended in an existential act of perception prior to poetic composition which the poem can later dramatize and reflect. But the poem itself is no longer the idealized locus of any subject/object encounter.[17] It is precisely the privileged status of the poem (accorded to it by a modernism intent upon the uniqueness of aesthetic experience) that Snyder's writing calls into question as part of its general rejection or redefinition of history, tradition, culture, myth and literature itself, all finally seen as irrelevant to a reality that is prior to language, custom and culture. For it is Snyder's ultimate and most radical assumption that he can break out of what Ernst Cassirer calls man's inevitably "symbolic universe" and work his way back to a purely physical one, reconstructing the "seamless web" of man and nature, the enveloping silence of their primordial relationship, that language originally shattered.[18]

The poems in *Riprap* which most clearly embody this assumption and which are written according to the strictures that it entails are primarily those dealing with experience in the wilderness, experience in which the speaker finds, first and foremost, that "I cannot remember things I once read," that ordinary mental experience has somehow been altered.[19] Here, for example, is the first and longest stanza of "Piute Creek":

> One granite ridge
> A tree, would be enough
> Or even a rock, a small creek,
> A bark shred in a pool.
> Hill beyond hill, folded and twisted
> Tough trees crammed
> In thin stone fractures
> A huge moon on it all, is too much.
> The mind wanders. A million
> Summers, night air still and the rocks
> Warm. Sky over endless mountains.
> All the junk that goes with being human
> Drops away, hard rock wavers
> Even the heavy present seems to fail
> This bubble of a heart.
> Words and books
> Like a small creek off a high ledge
> Gone in the dry air.

Given the presence here of such explicit, direct statement as "The mind wanders," suggesting the sort of narrative consciousness at a distance from the scene that Snyder will eliminate from his later work, this is clearly a much more discursive rhetoric than that in "Mid-August at Sourdough Mountain Lookout." Characteristically the definite article prevents us from reading the line as merely a subjective comment and turns it into a general statement about the behavior of mind under the given circumstances. But the focal experience in both poems is essentially the same. Under the impact of an immense nature, "All the junk that goes with being human/ Drops away," "junk" here meaning primarily, as Snyder puts it elsewhere, "the ancient, meaningless/ Abstractions of the educated mind,"[20] so that nature itself in these early poems performs the function of clearing the mind that Snyder will later ascribe to meditation. And when the mind is cleared it is "Words and books" that are "Gone in the dry air," leaving the mind in a state of disciplined attentiveness that allows it to interpenetrate with physical reality, as in the poem's concluding stanza:

> A clear, attentive mind
> Has no meaning but that
> Which sees is truly seen.
> No one loves rock, yet we are here.
> Night chills. A flick
> In the moonlight
> Slips into Juniper shadow:
> Back there unseen
> Cold proud eyes
> Of Cougar or Coyote
> Watch me rise and go [R, 12].

The sign of transformed consciousness here lies neither in the rhythmic firmness of these lines nor in their unobstrusive play with sound but rather in the way the speaker's point of view, by the very end, has moved outside himself. Yet is is the problem of readying the mind for such interpenetration more than the interpenetration itself that these poems, for the most part, seem to dwell upon. They are almost celebrations of those moments when the mind's resistances have been overcome and the difficult transition has been made from ordinary consciousness to a state in which the mind has dropped its symbolic burden of words, books, abstractions, even personal history and identity—whatever might stand in the way of a direct, unhampered perception of things. Of course this is precisely the kind of perception that Cassirer denies is any longer possible for man, who, he says, "has so enveloped himself in linguistic forms, in artistic images, in mythical symbols or religious rites that he cannot see or know anything except by the interposition of this artificial medium."[21] Snyder's position, on the other hand, despite the fact that its difficulties, particularly in these early poems, are acknowledged and dramatized, implies that it is these very artificial media that must be removed before any real perception can take place; and these media include, we might note, such "linguistic forms" as poems. In this sense the possibilities of poetry have indeed been reduced for Snyder, but such a reduction seems to be demanded by an epistemology radically at odds with the neo-Kantian assumptions of a philosophy like Cassirer's a philosophy for which no relationship between self and world is possible without the mediation of symbolic forms that reconstitute the world in their own terms and thus make it available to human consciousness.[22]

Snyder's epistemological radicalism, however, is most crucial in its implications for poetics. While Cassirer's philosophy, in its compatibility with modernist, specifically symbolist notions of the poem as a cognitive structure affording access to an otherwise hidden reality, demands poetry, so to speak, as one of several precious avenues to truth, Snyder's stance, as we have seen, verges more and more towards silence and suggests that the poem, far from constituting a medium of relationship between self and world, actually interrupts such relationship. Given his preference for a notion of experience as presence, as opposed to any sort of mediation, and insofar as literature itself is a symbolic form, Snyder's early poems are inescapably anti-literary—metonymic and elliptical in style, impatient with language, especially in its literary seductiveness, and always aware of a reality beyond verbal reach. But even more radically, they would seem, if only by implication, to be structures impatient with themselves, denying their own validity, and if this is the case, why write (or read) at all? What value can the poem possibly have? Can it be anything more than a self-indulgent exercise in transforming a primary experience of the world into linguistic symbols?

What value the poem has is suggested, in part, by a witty lyric like "Thin Ice," which raises these very questions:

> Walking in February
> A warm day after a long freeze
> On an old logging road
> Below Sumas Mountain
> Cut a walking stick of alder,
> Looked down through clouds
> On wet fields of the Nooksack —
> And stepped on the ice
> Of a frozen pool across the road.
> It creaked
> The white air under
> Sprang away, long cracks
> Shot out in the black,
> My cleated mountain boots
> Slipped on the hard slick
> — like thin ice — the sudden
> Feel of an old phrase made real —
> Instant of frozen leaf,
> Icewater, and staff in hand.
> "Like walking on thin ice —"
> I yelled back to a friend,
> It broke and I dropped
> Eight inches in [R, 20]

In a rhythm that seems to hurry us through it and a language insistently ordinary and prosaic, the poem dramatizes an experience of reification, "the sudden/ Feel of an old phrase made real," in which language becomes reality. But the focus is on the differences, and the distance, between language as a conceptualizing medium and the reality which it conceptualizes, so that language is defined as the absence or displacement of that to which it refers. The fact that the speaker's action can be summed up in an old phrase distracts him from the reality that the phrase has displaced. Conceptual or linguistic experience literally takes the place of physical experience, until the latter reasserts itself as a reality prior to or at a distance from language, a reality, moreover, with consequences against which a mere phrase can offer no protection. This is why, for Snyder, language cannot be a substitute for reality and why these poems do not participate in the modernist pursuit of the thing itself. They are precisely about the dangers (here quite literal) of mistaking language for experience, of assuming that the poem can be the thing itself. Instead they seem to accept their referentiality, their representational nature, and that acceptance constitutes their value, a value which can be defined as their refusal to be valued in and for themselves. Indeed, as poems which forego any literary gleam and glitter and thus try to avoid calling attention to themselves, they preserve the inviolability of experience which originates in the "utterly incommunicable," suggesting, nevertheless, that such experience is available non-verbally.

At their own expense, then, these poems promote the value of the external world and of immediate experience. They do so, that is, by subordinating themselves to the world and by insisting on their own inadequacies, as well as those of language, to do anything more than represent. Paradoxically, however, their failure is also their success. For just to the extent that they can achieve transparency, without calling attention to themselves, and thus make vivid and real what they claim to be able merely to *re*produce, they tend to become what they mean, to constitute experience rather than simply refer to it. The art of these poems, in fact, often lies in the way they convince us that certain kinds or uses of language are more "concrete," and therefore less abstract or conceptual, than others. If the distinction in "Thin Ice"[15] is between a common cliché and the reality it hides, then in "Above Pate Valley" we move from the abstract mental concept of "Ten thousand years" to a realization of the awesome historical reality that the concept stands for, the realization prompted by the speaker's direct contact with the evidence of the passage of time:

> ... I spied
> A glitter, and found a flake
> Black volcanic glass — obsidian —
> By a flower. Hands and knees
> Pushing the Bear grass, thousands
> Of arrowhead leavings over a
> Hundred yards. Not one good

> Head, just razor flakes
> On a hill snowed all but summer,
> A land of fat summer deer,
> They came to camp. On their
> Own trails. I followed my own
> Trail here. Picked up the cold-drill,
> Pick, singlejack, and sack
> Of dynamite.
> Ten thousand years [R, 15].

In both poems we seem to be led through a process of deconceptualization; we move from language to reality, from the abstract to the actual. A more elaborate example is provided in "Milton by Firelight," where the speaker cleanses his mind of *Paradise Lost* and the Christian myth, with their concepts of paradise and fall, by turning to the more immediate "realities" of climate and geology: "No paradise, no fall,/ Only the weathering land/ The wheeling sky...." And the poem's final lines, with their reference to Milton's Mulciber (*Paradise Lost*, Book I, ll. 738-51), illustrate how the Miltonic version of Christian history, itself a deliberate displacement of pagan myth, is displaced in turn by a new myth (though Snyder himself might not regard it this way), that of the poetry of reality:

> Fire down
> Too dark to read, miles from a road
> The bell-mare clangs in the meadow
> That packed dirt for a fill-in
> Scrambling through loose rocks
> On an old trail
> All of a summer's day [R, 14].

This whole process becomes explicitly clear in one further example, "Migration of Birds," where the poet, characteristically, is distracted from his reading by an empirical event. The title of a book and the abstraction it contains become actualized as a series of real, visible, on-going activities, as though the speaker looked up from his book to find a translation back into realtiy of its linguistic signs:

> It started just now with a hummingbird
> Hovering over the porch two yards away
>   then gone,
> It stopped me studying....
> Yesterday I read *Migration of Birds*;
> The Golden Plover and the Arctic Tern.
> Today that big abstraction's at our door
> For juncoes and the robins all have left,
> Broody scrabblers pick up bits of string
> And in this hazy day

Of April summer heat
Across the hill the seabirds
Chase Spring north along the coast:
Nesting in Alaska
In six weeks [R, 23].

Here, as in all of these poems, we have a reversal of the usual civilized process by which the world is transformed into symbols so that it can be dealt with and manipulated conceptually, a process that is itself, according to Cassirer, a "reversal of the natural order" by which the "direct and immediate answer ... given to an outward stimulus" in organic reactions is interrupted and delayed by thought. Snyder apparently would reinstate the organic reaction to its pristine form and thus return to the natural order, agreeing with Rousseau that thinking is a kind of depravity, a human violation of natural limits. Yet, as Cassirer also points out, "Man cannot escape from his own achievement,"[23] his symbolic activity, and so although we find Snyder writing poems that ultimately question their own desirability and even legitimacy, that implicitly call for their own extinction as unnecessary devices of mediation breaking the continuity between mind and world, we find him writing poems nevertheless.

In one of the first critical articles on Snyder's work, Thomas Parkinson suggested that there is one abstraction, after all, that a poet cannot help but accept, and that is language.[24] Yet Snyder persists in his efforts to counter its abstract force. If he works hard in most of the poems of *Riprap* to convince us that his uses of language actually represent a reversal of the symbolizing process, there is at least one poem in the book, the programmatic and uncharacteristic title-poem, in which he adopts the alternative strategy of invoking the familiar modernist notion of words as things and of poems as objects constructed from those things. Here, in a verse-layout that is reminiscent of Williams' later style, we are not only provided with instruction in how to read the poems but are given a rough definition of poetry that is relevant to the general issue of its value, an issue that, given Snyder's attitudes, continually raises itself:

Lay down these words
Before your mind like rocks.
     placed solid, by hands
In choice of place, set
Before the body of the mind
     in space and time:
Solidity of bark, leaf, or wall
     riprap of things:
Cobble of milky way,
     straying planets,
These poems, people,

```
        lost ponies with
Dragging saddles —
        and rocky sure-foot trails.
The worlds like an endless
        four-dimensional
Game of Go.
        ants and pebbles
In the thin loam, each rock a word
        a creek-washed stone
Granite: ingrained
        with torment of fire and weight
Crystal and sediment linked hot
        all change, in thoughts,
As well as things [R, 36]
```

Although the essentially narrative and mimetic qualities of the poems in *Riprap* as a whole make it difficult to regard them as modernist objects, this is precisely the status that Snyder's compositional methods and metaphors here would impose upon them, and we seem to be asked to think of them in just this way. As Sherman Paul remarks in his discussion of the poem, its "imperatives of composition are modernist: the unit of composition is the single word, like rock, a solid particular thing of weight and texture that exists in place and time and appeals to the senses...."[25] To be sure, the poem proposes a series of metaphors in which words are rocks, poems are trails or paths, and reading is walking or riding, all in accord with the definition of riprap that Snyder provides on the book's title-page: "a cobble of stone laid on steep slick rock to make a trail for horses in the mountain." Riprap, then, is an implicit analogy for poetry and becomes an overt one in this later definition from *Myths & Texts*: "Poetry a riprap on the slick rock of metaphysics."[26] Both definitions suggest, however, that if the composition of poetry is a kind of physical handiwork, its ultimate purpose is less to produce beautiful objects that are admirable in themselves than it is to produce useful or functional ones, the function in this case being the provision of a path over difficult mental terrain. Snyder is still insisting that the "cobble" constituted by his uses of language will somehow be different in kind from the "steep slick rock" of metaphysics that lies beneath it, that his poetic (or anti-poetic) disposition of words can somehow avoid the abstraction of language or thinking that is more obviously conceptual in character.

What is most important, though, is the assumption about the purpose and value of the poem that emerges from all of these metaphors. They imply, clearly enough, that poetry is a craft and that the poem is an object in the world, but it is not the primarily autotelic object, the aesthetic or meditational locus, of traditional modernism. Rather than such an isolated enclosure or point of rest, it is an opening to the world, a path leading outside itself, a linguistic form that is analogous in structure to the physical world and that exists alongside it but without being closed off from it. Indeed, as something to move through, its purpose is to make such movement possible, and its value lies precisely in its function as a bridge back to impirical reality, "quite as though," as one writer puts it, "the intelligibility of words were always to disappear before the superior intelligibility of things."[27] In this sense, too, however, the value of the poem, which is made of words and not things, is always disappearing before the superior value of the world, and this raises the question of whether a writing career can sustain itself upon such an attitude for very long without being entirely subverted. Perhaps the writer has no choice in the matter. For if poetry *is* before it *begins*, as Snyder has suggested,[28] then it also *is* after it *ends*, a proposition implying that poetry both comes from the world and returns to it, the poem that the poet writes and that we read being merely a bridge between this origin and this destination, which are the same. The positive point here is that while the poem can interrupt our silent relationship with the world, it can also, in its function as a bridge, renew it. But in this case we may not need the poem and at times we may even be better off without it, though at its best this is precisely what the poem teaches as it leads us back to the world. Still, assuming that the writer is maker as well as medium, is this "best" enough?

From the perspective of his subsequent books it is clear that Snyder has carried over many of the features of his early poetics into his later work. Yet it also seems as if there has been a relaxation of the severity of his limited approach to the poem and to poetic value, particularly in terms of his willingness to open his work to what he calls "the two sources of human knowledge — symbols and sense-impressions."[29] His next book after *Riprap* is *Myths & Texts* (1960), a fabric of personal experience, Buddhist mythology and American Indian lore, and it is here, apparently, that this accommodation is made. For even a cursory consideration of its poetry reveals enormous differences between the two books and suggests that *Myths & Texts*, as its very title implies, is a deliberate attempt to combine the two sources of human knowledge, to work with "myths and symbols and ideas ... old traditions and insights,"[30] — in fact, all the abstract symbolic media that *Riprap* largely rejects as epistemologically obstructive and tries to bury under its concrete surface texture. Yet when we come to the end of the book and discover its dates of composition — "Crater Mt. L. O. 1952 — Marin — an 1956"[31] — discover, that is, that it must have been composed more or less simultaneously with *Riprap*, it becomes difficult to maintain any argument that there has been a development or change in Snyder's outlook, that he has moved in any simple way from a denial to an acceptance of the symbolizing process and its products as valid sources of human knowledge. What is suggested, on the other hand, is the extent to which *Riprap* constitutes a calculated response to the modernist imperative, a deliberately initiatory gesture whose purpose is to clear a space for itself and whatever might follow. As such, it could not be anything but a first book, a radical but necessary answer to the paradoxical demand for originality as the only valid tradition that proceeds not only by denying the past but by submitting literature (and itself, in effect) to a critical interrogation of its very claims to ontological validity. It is, in Sherman Paul's phrase, "a decisive beginning,"[32] a book that aims to clear the ground, to deconstruct the given literary environment and reinhabit it, as it were, from scratch, denying all example and all precedent, with one inescapable exception: the modernist imperative itself.

[1] Quotation on the dust jacket of *Regarding Wave* (New York: New Directions, 1970).

[2] *Poets of Reality* (New York: Atheneum, 1969), p. 1.

[3] The discussions of Snyder's work that I have in mind here are primarily those by Charles Altieri and Alan Williamson. Altieri's "Gary Snyder's Lyric Poetry: Dialectic as Ecology," *The Far Point*, No. 4 (1970), 55-65, is an essential article on Snyder and the best brief treatment of the philosophical implications of his style. Williamson's two essays, "Language Against Itself: The Middle Generation of Contemporary Poets," in *American Poetry Since 1960: Some Critical Perspectives*, ed. Robert B. Shaw (Cheshire: Carcanet Press, 1973), pp. 55-67, and "Gary Snyder: An Appreciation," *The New Republic*, 173, 18 (November 1, 1975), 28-30, dwell more on Snyder as a craftsman and a "moral thinker." But both Altieri and Williamson rely on *The Back Country* almost exclusively as the basis for their judgments.

[4] See Robert Boyers, "Mixed Bag," *Partisan Review*, 36 (1969), 311-13, for a negative review of *The Back Country*.

[5] See "Literary History and Literary Modernity," *Blindness and Insight* (New York: Oxford University Press, 1971), pp. 142-165.

[6] Roy Harvey Pearce, *The Continuity of American Poetry* (Princeton: Princeton University Press, 1961), p. 5. For Williams' thinking about the relationship between American writing and the newness of the New World, see *In the American Grain* (New York: New Directions, 1956), particularly the chapters on Daniel Boone and Edgar Allan Poe. My comments here are based on the more elaborate argument presented in my essay "Williams, Brautigan and the Poetics of Primitivism," *Chicago Review*, 27 (Summer 1975), 47-57.

[7] *Ezra Pound: Poet as Sculptor* (New York: Oxford University Press, 1964), pp. 44-5.

[8] Quoted by Hugh Kenner in *A Homemade World* (New York: Knopf, 1975), p. 57. For a valuable treatment of "The Red Wheelbarrow" as metonymic, see Charles Altieri, "Objective Image and Act of Mind in Modern Poetry," *PMLA*, 91 (January 1976), 111-12.

[9] *Riprap & Cold Mountain Poems* (San Francisco: Four Seasons Foundation, 1965), p. 7. Further quotations from *Riprap*, designated R, will be cited in my text.

[10] Especially applicable to Snyder's poem are Jakobson's remarks on the similarity-deficient aphasic's dependence on context or actual situation for his cue to utterance: "The sentence 'it rains' cannot be produced unless the utterer sees that it is actually raining." See "Two Aspects of Language and Two Types of Aphasic Disturbances," in *Fundamentals of Language* by Roman Jakobson and Morris Halle (The Hague: Mouton, 1971), pp. 77-8. For an interesting argument, more

elaborate than but somewhat parallel to mine, applying Jakobson's categories to modern poetry, see Herbert Schneidau, "Wisdom Past Metaphor: Another View of Pound, Fenollosa, and Objective Verse," *Paideuma*, 5 (Spring 1976), 15-29. It is interesting to note, in this context, that although Jakobson points out that the similarity-deficient aphasic turns to metonymic expression out of a need to avoid the "sameness" or redundancy of calling a thing by its name, Ernst Cassirer suggests that names themselves perform metonymic functions: "The function of a name is always limited to emphasizing a particular aspect of a thing, and it is precisely this restriction and limitation upon which the value of the name depends. It is not the function of a name to refer exhaustively to a concrete situation, but merely to single out and dwell upon a certain aspect." See *An Essay on Man* (New Haven: Yale University Press, 1944), p. 134.

[11] John T. Irwin, "The Crisis of Regular Forms," *Sewanee Review*, 80 (Winter 1973), 161.

[12] "General Aims and Theories," *The Complete Poems and Selected Letters and Prose of Hart Crane*, ed. Brom Weber (Garden City: Anchor Books, 1966), pp. 220-21.

[13] "Poetry and the Primitive," *Earth House Hold* (New York: New Directions, 1969), p. 118.

[14] David Kherdian, *A Biographical Sketch and Descriptive Checklist of Gary Snyder* (Berkeley: Oyez, 1965), p. 13.

[15] *Conceptions of Reality in Modern American Poetry* (Berkeley: University of California Press, 1966), p. 3. In his introduction, Dembo outlines the "objectivist logic" that underlies the aesthetics of modern poetry.

[16] "Projective Verse," *Selected Writings of Charles Olson*, ed. Robert Creeley (New York: New Directions, 1966), p. 24.

[17] Cf. Frank Lentricchia in *The Gaiety of Language* (Berkeley: Univ. of California Press, 1968), p. 16: "In romantic theory only the act of perception is organic or self-sufficient, and the poem's ultimate function is to window that act. Thus, poetry yields the highest knowledge because *through* its language we can see the interpenetration of poetic mind and nature...." If for the Romantics, however, the coherence of subject and object is guaranteed by their mutual grounding in the "Absolute," or Wordsworth's "something far more deeply interfused," for Snyder their coherence depends on ecological and Buddhist models of reality.

[18] See *An Essay on Man*, p. 25. See also Stanley Burnshaw, *The Seamless Web* (New York: George Braziller, 1970), where it is argued that the poem constitutes "a re-enactment of unification" between man and his environment, despite the fact that the poem consists of the linguistic symbols "that were and are involved with divisiveness" (p. 184).

[19] I take these wilderness poems to be Snyder's central achievement in *Riprap*. The poems about Japan and life at sea seem lightweight in comparison and less than fully expressive of his most authentic poetic impulses. Even so ambitious a poem as "A Stone Garden," from the perspective of later work, seems somewhat off the track for Snyder.

[20] *Myths & Texts* (New York: Corinth Books, 1960, p. 7.

[21] *An Essay on Man*, p. 25.

[22] I am indebted here to Lee T. Lemon's brief but useful outline of the implications of Cassirer's thinking for poetics in *The Partial Critics* (New York: Oxford University Press, 1965), pp. 205-9. For an interesting contrast between Cassirer and another poet (in this case, Valéry) on the issue of language as substance and as function, see Gerald L. Bruns, *Modern Poetry and the Idea of Language* (New Haven: Yale University Press, 1974), pp. 11-15.

[23] *An Essay on Man*, pp. 24-5.

[24] "The Poetry of Gary Snyder," *The Southern Review*, 4 (Summer 1968), 619.

[25] "From Lookout to Ashram: The Way of Gary Snyder" (Part I), *The Iowa Review*, 1 (Summer 1970), 86.

[26] *Myths & Texts*, p. 43.

[27] Gerald L. Bruns, *Modern Poetry and the Idea of Language*, p. 235.

[28] "An Interview with Gary Snyder," *Road Apple Review*, 1 and 2 (Winter 1969 – Spring 1970), 63.

[29] See Snyder's "statement on poetics" in *The New American Poetry*, ed. Donald M. Allen (New York: Grove Press, 1960), p. 421.

[30] "An Interview with Gary Snyder," *Road Apple Review*, 65.

[31] *Myths & Texts*, p. 48.

[32] "From Lookout to Ashram: The Way of Gary Snyder" (Part II), *The Iowa Review*, 1 (Fall 1970), 70.

The Development
of the New Language:
Michael McClure, Philip Whalen,
and Gregory Corso

by Geoffrey Thurley

Even if we see Ginsberg as a wren who used the cover of Whitman's wingspan to fly higher than he could have flown unaided, the fact is that he *did* fly higher — higher than he could have flown had he not had the intelligence and the energy to exploit the various influences that lay in the background; higher than his older contemporaries, the liberal academics who were still cramped and twisted up with the self-consciousness endemic to the ironist tradition. He evaded the grip of the attitudes which were stifling the creative forces of American and English poets — the obligatory alienation, the by now stultifying isolationism, the cowardice of irony, the negativity which eventually congealed into the poetry of nervous breakdown. Ginsberg's breakthrough, such as it was, was a matter not so much of technique as of ideology. The cult of the nervous breakdown is, I have suggested, a phenomenon of affluence, like the extreme self-consciousness of modern America.[1] In this sense it seems relevant to describe the cult of the nervous breakdown in poets like Lowell, Berryman, Roethke, Sexton[2] as ideological symptoms; their varying academicism is only secondarily a technical matter. It is primarily a question of outlook, purpose and belief. If we turn to Allen Ginsberg's poetry or Kerouac's fiction we shall not need to look far for evidence of the spiritual suffering and nervous exhaustion which are part of life in an over-organized but chaotic society like America. The first line of *HOWL* prepares us for the saga of sickness and pointless debauch we duly get; Kerouac's novels are the reverse of orgiastic: *Big Sur*, for instance, offers one of the most harrowing experiences available to the modern reader. Yet still, *HOWL* is as different in purpose and impact from Berryman's *Dream Songs*, or a more recent work, like Galway Kinnell's *Book of Nightmares*, as *Big Sur* is from *Herzog*. Ideologically, Ginsberg

165

and Kerouac are in a different age from Berryman and Bellow. And this
difference is to be understood less through technical analysis than through
an appreciation of a subtle, decisive shift in emphasis and direction. The
nightmare is no longer hugged, as providing identity; the isolation no
longer clutched, the alienation no longer cherished, the agony no longer
needed.
       [...]
       The use so many Beat poets made of drugs clearly formed part of
its basic orientation towards non-striving, passivity and femininity. The
experimentation with different drugs carries on the long tradition of
avant garde spiritual exploration. But the ideal of the narcotic mandarin
is a passive world, in which people do nothing because there's nothing
they want to do but turn on.[3] It's at this point that one usually starts
talking about a new consciousness. It would be better to talk about a new
orientation than a new consciousness. Consciousness does not alter: the
psychedelic facts still have to be sorted somewhere in the human control-
tower. An interesting confirmation of this is Michael McClure's first
"Peyote Poem," written down the day after the experience:

> I KNOW EVERYTHING! I PASS INTO THE ROOM
> there is a golden bed radiating all light
> the air is full of silver hangings and sheathes
>   I smile to myself. I know
> all that there is to know. I see all there
>   is to feel. I am friendly with the ache
>   in my belly. The answer
>   to love is my voice. There is no Time!
> No answers. The answer to feeling is my feeling.

It is exhilarating and the moral authority assumed by the poet guaran-
tees a consistent air of seriousness. It also brought McClure a following:
he seemed in the mid-1960s the poet closest in intention to Timothy
Leary. But this poem is really not typical of the sort of effusion it helped to
encourage from so many other poets.
       There is of course a sameness about all mystical and narcotic ex-
perience — or at least about the reports mystics and drug-users have given
of it. Whether the experience is gained through a natural oddity of bodily
chemistry, whether it is deliberately induced or involuntary, whether it is
celebrated in awe or suffered in terror, whether it is mystical or
schizophrenic — the experience of the world we are here concerned with
has certain unvarying properties: we may be familiar with McClure's intense lighting effects, his sense of great significance and his feeling of
being at the center of the universe from the works of Blake, De Quincey,
Boehme, Swedenborg, Strindberg — or from a psychiatrist's casebook.
Mysticism and extreme schizophrenia depend as much on the body's

chemistry as the hallucinations of the drug-user. The important variable is the intellectual context in which they take place—the use, in other words, which the victim of these bodily states makes of them. This is not the place to discuss the implications of these ideas. Whether a poet uses hallucinogens or not, the only question that concerns the reader of what purports to be poetry is, is the poetry produced good, bad or indifferent? Nor need this inquiry stay academic. It may be more significant than at first appears likely, for instance, that Michael McClure's poetry is by no means always as good as its tone suggests it must be. Poetry—for Michael McClure as well as for F.R. Leavis—is important beyond the performance of certain linguistic skills. If, to put it bluntly, poetry fails certain acid-tests, the conclusion critic and reader are justified in drawing is that there is something more radically wrong with the utterance than some technical incompetence. This is commonplace. But it needs re-stating here, I think: for Michael McClure, in the volumes that followed the poem quoted above, makes certain assumptions, certain claims, which, if justified, undercut a great deal of conventional intellectual and spiritual life: the poet, it is claimed, is able with the use of hallucinogens to penetrate to a layer of experience, of reality, which lies within or beneath "normal" vision, and is in some sense "more true," more real. So the normal version of the dogma runs. I have already indicated my opinion of the metaphysical bases of this dogman: hallucinogens cannot be said to make contact with reality, or truth. They simply change the body's chemistry and thereby its perception, which reverts, unless the equipment is damaged in the process, back to its former state (which we may therefore call "normal") upon the cessation of the narcotic effect. The most that could be claimed is that it is somehow morally better or healthier to perceive and experience hallucinogenically than in the ordinary way. Rimbaud's *Une Saison en Enfer*, the decline of Coleridge, and the testimony of William Burroughs suggest otherwise, but this is not, as I have said, the place to discuss that question. What is relevant here is the question, how do the aesthetic facts bear out the metaphysics? Why, and how, does McClure's verse fail? What are the moral implications of the aesthetic facts?

If McClure had been right, he ought to have hit a poetic gusher: there ought to be no difference between one poem and the next, whereas in fact there are enormous differences—of quality, tone, effect—even within one passage of one poem. Excellent as McClure's best drug poems are, there is little evidence of his having achieved the goal of every poetic mineralogist: the level of his verse fluctuates wildly, it moves from near-sublimity to near-bathos from one one to the next. This is so in the peyote poem already quoted. This, for instance, is the note hit so monotonously by psychosis—"I KNOW EVERYTHING!" McClure's poetry, like Christopher Smart's, moves into and out of relevance, while itself apparently remaining convinced of its own oracular profundity. The nuttiness of "I KNOW EVERYTHING!" is familiar to many users of hallucinogens, to say nothing of alcohol. Everyone who has ever been drunk or high knows this feeling of *significance*: the things said in this state — afterwards recollected to have been quite trivial — seem at the time to be tremendously, ultimately, profound. Later, in the same poem, McClure tones it down and drops the block capitals — "I know all that I need to know" — arrogant still perhaps, but not absurd. The second statement occurs after a passage of considerable beauty —

> The dark brown space behind the door is precious,
> intimate, silent, still. The birth-place
> of Brahms.
>   [Peyote Poem]

That is an adjective sequence, we feel, which might have come into being without the peyote, though it's unlikely that the actual instigation — the space behind the door — would have caused it. Not so the Nerval-ish pretensions of "I read the meaning of scratched walls and cracked ceilings." This is surely private — an attestation only. Poetry comes into existence in the space between the poet and the world, between his experience and ours. McClure's over-use of upper-case type is a telltale sign of exasperation, an inability to communicate. But poetry, to say it another way, is not — much pseudo-symbolist claptrap to the contrary — concerned with the incommunicable, but with the *otherwise incommunicable*. Chairs are inexpressible, if you like, but our experience of them, or what this experience means to us, is not. In the same way, McClure's poetry succeeds when it is not trying to gesticulate towards the INEXPRESSIBLE, but precisely when it concerns itself with the frontierland between the experience of drugs and his own waking consciousness, between his extraordinary experience and our own more ordinary. It is, in other words, half-critical, half-comparative. It is blasphemous to seek to "say" God, to say what should be left unsaid. The true mystic's concern is what his experience teaches him and his readers about the whole meaning and conduct of life itself. Much of McClure's poetry invalidates itself in trying to declare the undeclarable. So, in the peyote poem under discussion, the interesting and comprehensible statement,

> Here in my Apartment I think tribal thoughts

(we think of Wise Indians smoking pipes of peace, of the wholeness the white man has lost), is followed by a straight line rules across the page, and then the single word "STOMACHE!!!" It is hard to know which is funnier, the upper-case type or the triple exclamation marks. Here, truly, is the absurd of drunkenness, the ludicrous conviction of *significance*. It is a phenomenon which could be illustrated at random from any of Mc-Clure's longer poems, those sprawling numinous extravaganzas. This is the sort of thing "poor Kit Smart" stumbled on in his madness: "STOMACHE!" In this instance, McClure immediately goes on to fish out a genuinely fascinating emblem from the unconscious—

> I am visited by a man
> who is the god of foxes
> there is dirt under the nails of his paw
>   fresh from his den.
> We smile at one another in recognition.

The episode is strangely meaningful, though its significance is hard to define without talking in Jungian terms about archetypes and collective memories. Anyway, McClure's memory becomes ours here: the weirdly alarming beauty of childhood is skilfully conjured up. Almost at once—so drastic are McClure's transitions—the scene vanishes: the poet closes his eyes—"Closing my eyes there are flashes of light—My eyes won't focus but leap." The reporting here is interesting and to the point: the physiological facts are relevant at this juncture. We want to know what it feels like, what actually happens, and he tells us, with a frank courage which is an important part of McClure's make-up. It doesn't seem important in the same way to know that he then felt he had three feet. But the odd detail—"I see seven places at once"—has a factual authenticity which tells us something we ought to know about the trip. Throughout this passage, indeed, the reporting is absorbing and pointful, probably because it keeps the inner narrative closely related to the outside world. "Seeing the loose chaos of words on the page"—we all know that aspect of language. In the middle of the passage there is another hilarious interjection—"STOM? ACHE!"—which must, but can't, be ironical; then, after another line ruled across the page, McClure again tells us solemnly of his feelings about his belly[4]:

> My belly and I are two individuals
>   joined together
>   in life.

The conclusion of the poem, however, returns to the archetypal world to which it is McClure's peculiar gift and privilege to be able to penetrate:

> I stare into clouds seeing
>   their misty convolutions.
>   The whirls of vapor
>   I will small clouds out of existence.

> They become fish devouring each other.
> And change like Dante's holy spirits
>   becoming an osprey frozen skyhigh
>   to challenge me.
>   ["Peyote Poem"]

Those ospreys, like the fox-man earlier and the lion men in the beautiful short poem "The Child," come from an impersonal realm, a timeless symbol-bank, which sets all the rest of the hallucination in a meaningful context. All McClure's best verse connects his drug-experience with some deeper, broader metaphoric layer, and in just this connection lies the poetry:

> COLD COLD COLD COLD COLD COLD COLD COLD
>   COLD AND FAR AWAY
> and we are not cold in our space and not cool
>   and not different. And I do
> not mean this as a metaphor or fact.
>   Even the strained act it is.
>
> Bending by the brook and filling cups.
>   ["Peyote Depression"]

The last line suddenly makes contact with Chinese religious thought; at the same time, it provides a metaphor for life itself which is at once ancient and original. The "fact-act" echo here reminds us again of McClure's verbal subtlety, subtlety evident more in a non-narcotic piece, like "Canoe: Explication" which reveals most strikingly McClure's provenance from Robert Duncan:

> it's the imagined song, the concept
>   of anarchy set to music
> Wavering, symmetrical, unsymmetrical
> Pointed and strange as a matchflame
>   Held in sunlight.

The almost invisible image (so much more apt than Olson's shot at the same thing) beautifully captures the elusiveness of the thought. The same delicacy is applied later to the motion of the canoe:

> A volta appears — the serene charged pause.
>   Thought alone wonders
>   At the connection
>   And the duet begins again.

The simple yet subtle physical event — canoeing — has been "explicated" by the metaphor of music, just as the experience of hearing music has been enlarged by the physical analogy. The slightness of the theme produces a poetry of equal delicacy. McClure is a poet with or without drugs.

Whether he has realized his enormous potential is another matter. Since he came down from his narcotics plateau — a decade ago now — McClure has written a great deal of good poetry. Its sheer quantity indeed makes it impossible for this kind of survey to do it anything like justice. It is enough to say that at its best it achieves a poise and a sinewy delicacy rarely to be found in recent American writing. Its essence is a clarification and refinement of the archetypal symbolism which emerged so excitingly from the highs and lows of his peyote poems.

His best poems balance on a needle-point, yet are as sure as rock. What we might perhaps question is that power to engage our deepest human interest. Here is a more recent instance of this quasi-Blakean mode:

EACH
MAMMAL
does
a
small perfect
thing
like
to be himself
or herself
and to hold a new creation
on a shining platter
as he
(or she)
steps towards
the waiting car.
["For Robert Creeley"]

A derivate of Duncan's pedestal pieces, this poem has the shape of a baroque fountain. But one wonders whether it doesn't also share that non-problematicness essential to Duncan's often rather bland celebrations. The central assertion of the poem — that each created mammal (especially, by implication, man) is in itself perfect and in need of celebration — is finely illustrated by the final clause — the step towards the waiting car. No matter how trivial or transient the act, the poem asserts, we are in ourselves at any point perfect. But little of that complexity of all good poetry is generated out of the combination of the two major elements of the poem: we look in vain for that tension of contraries that gives Blake's smallest poems such force. Beat poetry offered Blakean celebration as opposed to existentialist nihilism. But it also offered at its best — in McClure's best peyote poems, in *HOWL*, in Corso's "Mutation of the Spirit" — an awareness of the foulness and complexity of the conditions against which the capacity for joy has to strive. I have noted above that Whitman himself shortcircuited exploration by the expedient of mass-acceptance — acceptance which really accepted nothing, since it did not *know* what it was claiming to accept. Much of Michael McClure's later poetry, like much of Duncan's, seems to me to limit itself by a desire to say "Yea," or, still worse, to tell the rest of us that *we* ought to say "Yea" — yet without admitting all the facts. There is a feeling that the affirmativeness has been too easily acquired.

That vital intelligence characteristic of the best Beat poetry of the 1960s has gradually gone under to an elegant and stylish blandness. The impression is reinforced rather than gainsaid by the obligatory abuse of easy targets — the Pentagon, the Man in the Grey Flannel Suit, and so on. But McClure is still — comparatively — young, and we have not seen his best.

No poet illustrates the sophistication of Beat poetry more strikingly than Philip Whalen. Whalen's stock-in-trade is an attractive self-awareness, a wry, biting humor, a negligent familiarity with the numinous that contrasts interestingly with Michael McClure's solemnity:

> The trouble with you is
> That sitting on a bench in the back yard
> You see an old plank in the fence become
> A jewelled honeycomb of golden wires
> Discoursing music, etc.
>   [Whalen, "Denunciation, Or, Unfrock'd Again"]

The subject-matter of the poem is much the same as in McClure's verse; but the psychedelic experience, the mind-changing effect of the drug, is not dashed down in rapt awe. It becomes a source of self-mockery:

> The trouble is aggravated by the grass
> Flashing alternately green and invisible
> Green and non-existent
> While the piano in the house plays
> *The Stars and Stripes Forever*

The self-mockery is more fertile, more purposeful than we had been accustomed to expect in modern verse. There is no covert self-satisfaction in the self-unmasking:

> The trouble with you is you keep acting
> Like a genius: Now you're not a genius
> You're nothing but a prick ... in fact you're
> Not even that, you're nothing but a son-of-a-bitch
>   GET OUT OF MY HOUSE!

Whalen obviously does find himself absurd, yet remains quite confident of the significance of what he has experienced:

> What plant put out those
> Tall thin stiff green leaves? Lines
> Drawn from the tip of each one
> Would describe the surface of what
> Regular solid polyhedron?
> You don't dare invent a name.

So closely are Whalen's satiric wit and his intellectual insight related. Once again, we are reminded of the significance of the new release of humor and wit: here something like the wholeness of sensibility it was the design of intellectualist criticism to guarantee with irony? Behind Whalen, as behind Leroi Jones, is the complex efficiency of Black Mountain imagism, with its subtle sense of vegetable life:

> Bud-clusters hang straight down from the sharply crooked
> Geranium stem like strawberries, the wild mountain kind
> These flowers almost as wild right here
> Barbarous thick-jointed tangle, waist-high
> Escaped once for all from the green-houses of the north
> A weed, its heavy stalks jointing upwards and winding out
> In all directions, too heavy to stand straight
> The neighbors clipped some out of their yard
> The stalks lay in the gutter and grew for days
> In the rain water, flowering
> Ignorant of their disconnection.
>   ["Soufflé — Take IX"]

The endless "takes" and jottings do, to some extent, betray a disorganized mind. Whalen has never produced the *magnum opus* he seems intellectually qualified to have written. Instead, there are the shorter ironic pieces ("For C," "Fond Farewell to the *Chicago Quarterly*") which are often perfect, and the longer, fragmented works which only occasionally achieve the moments of penetrating insight:

> The wind increases as the sun goes down
> The weight of that star pulling air after it
> Naturally the prune trees blossom now
> And some kind of bush with pink trumpet flowers
> All the other trees except acacias have quit.
>   ["Soufflé — Take III"]

It seems to have been Whalen's destiny, his function perhaps, to accept a kind of failure. We may speculate once again on the influence of the feminization of the mind encouraged by Buddhism. It is unlikely that a

forthright Christian ethic of duty, obligation and striving would have
been able to give us the things Whalen has given. If we compare him with
Roethke, for instance, whom he resembles in many ways (they write the
tragicomedy of obesity), Roethke's labor and strain seem inadequate
recompense for the loss of the humor and the play of mind Whalen's
detachment affords him:

> All day Christmas the sea whirled this tangle—
> Spruce logs, redwood stumps, fishboxes and lightglobes—
> A big eddy at the creek mouth
> Carting back several tons of debris back and forth
>   across a hundred feet of beach
> In water maybe a foot and a half in depth.
>   ["Letter to Mme E T S, 2.1.58"]

Curiously, many of Whalen's most strange and powerful perceptions are,
like this, entirely unmetaphoric. It is enough, he intimates, merely to ob-
serve. There is, in my opinion, nothing in Carlos Williams or Olson to
match the eerie reality of these things in Whalen. "All that comparison
ever does," Olson had observed,[5] "is set up a series of reference points: to
compare is to take one thing and try to understand it by marking its
similarities to or differences from another thing." Yet Olson's own verse
swills around pointlessly, unless some metaphor creeps in.[6] It is to
Whalen that we must turn for evidence of the power of annotated reality.

This is especially true of the earlier work. *Like I Say* (1950-58) still
seems his best collection. The wryness is already there. But the intelligence
about himself (what we have come to regard as intelligent behavior in
a poet this century being largely a matter of laughing at himself) is
displayed as much in the mental energy that vaults beyond itself in order
to see itself as it is in the self-depreciation. Whalen notes his failure—his
obesity, his never getting anything done—with an athletic intellectuality
strangely inconsistent with it and with the image of himself that he
otherwise projects in his verse. This intellectual energy was what made
possible the notation of unadorned reality just noted as being so important
in Whalen's verse: the logs swilling about in the tide, the cut-off flowers
still growing—these things are comprehended by an act of the
imagination, in Coleridge's understanding of the term, not copied by a
prose-camera. In his best pieces Whalen sets these natural images in a
sound-pattern of considerable subtlety and a very complex intellectual
frame. "Homage to Lucretius" (written in 1952, printed in the *Evergreen
Review* of 1956, included in *Monday in the Evening*, 1961) suggests a
systematic scheme in the title which is belied in the characteristic throw-
away manner:

> It all depends on how fast you're going

> Tending towards light, sound
> Or the quiet of mere polarity

But the casual manner is supported here (or it supports) a very wide-ranging and economically presented argument. "We want crystals," he observes, but "can't easily imagine another world" — and the reason is that this one (we remember at this point the atoms of Lucretius) is itself "barely/ Visible." Enough to say that this genuinely philosophical inquiry lacks altogether the portentousness of Robert Duncan's pronouncements, but also that it succeeds in giving the abstract speculation a natural expression: the root-experience, which, I imagine, gave rise to the poem in the first place, is now disclosed, to fill out and illustrate the Lucretian speculations which were in fact suggested by it:

> We lined up and pissed in a snowbank
> A slight thaw would expose
> Three tubes of yellow ice....
> And so on.....

The last phrase is disarming, and — of course — charming: we are meant to be delighted by the performance, and we are. This seems to me to be close in many ways to William Empson's more successfully philosophical explorations. What is characteristic of Whalen is not just the colloquial casualness which he shares with Empson, but the ease with which he succeeds in giving the insights — the piss frozen into tubes yields an insight into "A world not entirely new, But realized..." — a greater context of meaning. And the point is this meaning, not the attractive casualness, which is merely instrumental.

At his best, Whalen succeeds in relating this order of intelligence to the random events of a life — wasted, according to the world's view, in meditations, reading, and staring out of the window — and in holding it all in one perspective. The best of these complex efforts to marshal everything is, in my opinion, "Sourdough Mountain Lookout" (1955-1956), which displays, in its moments of inertia and fatigue, as much as in its explosions of mental energy, a wholeness rare in contemporary writing:

> Then I'm alone in a glass house on a ridge
> Encircled by chiming mountains
> With one sun roaring through the house all day
> & the others crashing through the glass all night
> Conscious even while sleeping....

The poem exercises a fine virtuosity of feeling, moving from sharp imagist observation, instinct with life, to the inward world, the relations between which are Whalen's real theme. The intellectual vitality which holds together the details and the percepts is revealed also in the apparently random reading which structures the poem: Heraclitus, Byron, Empedocles, Buddha — the sources and influences file into and out of the poem according to a rhythm of walking, resting, climbing and reflection. When he is tired ("pooping out, exhausted"), the ironic awareness of himself comes to the surface ("Remember smart guy there's something/ Bigger, something smarter than you"). And this wry self-ridicule — what a reader fresh to Whalen is most likely to take away from the experience — is a product of his intellectual vigor as much as the ability to "get round" — come round the back of — his wider intellectual interests. He concludes with a generalization that holds the whole of what has gone before easily within itself:

> What we see of the world is the mind's
>   Invention and the mind
> Though stained by it, becoming
> Rivers, sun, mule-dung, flies —
> Can shift instantly
> A dirty bird in a square time....
>   ["Sourdough Mountain Lookout"]

Such reflections upon the relations between the mind and the outer world constitute Whalen's major theme. It is a slippery ramp to get on: it is easy to feel, in moving through *On Bear's Head*, that Whalen is too clever for his own good. He does not work up the excitement in the face of the world which we see in the best of McClure; he cannot, it could be, put all the bits together right. He finds it easier to negate what he has just said than to find reasons for moving from it onto something greater. Scepticism is his essence.

It was Gregory Corso, perhaps, who suggested most powerfully what Beat was to be capable of. He stands in relation to Allen Ginsberg as Burroughs does to Kerouac. Where Ginsberg is all expression and voice, Corso is calm and quick, whimsical often, witty rather than humourous, semantically swift rather than prophetically incantatory. His early verse carries on the wit of Dickinson, with a fine surrealist fantasy:

> The light that makes us a friend of eagles
>   has made our poor wounds an interval of clouds,
>   slow and creeping, calm and sad,
>   in the skyful dungeon of things.
>   ["One Day"]

The surrealism is taken as lightly and deftly as it should be: collocations like "pie glue,"[7] "telephone snow," "cat shovel," "Firestones! Gas! Couch!," "old Dutch shoes," "nineteen twenties Norwegian stamps," "twig smear," "Roman coin soup," "Christmas teeth," "apple deaf," are meant to throw light on things, to illuminate the experiences of which they are severally composed. This has been commonplace poetic practice since the symbolists: Rimbaud's violent yoking together of opposites was applied systematically by the surrealists, and in essentially the same spirit. But Corso's orientation is quite different: the surrealist, following the symbolist, built up a hermetic wall around his sensibility: his creative identity depended upon the mysteriousness of his own words. He was afraid he would cease to exist — in his own mind — if his utterances became less cryptic. The Romantic poet's claim to be an unacknowledged legislator of the world had become strangely transmuted over the intervening hundred years. From the time of the symbolists, the poet had taken to cherishing his alienation as his last surviving claim to existence. The *avant garde* — for all its affectation of disgust for bourgeois obtuseness — had in fact always striven rigorously to repulse any attempted bourgeois fraternization: the public's acceptance of an *avant garde* idiom was always the sign for a rapid withdrawal to higher ground. The artist since Flaubert and Baudelaire has not tried to make himself understood by the bourgeois: on the contrary, he has worked hard to preserve his obscurity, while all the time capitalizing on the bourgeois's sociopolitical guilt to make the bourgeois itself feel responsible for the "gap." The gap has now been obliterated: there was no going beyond Pollock's painting and Cage's "music." It was the Beats who first made possible the *rapprochement* which has transformed art and literature over the past decade. The Beats were never an alienation movement in the *avant garde* tradition. On the contrary, theirs was primarily a spirit of acceptance, of celebration, of optimism. It was openly enthusiastic for a way of life of the yielded more spiritual sustenance, more sheer well-being than the life of the organization man. But it avoided the limiting non-alignment of the liberal intellectual; because he really subscribes to (that is, coheres with, lives in, fails radically enough to dissent from) the values of the society he is intellectually committed to deploring, the liberal intellectual is thrown back upon irony. The question is, again, basically ideological. The tortuous (ironical) writings of writers like Bellow, Lowell, Roethke, Auden and Empson can be explained satisfactorily only in terms of ideology. And only ideological considerations can make complete sense of poetry like Gregory Corso's.

This could be illustrated in some of the poems from which the already cited neo-surrealist collocations are taken — "Marriage," for instance or "One Day." In the first, we find that the relations between poet and society are quite different from what we find to be the case in T.S. Eliot: the poet's satiric humor allows compassion for "Mrs. Kindhead," whose community chest *is* well-meaning and, as far as it goes, admirable. The poet's rejection of marriage does not have the muted bitterness of Eliot's "Prufrock." Its laughter is, indeed, infectious.

But the point will emerge more impressively from a consideration of a later, more mature poem.

Mutation of the Spirit (1967) synthesizes his best qualities with a new seriousness. It opens with a breathtaking paragraph that seems almost the only verse since written to rival the ease, poise, sophistication and rapidity of *The Waste Land's* opening run-in:

> Last night a white apple fell from the loneliest
>   tree in the world.
> Today the field is green the sun bright and warm knit
> Children attend their spirits the old knit knit
> Chicken cries Sacramental sobs from the chapel a
>   window closes
> Loneliness grandeur and blue lambs whorled eyes
>   rinsed light
> Swimming deer and now the long hike back to the city
> Smells of rats and pasty poisons horizons of fuming
>   domes dynamos
> Vast sick sense smudgepots gasping black-smoke
> Cheese-cloth faces dead carts bells a white arm
> A long pale arm falls across the port.

The section that follows provides a list of Blake-Smart definitions that imply a maturation of Beat ideals: instead of the usual opting for craziness and the mad, Corso's definitions insist on a severe normality:

> Imperfection may discredit the rare the odd
> Yet shall perfection honor the typical
> Blemishes humiliate the outlandish the unique the strange
> Yet excellence extols the orthodox the natural

Corso's direction at the head of the poem claims that these pages of verse may be read in whatever order one chooses. Yet I fancy he would rather have it read in the order in which it is printed. The first line *is* a first line if ever there was one, and the alternation of lucid density in the first paragraph with the abstract norms of the second recalls the procedures of *The Waste Land*. The action of the poem is also a setting of lands in order, like Eliot's poem:

> It's no longer When will I break through this dream
>   suddened upon my by questioning life
> No longer is it A life unquestioned
>   did well enough unquestioned
> No the signals are clear I can hear
>   and I can ask
>   Who is that man whose snip-snap
>   makes him more than that mark madcap
>   Please who is he tell wild salvo

The mutations involve pop mythology ("Dusty Bright" — a sexually ambiguous figure who "is to the sun what the sun is to the earth the sun's sun") and sinister figures from the declining days of Rome. In fact the whole poem is poised between a sense of civic disaster ("S is axed from P, and Q from R is tore") and an extraordinary elation of spirit, exulting in symbols and images of ecstatic cool transcendence:

> O there is burning snow flickering the air
> and white velvet sloths in the falling sun
> and flamewhite bears tip-toeing across the trees
> and oh there are streams of luminous fish in mountain winds
> and seldom beasts winking in snowclouds
> O zero zoo invisibility

There is throughout a sense of having to make the final decisions — "come standby spirit my spirit fails" — in other words, a mature but not disabused reckoning, the kind of spiritual setting forth John Bunyan made once. As in Kerouac's *Big Sur*, the Beat life itself, which is what is in a way being placed (if not rejected,) enabled Corso to get to this starting-out point.

The basic elements of his earlier work appear transformed in this poem. There are the mythic personages — the Ares, for instance, of "Ares Comes and Goes" becomes "real opportunity," the new friend the poet says he's "gonna follow to the end." By means of such devices Corso has much freer access to regions of behavior and decision than is afforded by conventional introspective methods. In fact Corso had always shown great sophistication in his use of archaism, allegorical figures, fantasy and wit. All these elements of his art lend their weight to *Mutation of the Spirit*. The peculiar balance of the poem — its intensity and coolness, its force and delicacy, its urgent expectancy and moral seriousness — expresses Corso's own sensibility. But it expresses as well the intelligent flexibility of the poetic tradition to which it seems at the moment something like an apogee.

Ten years before it would have been unrealistic to expect from poetry in English a statement as mature and yet as joyously alive, as generally relevant and yet as unpompous as this:

> Everywhere here and way beyond there
>   suns glow with accordant liberties
> Paradise even pervades Hell cleansing like a bell
> The final gong deafens the sacrosanct room from its door
>   from its halls its rooms Paradise evermore
>   glowed with laughing liberties
> A hell-less universe is on its knees
>   [*Mutation of the Spirit*]

This seems to me to possess the classic strength, the clear joyous clash of great poetry. Every poem today is written under the eye of the Bomb. Between the fake demonic celebrations of Doom, and the sturdy pretense that it isn't there, between shaggy Beat gloom-consciousness and square commonsense, Corso's poem finds what seems to be the only true path. It is saturated with an awareness of imminent destruction, that emerges in a halo of ultimate purity (the "burning snow," "blue lambs," "rinsed light," "swimming deer"). Yet it enjoins neither *carpe diem*, nor despair, nor carelessness, nor irresponsibility. "Come adorned in sun foliage in the final mutation in this God-closed age," Corso exhorts. "Ahead is black" and "The decencies of life have lost their way," but still, total engagement is all that can be urged. As the poem begins, surely and beautifully, so it closes on a sure final cadence:

> Arise new spirit unroll a nadir wool
> From tip to top the source is measured full
> The eternal exists as well in the ephemeral
> Air is everywhere and life is changeable
> In the yard of the old sun retired spirits sleep
> Into the pool of night the swimmer of light leaps.
> [*Mutation of the Spirit*]

[1] In an earlier chapter of his study, Thurley had written that in the poetry of Anne Sexton "it is even more difficult with her poetry than with that of Lowell and Berryman to resist the inference that its *raison d'être* was the nervous breakdown, and that the breakdown itself ... provided structure not only for the individual poems and sequences, but for the *oeuvre* itself" (p. 86) [editor's note].

[2] This list of names may suggest to some readers A. Alvarez's *The Savage God* (London, 1971). It was not meant to, and I should regard that book too as itself symptomatic. Sylvia Plath's apparent self-sacrifice to this cult is only a particularly fierce example of the feedback: nervous breakdown, the post-Freudian version of Romantic agony, becomes itself not a symptom but a cause of behavior. Mr. Alvarez fails to see the difference between the poetry of nervous breakdown and that of Ted Hughes.

[3] See Aldous Huxley, *The Doors of Perception* (London, 1954).

[4] Peyote characteristically produces intense stomach pains, which McClure has duly — but unpoetically — honored.

[5] "Towards a human universe," 187.

[6] Viz. "what blows about and blocks a hole where the wind was used to go?"

[7] "Pie glue" is exceptional, in fact — a satirical version of "I do."

Afterword

Dionysus and the Beat Generation
and
Four Letters on the Archetype

by William Everson

Dionysus and the Beat Generation

The Beat Generation is perhaps the most significant American example of a universal trend: the reemergence in the twentieth century of the Dionysian spirit. Its mood of positive repudiation, as summed up in the phrase "I don't know; I don't care; and it doesn't make any difference," is counter-balanced by an opposite mood of negative affirmation: "Beat means beatitude." Before Dionysus was depotentiated in Greek culture to the status of a cheerful wine-god, his was a primordial orgiastic mystery-cult infiltrating from Thrace, disputing the worship of various local deities, and cursing with orgiastic madness those who refused him propitiation.

The art form principally associated with Dionysus was dithyrambic verse (a wild poetry of spontaneous enthusiasm). Thus the insistence of the Beat Generation to combine jazz and poetry is quite symptomatic of the Dionysian tendency. Even the Beat novel is an open effort to sustain lyric intensity over the whole course of the work. Kerouac's essay, "The Essentials of Spontaneous Prose," in the *avant garde* quarterly, *The Evergreen Review*, which was, characteristically, held up for ridicule by *Time*, is a transparent technique for achieving the true dithyrambic deeps: "If possible," he says, "write 'without consciousness' in semi-trance ... allowing subconscious to admit in own uninhibited interesting necessary and so 'modern' language what conscious art would censor, and write excitedly, swiftly, with writing-or-typing-cramps, in accordance (as from center to periphery) with laws of orgasm." Nothing could be more explicit.

181

The end of the Dionysian movement is always ecstasy, a going out of oneself, the loss of Ego to forces greater than it. Dionysus in his own realm of field and forest is nothing dangerous; he represents simply the flow of unconscious life in the whole psyche. But over against him stands Apollo, god of light and consciousness, the guardian of civilization and culture, education, commerce and civic virtue. To the civilizing Apollonian attitude, with its premium on rational consciousness and ego-integrity, nothing is more abhorrent, and hence more dangerously seductive, than the dark irrational urge. Ego fears to lose everything before the ecstatic force, and it organizes all its powers of persuasion and coercion to check the spontaneous effect.

Refusing any concession it seeks first to persuade, to admonish and convert, but it rarely knows how. Trying to be rational it simply rationalizes. The god of light does not understand the darkness, and, finding persuasions ineffectual, only repressive action remains. Dionysus is locked up. But locking him up, repressing the irrational unconscious, is not the end of the matter, only its postponement. Man is a rational animal, but an animal for all that, and Dionysus is unkillable. Unless his voice be heard, unless the irrational be given its healthful place in the whole psyche, sooner or later the god will break out. And the humiliated outrage with which he makes his emergence bodes ill for consciousness and Apollo when darkness drops over the earth. The terrible and magnificent might of Apollonian Rome fell once, and it fell forever.

If rational persuasion, or enforced repression, is so often ineffectual in dealing with the feared influx, it is because the latter is usually a sign, in advanced cultures, of some deficiency in the Apollonian attitude itself, some awful skeleton in its own closet. The annihilation of the American Indian, the enslavement of the African Negro, the hysterical atom-bombing of the Orientals, persist as a terrible fear and a compulsive guilt in the American unconscious. The solution, after a thorough examination of conscience, true contrition followed by a heartfelt confession, would call for the incorporation of genuine ecstatic and mystical needs in the interplay of the collective psyche. The Apollonian, however, in his civilized fear, calls ecstasy Satanic, and stands ready to strike again.

Now it is a theological truism that Satanic influence over the mind of man is maintained principally by virtue of human blindness, human ignorance; and though Dionysus is indeed blind, he is never ignorant: he knows himself thoroughly. It is the Apollonian refusal to recognize its own variety of blindness—*hubris*, pride—that enables the Satanic spirit to exploit any ecstatic impulse against it. This is the real sin of the civilized. It was not Dionysus, remember, who crucified the Christ, but a rational Apollonian Roman governor and his religious counterpart the high priest. Perhaps depth psychology's greatest contribution is to have discovered that the desperate failure of Apollian culture to effect any genuine synthesis with the unconscious is bringing its own doom down on its head.

But apparently this is something neither Pilate nor Ciaphas is ever prepared to concede: it is safer to crucify. In the upshot Dionysus and Agape, the Good Thief and the Christ, share the cross together, and Barabbas goes free. For though it is the purpose of this paper to distinguish between Dionysus and Christ rather than identify them, one fact they do share in common. In some places the cult of Dionysus took the form of Zagreus, meaning "torn-to-pieces," the god whose dismembered body rose each spring to redeem the people from the ravages of winter. "Beat means beatitude" indeed — but in a sense which perhaps neither the City Hall nor the Beats have sufficiently grasped.

Genuine religious cultures, cultures not utterly dominated by the Apollonian attitude, are not so vulnerable to the inroads of the ecstatic, for their authentic mystical character militates against the sharp crystalization of the ego-centric attitude, and permits a more balanced interplay between the instinctual, rational and intuitional elements of the psyche. Nazism, the major revival of the Dionysian spirit in our time, is indicative of the fate awaiting a highly developed technology when its atheistic humanism denies the validity of any ecstatic outgoing — especially the subsuming mysticism of religious aspiration in which the twin forces of the Apollonian and the Dionysian attitudes are most properly harmonized and annealed. The twentieth century is Apollonian to a painful excess, and the war between the two forces is everywhere discernible. It is a commonplace that the repressive action of Prohibition led straight to an orgy of alcoholism. And though this Protestant example comes conveniently to mind, secular Catholicism is not without instances of its own Apollonian blindness. Such an episode as the protestation against the naming of Walt Whitman Bridge is only the most trifling, if indeed the most embarrassing, of an all too frequent trend. It is their utter lack of perspective which makes these episodes such dangerous symptoms.

The problem is complete because of the double character of the "unconscious" forces paired below and above the Ego. There is a God far greater than Apollo, that master of the finite world of humanized effects. Transcendently greater is *Yahwah*, He Who Is, incomprehensible in His infinity and incommunicable in His otherness. Ego stands against the uprush of Dionysus from below and the downrush of the Spirit from above — both ecstatic factors, and both feared by it. For Ego is actually a kind of conscious differential, militating between the instincts and the intellective intuition, subject to tremendous invasion from either quarter. On Pentecost the populace took the disciples to be drunk. It was an easy mistake to make — to Apollo both Eros and Agape are fools. King Pentheus, taken for a beast and killed by his own mother at the Dionysian revels, and St. Paul, struck from his horse and rendered impotent on the road to Damascus, are both types that Ego dreads to contemplate. Confronted with these fearful alternatives it compulsively freezes, rigidifies around such static civilized norms as it has acquired, and depends upon common sense and coercion to carry it through, projecting with anxious hostility against the reveler and the prophet wherever it finds them. But in the end it will give in or go down. Proud King Pentheus and the Pharisee Saul each in his own way witnesses to the fate of the Apollonian attitude.

In fallen man the problem is endemic, and has but one solution: voluntary expiation of the Ego. On the Cross we see the true Person, symbol of the perfect synthesis between body and soul, instinct and intelligence, Eros and Agape, crucified between the demonic mob and the pharisaical Ego. The role of the Christian in any age is precisely this, which is nothing less than the functionalism of the Cross, taking into himself in an act of ego-annulment the brutalities of each. If it is not accepted willingly, then it follows as a matter of course, consequent upon a kind of divine archetypal necessity. There will always be a victim. Was it not the inability of the Jews to grasp this functionalism which led to their repudiation of Golgotha, and which accounts for their subsequent tragic history? But for the Christian martyr it is not much different—the same law is at work. St. Bernadette of Lourdes underwent a "trial" before incredulous Apollonian judges and "crucifixion" by a contemptuous Apollonian superior in order to conform to that Christ-archetype, and expiate the materialistic sins of her century. And we breath a sigh of relief that our egoistic culture was saved, and hope for another saint to stand up and save it again—anyone but ourselves.

These are terrible fates to the Ego, the willing and the unwilling alike. But what will become of that true Apollonian, the solid citizen, that "square" of the Beats, be he statesman or churchman, who complacently overlooks the conventional sins of his time: racial injustice, institutionalized graft, legalized pornography, administrative corruption, convenient prostitution, yet contemptuously rejects any genuine manifestation of the spirit, whether it be Dionysian or of the Holy Ghost, lest it upset the customary equanimity of his life? Christ forgave both the hot and the cold but for the lukewarm he poured out the apotheosis of his scorn.

So once again we see, along with the revival of the religious spirit, the rise of the repressed Dionysian. It is the endeavor of the Beat Generation to fuse Eros and Agape in a profane synthesis, but by settling for ecstasy at any price, it roves restlessly from the delirium of sensational licentiousness to compulsive flights at the infinite through drugs or dithyrambic aestheticism. It has in its favor the repudiation of all philistine values, a salutary contempt for the attitudes of "this world" to a degree that puts many a Christian to shame, and an earnest quest for actual existential engagement. But because in its protest against stodginess it repudiates true order, not simply the Apollonian order of contingent effects, but the veritable order of interior synthesis, it oscillates between an orgiastic sexuality and an incoherent elation. The way of perfection is hard, rigorous, and disenchanting, as the great religions have ever taught.

All efforts to find a means to circumvent the desperate straits of Ego in some experimental transcendent participation must fail. Were such gnostic endeavors truly efficacious, God would never have instituted the sacrifice of Golgotha. It is not possible in fallen man for the Dionysian and Apollonian attitudes to make a natural resolving synthesis—even a tragic one, as Nietzsche thought he saw in the birth of tragedy. Aesthetic resolution to tragic drama, the Greek catharsis, is indeed a genuine climactic, but it is obvious from the course of history that it could not effect the deliverance of man from the opposed tensions within him. Only in the Tragedy of Calvary was the final catharsis achieved, assumed by the divine promethean, the God-Man of universal expiation. And if Christian history seems as sorry to the sceptic as any other, it is the individual Christian's failure to accommodate himself to the truth in which his faith is hearted that must be blamed. For it is only in the efficacy of that total Archetype that each man can approach, through his own interior abnegation, the expiatory act that achieves his beatitude. Only when through contemplation he understands and realizes and *knows* that each day that Sacrifice must be relived within himself—only then can he accommodate his actions to the divine reality at work within his soul, truly participate in his own perfection.

Yet the fact that the Beat Generation, in spite of its dangerous recklessness, has produced valid art testifies at least to its essential seriousness, its preoccupation with the real, rather than the pseudo. For by the very fact of delivering itself over in a kind of trust, to the deepest forces of the psyche, it has, in some instances, succeeded in liberating art from the preoccupation with surfaces which has dominated it since the Renaissance. In so doing it has, be it ever so blindly, exposed the essential seriousness of the disordered human soul. Those who are saddened rather than ostracized to see young men and women damage themselves in an effort to achieve authenticity must understand the need of youth for self-immolation will manifest itself, if not in good ways then in bad ones; that the world of "civilization-as-usual" (offered as the chief preoccupation of reasonable men) is no longer capable of stemming the uprush of ecstatic forces from the repressed instinctual and spiritual life of man. In the end, both the Apollonian and the Dionysian must learn that only a supernatural culture, the culture of basic Christian mystical life, hearted in the sacraments, subsumed in collective ritual, the Liturgy, and cruxed on the profound knowledge of expiatory self-sacrifice in the Christ-immolation,

is capable of healing the disordered human psyche, torn since Adam between the counter-claiming forces of Instinct, Ego and Intuition. If the
twentieth century is breaking up, it is because nowhere on earth has it
been able to effect any such synthesis.

Four Letters on the Archetype

NOTE: *In late July, 1975, William Everson and Lee Bartlett spent
an evening together in Davis going over a manuscript Bartlett was
editing,* Earth Poetry: Selected Essays & Interviews of William Everson
(Oyez, Berkeley). *During the course of the discussion, they talked at
length about a critical study Bartlett was starting — a Jungian analysis of
the Dionysian archetype in 19th- and 20th-century American
poetry — which was to take as its starting point Everson's essay "Dionysus
and the Beat Generation" (Fresco, Summer 1959). His basic contention in
that essay, and in their discussion, was that the frontal attack of the Beats
on Modernist poets and New Critics was a re-enactment of the archetypal
conflict between the Dionysian impulse toward the primitive, the ecstatic, and the unconscious, and the Apollonian tendency toward culture,
education, and the ego. In poems like "Howl," Everson saw the re-
emergence of the Dionysian attitude in American poetry. A few days after
their talk, Bartlett received the following note.*

                                             Aug. 2, 1975
          Dear Lee:
                    The cruciality of the shift from Newtonian to Ein-
          steinian physics for contemporary art came to me on reading
          "Frost as Modern Poet" in *The Pastoral Art of Robert Frost* by
          John L. Lynen, Yale, 1960.
                    Of course the assertion that these facts cut the whole
          ground out from under Modernism is an extension of my own.
                    Bill

          The shift validated the subjectivization of value over against
          Newtonian objectivization — hence the validation of the
          Dionysian vs Apollonian psychological perspectives. Right? But
          of course the American *experience* was prior to the proof.

*Then, between August 2 and August 8, came the following four letters
rapid-fire.*

1

August 2, 75
Swanton

Dear Lee:

In my card (just posted) I pointed to Lynen on "Frost as Modern Poet" as giving a provisional sketch of the situation in science which produced Modernism. The quote is from Whitehead:

> There persists ... throughout the whole period [from Copernicus to Einstein] the fixed scientific cosmology which presupposes the ultimate fact of an irreducible brute matter, or material, spread throughout space in a flux of configurations. In itself such a material is senseless, valueless, purposeless. It just does what it does do, following a fixed routine imposed by external relationships which do not spring from the nature of its being.

He notes that Frost accepts this view and meets it through stoicism. So did Williams. Both rejected Symbolist solutions. What Williams did was to adopt grass-roots American positivism; and regionalism as the positivistic basis of culture, no more. I spoke of him as a key figure due to his approximate relationship to the Beats, which is deceptive, and has made the scene so hard to get straight. He was a formative influence on Ginsberg, Snyder, and Whalen, yet he was not a dionysian. Nor was he a precisionist in the refined aesthetic sense of Zukofsky. But much more a precisionist than symbolist, which is what I take to be the two sides of Modernism (imagism & symbolism) both exploiting high-consciousness, Apollonian clarity.

(I'm beginning to believe it must have been Einstein who opened up the cosmos for Jeffers, enabling his Emersonian transcendentalism to find an objective scientific basis. For pantheism enabled him to accept the scientific world view and at the same time retain the dionysian perspective. But it's something I'll have to develop elsewhere.)

I became a dionysian through Jeffers, but it was Lawrence who enabled me to make it whole within myself — subjectivize the Jeffersian cosmos as the pattern of my soul. In your study your problem will be to get from the Modernists to the Beats. I think the line is through Lawrence via Rexroth. "The line" in the sense of a short-circuit. The *real* line, decreed by the archetype but missed because of the cultural warpage, was Emerson — Whitman — Jeffers — Everson. When I discovered Lawrence I had yet to hear of Rexroth, but it was Lawrence who brought us together. It was as Lawrentians we faced the world of the formalists. Rexroth, like Williams, was an "experimentalist," if objectivist, etc. first, then discovered the dionysian when he came West — avowedly through

Lawrence but actually through Jeffers. When I spoke of Williams as a key figure I meant one to be wary of. Rexroth is to the Beat Generation what Williams is thought to be: the real link to the authentic dionysian root in Lawrence. (But it was the impact of Whitmanian America that shaped and liberated that dionysian strain in Lawrence. Today it is hard to credit the passion with which Lawrence took on the whole continental precisionist Establishment, and did it in terms which the American counter-culture today validates).

Lawrence  High Culture/European
(civilized)

Low Culture/American
Pound/Eliot (aboriginal)

To get back to Rexroth. The split in him between objectivist precisionism and dionysian orgiastic-celebration is awesome. This is why he was able to weld together the precisionist-derived Pound-Williams-Olson side of the attack on the formalists (the attack on stasis), and the Whitmanesque-Lawrentian-Reichian side of the same confrontation. But after the emergence he was unable to hold it together — the precisionist triumphed because it was the only side high-conscious enough for the academic poets, poets jarred loose and shaken off by the Beat triumph, to relate to. If you are an iron-filing and some lightning bolt sparks at your magnet, the only other magnet you can gravitate to can be some other corresponding iron-filing precisionist, with Father Pound pumping away at the generator. That's why the dionysian-apollonian equation is so basic — it separates the sheep from the goats.

Yrs,
Bill

2

August 7, 1975
Swanton

Dear Lee:

If we think of the pre-Einsteinian scientific situation as imposing an increasing pressure of objectivization in consciousness, then the response of Modernism was to refine the image in direct conformation (brilliance, crystalization, sharpness, precision, definition, etc.) and the objectivization of the symbol in indirect conformation. The objectivized symbol was used to telescope the time-span to present science with a verifiable art-function which its (science's) norms could authenticate. Thus the symbol was not used properly, as in dionysian art, as the aperture to the energies of the unconscious, but objectively and controlled to afford measure to the mind, to make decisive judgements on history and time, to achieve a stasis that could be verified judgementally.

I never read *Time & Western Man* — just picked up the quote I mentioned somewhere. Will have to check this out.

Actually, the two Englishmen who brought the dionysian back into American awareness in the pre-Beat era were Lawrence and Dylan Thomas. When Rexroth blurbed *The Residual Years* in 1948, he used Lawrence as the opening wedge. When Leslie Fiedler rose to the bait in August 1949 *Partisan Review*, he mostly attacked the blurb; it is significant that he coupled me with Dylan Thomas as my fellow "traveller in emotional excess." The sensational life and death were directly responsible for a shift in perspective, and helped pave the way for the Beats. It is significant that Bob Dylan took his name.

Thomas had been published before the war but his impact had not been all that great. It was his platform appearances that did it. He had a Shakespearean manner which gave him immense authority and enabled the dionysian aspect to ride in behind its prestige. His first American tour was immensely successful (1950?). Then his legend began to grow and he emerged as a true dionysian, so that by the time of his death it had become his image. The *impact* of Lawrence actually came later with legalization of *Lady Chatterley's Lover*. As a poet he never has had in the States the renown that Thomas has. Nevertheless, he is a more root figure. He developed his dionysian platform in the pre-Einsteinian era and came by it through painful thought and conflict. Thomas you might say was one of the first fruits of the Einstein revolution. He quickened in its soil. Lawrence's *concepts* are more enduring, thus he is the more important long-range influence.

Yrs,
Bill

3

August 8, 1975
Swanton

Dear Lee:

In my sketch yesterday I should have mentioned Rexroth's issuance of Lawrence's *Selected Poems* in 1946 or '47. It was Rexroth's opening Salvo — his Introduction, I mean — and it took them by surprise. "Intellectual truancy!" I remember one reviewer squeaked. Rexroth had been quietly perfecting his polemical skills in the small anarchist publications, but this one was his opening blast, and it's still around today. This issuance has to qualify what I said about Lawrence's impact on the counter-culture coming with *Lady Chatterley* a decade later.

This was followed rapidly by *Paterson* — or maybe the two hit together, I don't remember the dates. Anyway, these two events were the prime dionysian strikes during the late forties. Then Dylan coming to sustain it across the New Critical triumph of the fifties until the arrival of the Beats.

Going back to the twenties — or, say, to the teens. It was Lawrence in England and Sandburg in America who carried what I call "the uses of imprecision" along with the precisionist breakthrough in the Revolution of the word — both wings striking at the dead past — Victorian formalism. In the twenties on the international scene, precisionism triumphed with *The Waste Land, Ulysses,* etc. Williams' *Autobiography* chronicles this period well, and his dilemma as an American author.

Actually, the precisionists didn't triumph all that much in America. I think of the power displayed by Sandburg, O'Neill, Jeffers, Millay, Thomas Wolfe, and others across the twenties — all dionysians. In *Exiles Return* Malcolm Cowley has written eloquently of the difficulties encountered by the expatriates (precisionist) in this period.

The Depression put a stop, or at least a severe check, to this up-welling tension of the twenties. Economic issues swept all fields of expression, but the dionysians kept their hand in through the populist roots from the teens that Sandburg had drawn on. Steinbeck emerged as Jeffers began to fall in the background under the charge of fascism. Steinbeck and Saroyan — powerful dionysian voices in the later thirties. At this time Rexroth changed from an objectivist-precisionist to a Lawrentian dionysian, and when the war came became a pacifist. Lawrence dies, but Henry Miller emerges in Paris ... one expatriate who is pure anti-precisionist/dionysian.

During the war Rexroth brooded deeply, wrote his best poetry, and began to put it all together. Looking back on it, it seems to me the only mistake he made was his rejection of Jeffers. Other than that, he saw the gleam of the future in the combination of Lawrentian passionate eroticism, populist-anarchist-pacifist collective surge and American precisionist adhesion through Bill Williams. I was to be his Lincolnesque populist pacifist — the "pome-splitter," Duncan a celebrative dionysian aesthete with formalist adhesions to the precisionists, Lamantia a dionysian surrealist. It would have worked if we could have held together but the personality problems blew it up. Thus San Francisco.

In the early fifties, the scene shifts to Black Mountain. Olson, Creeley, et al. Precisionism refinding itself against the stuffy New Critical academic triumph. Pound, the master. Duncan admires and falls under Olson's spell.

Late fifties. The scene shifts back to San Fran. Snyder, Whalen, & Welch arrive from Reed, Williams their mentor. Ginsberg and Kerouac arrive from New York. Duncan returns. Lamantia has converted back to Catholicism. I am in the Dominicans. Rexroth pulls it together, provides just the right touch to make it coalesce. The feuds of the forties are forgotten. The S.F. Renascence and on its heels the Beat Generation.

The problem is compounded by the universal and ever-present problem of formalism. Formalism might be defined as the codification of the precisionism of the past. When this happens, both the neo-precisionist avant-garde and the dionysian ecstatics combine to overthrow it. Thus Pound and Lawrence both assailed post-Victorianism, exhausted formalism. Thus too Olson, Creeley, et al., neo-precisionists, combined with Ginsberg, Corso, Kerouac, et al., imprecisionists with gusto, to overthrow New Critical formalism.

> Post-Victorianism was a formalism of *practice*.
>
> New Criticism was a formalism of *method* — its best achievement in practice was the early Lowell.
>
> I remember when I first met Olson in 1947 he had just come from Pound at St. Elizabeth's. He was calling for a new approach to Pound even then, saying that New Critics like Tate had nothing more to say, whereas he and Kenner offered a fresh approach.

But once the revolution is won, the movement tends to fragment, and the neo-precisionists usually capture the control because their methods can be codified, whereas the dionysians depend on subjective spontaneity. The triumph of projective verse broke down the New Critical progeny and compelled them to adopt its methods in order to advance. The Beats fell away, only Ginsberg by sheer personal charisma and platform skill maintained his place. But Bukowski followed close in the dionysian strain, versifying Henry Miller's crude sexuality.

Something tells me I've covered all this in earlier letters.

Yrs,

Bill

P.S. I'm thinking now about my place in this development. As a dionysian, I moved in with the Beat sweep, and especially on platform and in sensational publicity ran with the pack. I espoused "erotic mysticism," and did it right up to my leaving the Order. That all fits together. But my deeper roots are in Jeffers, another problem. If Rexroth had welded Jeffers into the movement it would have gained power and substance. As it was, his offering had to go forward through me. Since leaving the Order my own place is compromised. I haven't found a new strain. My peers are more comfortable with me, but hardly know how to fit me in. Except in the group readings, where I'm a natural. But my resistence to projectivism bewilders them. Actually, I'm still ingesting the past, getting it together for a new emergence. But I don't think it will be a *group* emergence for some time. The new formalism is not yet jelled enough to produce a revolt. Actually the women poets are carrying the new creative tension right now, but how permanent it is is hard to say.

The place of Jeffers in the dionysian movement is to bring a strain of negativity over-against the populist utterance. If we think of Emerson as the fountainhead, and Whitman and Thoreau as the twin strains of positive and negative, then Jeffers follows Thoreau. It downgrades humanity in order to upgrade Nature and God.

EMERSON

(—)   /\   (+)

Thoreau   Whitman
Melville   Lawrence
Frost   Ginsberg
Jeffers   Wolfe
                                                       Saroyan
                                                       Thomas
                                                       Steinbeck
                                                       O'Neill
                                                       Miller
                                                       Bukowski
                                                       Corso
                                                       Williams
                                                       Rexroth
                                                       Sandburg

4

August 8, 1975
Swanton

Dear Lee,

In this morning's letter, already sealed, I drew up two lists under the dionysian setting: positive & negative. These two lists tend to themselves divide, the negative side between the sceptical and religious, the positive side between the passionate and critical.

DIONYSIAN

Other Worldly			This Worldly	
Religious (—) *Sceptical*			*Hot/Passionate* (+) *Cool/Critical*	
Melville	Thoreau		Whitman	Williams
Jeffers	Frost		Lawrence	Olson
early Everson	Robinson		Ferlinghetti	Snyder
			Wolfe	Creeley
			Thomas	Duncan
			Sandburg	Levertov
			Corso	Whalen
			Ginsberg	
			Rexroth	
			Miller	
			O'Neill	
			Cummings	
			Patchen	
			Bukowski	
			Steinbeck	
			late Everson	
			Lew Welch	
			Kerouac	
			Kesey	
			McClure	

This side takes a pessimistic view of human life.

This side takes an affirmative & optimistic view of human life.

To get some background on this way of looking at things, see the diagram of the Archetypal Feminine in Eric Neuman's *The Great Mother*. See also his *Origins and History of Consciousness*.

Yrs,
Bill

* * *

Sept. 21, 1977
Swanton

Dear Lee:

I have yours of the 19th suggesting publication of my 1975 letters to you on the tension between apollonian and dionysian tendencies in recent American poetry. I do not know how persuasive these letters will be since I did not document my contention that modernism is the product of nineteenth century scientism and was rendered obsolete by the Einsteinian revolution in physics.

Modernism dies hard. Only recently Denis Donoghue in *The New York Review of Books* attacked Yeats for his departure from modernist tenets — his interest in the occult, his emphasis on lifestyle as opposed to aesthetic detachment, his dependence on regionalist incentives, his imprecisionist technique — all factors validated by Einsteinian perspectives. It's as if Shakespeare, seventy-five years after Copernicus, were being assailed because his practice did not accord with the Music of the Spheres!

Publication would also seem imprudent for other reasons. For one thing I brag on myself, making myself the issue of a new American mainstream: Emerson-Whitman-Jeffers-Everson! For another, I play fast and loose with categories, arbitrarily assigning people in ways they might resent. This seems to be part of the teaching process — all right in the classroom, but best not publish! Still, perhaps these letters will stand as sketches merely, loose formulations intended to be suggestive rather than final. So let it roll!

> Yrs,
> Bill

The Beat Generation:
A Selected Annotated Bibliography

The following bibliography is divided into two parts. Part one centers on the Beat Generation as a whole, containing sections listing bibliographies, anthologies, full-length works of criticism, and shorter critical studies. Part two contains checklists for each of the writers represented in this collection: books and pamphlets, interviews, bibliographies, full-length works of criticism, and shorter critical pieces. Save for the authors' primary checklists and the list of anthologies, all entries are annotated.

The order of entries is chronological with each section or subsection.

Part One. The Beat Generation

Bibliography

Parkinson, Thomas, ed. *A Casebook on the Beat.* New York: Crowell, 1961. Includes as an Appendix the earliest Beat Generation bibliography: magazines, primary works by Burroughs, Corso, Ferlinghetti, Ginsberg, Kerouac, Lamantia, McClure, Snyder, Whalen, and Wieners, anthologies, and "secondary works commenting on Beat writers, Beatniks, the Beat Generation, etc." The list of secondary works is a treasury of contemporary opinion (both popular and scholarly) on the Beats.

Kherdian, David. *Six Poets of the San Francisco Renaissance.* Fresno, Calif.: Giligia Press, 1967. Includes annotated checklists of books, pamphlets, broadsides, periodical contributions, ephemera, foreign editions, films, and secondary criticism for Ferlinghetti, Snyder, Whalen, David Meltzer, McClure, and Everson (Antoninus). Each checklist is preceded by a brief biographical sketch/interview.

Wirshup, David S., ed. *The Beat Generation & Other Avant-garde Writers.* Santa Barbara, Calif.: Anacapa Books, 1977. A sale catalog with a very extensive list of works by and about Beat writers, anthologies, and little magazines. Also includes descriptions of various manuscripts and letters (including the ms. of Ginsberg's *Iron Horse,* the first book-length ms. of Ginsberg's to be offered for sale in a catalog or at auction).

Lepper, Gary M. *A Bibliographical Introduction to Seventy-Five Modern American Authors*. Berkeley, Calif.: Serendipity Books, 1976. Extensive bibliographical checklists of separate publications by 75 post-modern American writers, including Burroughs, Everson, Ferlighetti, McClure, Snyder, and Whalen. A thorough and accurate listing of works through 1974.

Anthologies

Feldman, Gene, and Max Gartenberg, eds. *The Beat Generation and the Angry Young Men*. New York: Citadel, 1958.

Beatitude Anthology. San Francisco: City Lights Books, 1960.

Ekner, Reidar, ed. *Helgon & Hetsporar: Poesi fran Beat Generation och San Franciscorenassansen*. Stockholm: Raben & Sjogren, 1960.

Allen, Donald M., ed. *The New American Poetry: 1945-1960*. New York: Grove Press, 1960.

Fisher, Stanley, ed. *Beat Coast East: An Anthology of Rebellion*. New York: Excelsior, 1960.

Krim, Seymour, ed. *The Beats*. Greenwich, Conn.: Fawcett, 1960.

Wilentz, Elias, ed. *The Beat Scene*. New York: Corinth, 1960.

Corso, Gregory, and Walter Hollerer, eds. *Junge Amerikanische Lyrik*. Munich: Carl Hanser, 1961.

Baro, Gene, ed. *Beat Poets*. London: Vista, 1961.

Parkinson, Thomas, ed. *A Casebook on the Beat*. New York: Crowell, 1961.

Jones, Leroi, ed. *The Moderns*. New York: Corinth, 1963.

Seaver, Richard, Terry Southern, and Alexander Trocchi, eds. *Writers in Revolt*. New York: Fredrick Fell, 1963.

Wholly Communion. London: Lorrimer Films, 1965.

Astronauts of Inner Space: An International Collection of Avant-Garde Activity. San Francisco: Stolen Paper Review, 1966.

Morris, Tina, and Dave Cunliffe, eds. *Thunderbolts of Peace and Liberation*. Blackburn, England: BB Books, 1967.

Rosenthal, M.L., ed. *The New Modern Poetry*. New York: Macmillan, 1967.

Fuck You! Underground Poem Untergrund Gedichte. Darmstadt: Joseph Melzer, 1968.

Meltzer, David, ed. *The San Francisco Poets*. New York: Ballantine, 1971.

Harvey, Nick, ed. *Mark in Time: Portraits & Poetry / San Francisco*. San Francisco: Glide, 1971.

James, Laurence, ed. *Electric Underground: A City Lights Reader*. London: New English Library, 1973.

Pellec, Yves Le, ed. *Beat Generation*. Rodez, France: Entretiens, 1975.

Barnatan, M.R., ed. *Antología de la "Beat Generation."* Barcelona: Plaza & Janes, 1977.

Note: *The primary magazines carrying work by writers of the Beat Generation are* Big Table *(Chicago, 1959-1960)*, Evergreen Review *(New York, 1957-1967; issue 2 was devoted to the San Francisco Renaissance)*, Yugen *(New York, 1958-1962)*, Beatitude *(San Francisco, 1959-current)*, Journal for the Protection of All Beings *(San Francisco, 1961-current)*. Caterpillar *(New York, 1967-1973)*, Origin *(Dorchester, Ashland, and Kyoto, 1951-1964)*, San Francisco Review *(San Francisco, 1959-1962)*, Some/Thing *(New York, 1964-1968)*, and City Lights Journal *(San Francisco, 1963-current)*.

The Unspeakable Visions of the Individual, *an ongoing journal of beat writing and related materials published and edited by Arthur and Kit Knight, has published eight numbers to date (including* The Beat Book, The Beat Diary, *and* The Beat Journey).

Criticism — Full Length

Lipton, Lawrence. *The Holy Barbarians*. New York: Julian Messner, 1959. A popular study of the Beat Generation through an examination of the Venice, California counter-culture. "The beat see themselves as outlaws from the Church, something like the first Christians who also lived in pads of a sort, in the slum quarters of slaves and outcasts, and were hunted down by the offical- dom of the church and the empire.... They have read their anthropologists and historians and are trying to cut back to something like primitive root sources for the meaning and function of true myth and ritual, before it was taken over by rulers and clerics and organized and institutionalized and wrung dry of every esthetic pleasure and every orgastic joy." Lipton devotes a chapter to a discussion of "The Literature, Art, and Music of the Beat Gen- eration."

Parkinson, Thomas, ed. *A Casebook on the Beat*. New York: Crowell, 1961.* An anthology of selections from the poetry and fiction of nine writers of the Beat Generation, followed by 12 critical essays on both the Generation and some individual writers, Parkinson's *Casebook* has remained the seminal critical text.

Cook, Bruce. *The Beat Generation*. New York: Scribner's, 1971. A casual and often journalistic, yet useful and informative, account of the Beat Generation. After a general discussion of the emergence of the Beats which relates it to the main- stream — "for the tradition of protest and dissent, of the beleagured minority against the majority, the individual against the community, this *is* the Ameri- can tradition" — Cook engages in an extended critical discussion of Kerouac "there can be no doubt that it was through Jack Kerouac and his book *On the Road* that the general public became instantly aware of the Beat Genera- tion"), Norman Mailer ("think of the hipsters as the Beat Generation's right wing"), Allen Ginsberg ("one of the most completely open and altogether decent people you are likely to meet among the great public personalities of our age"), Black Mountain poets (Olson, Creeley, Duncan), Gregory Corso (for whom the "simple act of choosing has always provided profound diffi- culties"), William S. Burroughs ("the Holy Monster"), Richard Brautigan, Michael McClure, and Lenore Kandel.

Meltzer, David, ed. *The San Francisco Poets*. New York: Ballantine Books, 1971. Contains five extensive interviews with Lawrence Ferlinghetti, Lew Welch, Kenneth Rexroth, William Everson, and Michael McClure. Much discussion of the Beats — biographical, historical, and critical — by poets who, according to Meltzer, "represent the history of poetry in San Francisco, in America, in the world."

Pellec, Yves Le, ed. *Beat Generation*. Rodez, France: Entretiens, 1975. Certainly the most substantial work on the Beats to be published in Europe, this is a special Beat Generation issue of the French *Entretiens*. It includes essays by and on the Beats, photographs, poems, and a bibliography. Perhaps the most in- teresting aspect of the collection is its inclusion of a series of seven interviews (all conducted in English, translated into French, and published here for the first time): "La Nouvelle Conscience: Allen Ginsberg," "Cafe à City Lights: Lawrence Ferlighetti," "Poète Zen: Philip Whalen," "Un Surrealiste on Californie: Philip Lamantia," "Une Gare Greyhound, le Retour des Tribus, et un Prof de Berkeley: Ron Loewinsohn," "Gahr, Groooor, Grayohh, pour

The articles Parkinson includes are described in the following section, indicated by "(In CB.)" after the annotation.

une poésie de la viande: Michael McClure," and "Amérique Ile Tortue: Gary Snyder." Other new pieces appearing here include Yves Le Pellec's introduction in which he discusses the origin of the term "Beat" and outlines the main postwar literary movements in America that have relevance to the Beat Generation, a long essay "Révolution dâns la Révolution dans la Révolution?" by Marc Chenetier (discussing the political content in the work of Ginsberg, Ferlinghetti, Snyder, Meltzer, and Kerouac, concluding that while in general the Beats paved the way for the radical political activism in the sixties, their primary concern was a "revolution morale," a revolution to "transform man from a creature of history to a creature of experience"), Leslie Fiedler's answers to questions put to him by the editor (he believes Ginsberg to be the most important figure of the Beat Generation, "the Ezra Pound of the movement," and that the Beat Generation signifies a return to the "grand tradition américaine" of anti-elitism in art), and others. A significant work.

Tytell, John. *Naked Angels: The Lives & Literature of the Beat Generation.* New York: McGraw-Hill, 1976. A full-scale, scholarly biographical and critical study of the Beat Generation, with an emphasis on Burroughs, Kerouac, and Ginsberg. Tytell's introduction, "The Broken Circuit," traces the emergence of the Beats, the "creative soul of the fifties." Three fairly detailed essays in biography follow, then three essays on the writings of Burroughs (He "continues the experimental tradition in fiction, the modernist movement of Gertrude Stein, Joyce, Gide, and others who sought to free fiction from the confining boundaries of the conventional novel. His novels court to the ultimate limits an idea expressed by William James in *A Pluralistic Universe* ... 'In the end nothing less than the whole of everything can be the truth of anything at all'"), Kerouac ("His true subject was America itself"), and Ginsberg (He "has focused his vision on the forces depleting the life of the spirit in the West. While his inspiration has been apocalyptic, he offers us compelling alternatives to the general disaster he sees"). A compelling book; its only drawback is that it gives the impression that the thrust of the Beat Generation resided pretty solely in the lives and work of Burroughs, Kerouac, and Ginsberg.

Saroyan, Aram. *Genesis Angels: The Saga of Lew Welch and the Beat Generation.* New York: William Morrow, 1979. A fairly slight, impressionistic account of the life of Lew Welch and his friendships with Ginsberg, Snyder, Whalen, and Kerouac. Interesting in that it is the first of the studies of the Beats to include Welch as one of their number.

Note: *There are a number of novels and books of memoirs which deal with the Beat Generation. These include Diane di Prima's* Memoirs of a Beatnik *(New York: Olympia Press, 1969), David Alexander's* The Madhouse in Washington Square *(New York: Collier, 1961), Frances Crane's* Death-Wish Green *(New York: Random House, 1960), Leslie Garrett's* The Beats *(New York: Scribner's, 1966), Ed Sanders'* Tales of Beatnik Glory *(New York: Stonehill, 1975), Jerry Kamstra's* The Frisco Kid *(New York: Harper & Row, 1975), Bernard Wolfe's* The Magic of Their Singing *(New York: Scribner's, 1961), Bruce Douglas Reeves'* The Night Action *(New York: New American Library, 1966), Nolan Miller's* Why I Am So Beat *(New York: Putnam, 1954), and David Markson's* Epitaph for a Dead Beat *(New York: Dell, 1961).*

Criticism — Shorter Studies

Rexroth, Kenneth. "San Francisco's Mature Bohemians," *The Nation,* 184 (February 23, 1957), 159-62. One of Rexroth's opening blasts. What Lawrence

Lipton calls the "underground culture" in America is, in San Francisco, the dominant culture. There are only two novelists who are part of the S.F. group: Henry Miller and Jack Kerouac (who, "behind all the jive, is really an outraged Puritan, an angry Hebrew prophet, Elisha sticking on the bears"). The best of the poets are William Everson (whose work "has the ultimate, agonized sincerity that makes for a great, truly personal style"), Robert Duncan ("a kind of Denis de Rougemont stood on his head"), Allen Ginsberg (who "has slain, with one little book in the Pocket Poets Series, *Howl*, any number of stuffed Goliaths ... technically it represents the first attempt since the early Carl Sandburg to handle the natural rhythms of American speech in a long strophic line"), Philip Lamantia, Lawrence Ferlinghetti, and Michael McClure.

"Big Day for Bards at Bay: Trial Over *Howl and Other Poems*," *Life*, 43 (September 9, 1957), pp. 105-08. The arrest and trial of Lawrence Ferlinghetti over the selling of "obscene literature" at City Lights in San Francisco provides the occasion for this photo-essay on the "San Francisco muse." Includes photos from the trial, plus photos of Ferlinghetti, Rexroth, Ginsberg, McClure, Everson, and others, with selections from their work.

Jacobsen, Dan. "America's Angry Young Men," *Commentary*, 24 (December, 1957), pp. 475-79. Discussion of writers represented in "San Fracisco Scene" issue of *Evergreen Review*. There are "few signs that these writers have been modest, disciplined, and serious enough to *look* determinedly and honestly at the America around them."

Rexroth, Kenneth. "Disengagement: The Art of the Beat Generation," *New World Writing No. 11* (New York: New American Library, 1957), pp. 28-41. Discussion of relationship between Charlie Parker and Dylan Thomas, modern art, poetry, and the San Francisco Renaissance. "As an old war horse of the revolution of the word, things have never looked better from where I sit." (In *CB*.)

Smith, W.R. "Hipcats to Hipsters," *New Republic*, 138 (April 21, 1958), pp. 18-20. "Mr. Ginsberg is not new in his cross-country research for epigrams drawn from gas-station latrine walls...." The original hipsters were black musicians who developed jazz and a special language as means of expression in an "ofay world"; Charley Starkweather and Allen Ginsberg are faddish, picking "up miseries like a crow picks up trinkets."

Burdick, Eugene. "The Innocent Nihilists Adrift in Squaresville," *The Reporter*, 18 (April 3, 1958), pp. 30-3. The Beat "vision has been invaded, mauled, over-studied, imitated.... Kerouac is a bad writer and often a silly one."

Podhoretz, Norman. "The Know-Nothing Bohemians," *Partisan Review*, 25 (Spring, 1958), pp. 305-11, 313-16, 318. Perhaps the most well-known attack on the Beats. Podhoretz takes Burroughs, Ginsberg, Cassady to task, then focuses his energies on Kerouac: "Kerouac manages to remain true to the spirit of hipster slang while making forays into enemy territory (i.e. the English language) by his simple inability to express anything in words." (In *CB*.)

Roberts, John G. "The Frisco Beat," *Mainstream*, 11 (July, 1958), pp. 11-26. A Socialist view of the Beat Generation. The "revolution" presents no danger to the Establishment as the Beats, like the Dadaists, advocate no specific remedies to social problems. The Beats have betrayed their professed values by failing to use their energies to fight specific political battles: McCarthyism, blacklisting, and nuclear warfare.

Daniels, Guy. "Post-Mortem on San Francisco," *The Nation*, 187 (August 2, 1958), pp. 53-5. Reply to Kenneth Rexroth. In reviewing works like *Howl*, the critics have allowed their "rage for rage" to blunt their literary judgment. According to Daniels, the talented members of the "Underground" are Gil Orlovity, Leslie Woolf Hedley, James Boyer May, Thomas McGrath, and others.

Ryan, Richard. "Of the Beat Generation and Us," *Catholic World*, 187 (August, 1958), pp. 343-48. "If they are Beat, so was Adam, and so will be that last, fragile child whose eyes will open to the sun. It is not a curse. It is not new. It is not their own precious trade-mark. It is Saint Augustine and 'The Hound of Heaven' *per omina saecula saeculorum.*"

Jones, Leroi; David Fitelson, and Norman Podhoretz, "The Beat Generation," *Partisan Review*, 25 (Summer, 1958) pp. 472-79. An exchange of letters among LeRoi Jones, David Fitelson, and Norman Podhoretz, prompted by Podhoretz's "Know-Nothing Bohemians" piece. "The language can be extended and enlivened by just such prosody as Kerouac's if we are not too snobbish to accept it" (Jones).

Hynes, Sam. "The Beat and the Angry," *Commonweal* (September 5, 1958), pp. 559-61. A comparison of the Beat Generation with England's Angry Young Men: "The best American writers under forty are not beat, and the best English writers are not angry." Both *On the Road* and *Howl* "demonstrate the obvious weakness of art made on Beat principles ... fixed forever in a gross and banal Romantic gesture of self-alienation, self-pity, self-destruction, and windy confession."

Prichett, V.S. "The Beat Generation," *New Statesman*, 56 (September 6, 1958), pp. 292-96. At first, the Beats seemed merely another version of the "Lost Generation." But there is a difference: where the writers of the 20's "were fertilised by contact with Europe in the latest glow of its genius," the Beats, despite their debt to Genet and Existentialism, are "purely American." In *On the Road*, the "bitterness and disgust which marked the American attempts at the picaresque novel in the 30's, the one-up-manship which mars Hemingway and makes him false, is absent."

Wolfe, Bernard. "Angry at What?" *The Nation*, 187 (November 1, 1958), pp. 316-22. "In twenty years the protest novel has shifted its attention from class struggle to sexual struggle," but "the Beats and the Angry Youngs have applied to the intensely personal matters rising to the surface to haunt people in the fifties a bag full of sociological cliches perfected and worked out in the thirties."

Sisk, John P. "Beatniks and Tradition," *The Commonweal*, 70 (April 17, 1959), pp. 74-77. "One cannot read Holmes, Kerouac, Corso, Ferlinghetti, or Ginsberg without realizing that their interest, even to themselves, is always in relation to the society that contains them. They depend upon the city, the physical symbol of society, to exacerbate in them the pearl of beatness." (In *CB*.)

Fleischmann, Wolfgang B. "A Look at the Beat Generation Writers," *Carolina Quarterly*, 11 (Spring, 1959), pp. 13-20. Kerouac and Ginsberg are the two best known writers of the Beat Generation. "Second string" writers include the "metaphysicals" (Brother Antoninus, John Logan, and Philip Whalen), the "ultra-terrestrials" (Lawrence Ferlinghetti and Michael Rumaker), the "experimentals" (Michael McClure, Philip Lamantia, Robert Duncan, and Josephine Miles). In his examination of Rexroth as "the literary apologist for the Beat Generation," Fleischmann compares *Howl* to "Thalassa, Thalassa" by James Neugass and *On the Road* to "Man on a Road" by Albert Maltz, seeing in the work of Ginsberg and Kerouac the reflection of 1930's American Marxist writing.

Van Ghent, Dorothy. "Comment," *Wagner Literary Magazine* (Spring, 1959), pp. 27-8. "The distinguishing characteristic of the Beat Generation is, it seems to me, the fact that they have a myth.... The hero is differentiated from the mass of the population of hell by his angelic awareness." (In *CB*.)

O'Neil, Paul. "The Only Rebellion Around," *Life*, 47 (November 30, 1959), pp. 115-16, 119-20, 123-26, 129-30. The article that brought the Beats to popular attention: "Bongo drums are beaten at Atlanta's all-night Beat parties, marijuana cigarettes ('left-wing Luckies' in the South) are sometimes smoked and, more daring yet, carefully selected Negroes are invited to rub shoulders with jean-clad white folks. After discussion of Ginsberg, Kerouac, Kaufman, Burroughs, McClure, and "the rare pad-sharing Chick," O'Neil ends by asking what "a hundred million squares must ask themselves: 'What have we done to deserve this?'" (In *CB.)*

Ciardi, John. "Epitaph for the Dead Beats," *Saturday Review*, 43 (February 6, 1960), pp. 11-13. "The fact is that the Beat Generation is not only juvenile but certainly related to juvenile delinquency through a common ancestor whose best name is Disgust.... Whether or not Jack Kerouac has traces of talent, he remains basically a high school athlete.... I cannot find that Ginsberg has written anything worth reading since *Howl*.... There remains William S. Burroughs, whose *Naked Lunch* is a powerful emphatic descent into the Hell of dope addiction.... He would have written exactly as he does write had there never been a Beat Generation." (In *CB.)*

Glicksberg, Charles I. "The Rage of Repudiation: Polemic of the Beats," *Southwest Review*, 45 (Autumn, 1960), pp. 338-44. The life of the Beats "is romantic in the worst sense — that is to say, undisciplined"; their work is "fragmentary, febrile, pretentious, confused." *Howl* "betrays, in form as well as content, not only the despair but the moral confusion of the group," while *On the Road* glorifies "psychopathic outlaws ... without at the same time revealing their basic limitations, their tragic flaw." While Holmes is a very talented novelist whose *Go* is "steeped in Dostoevski" and compellingly complex, and Kerouac is "gifted," in general the Beat Generation holds no promise as a literary movement.

Butler, F.A. "On the Beat Nature of Beat," *American Scholar*, 30 (Winter, 1960-61), pp. 79-92. The Beat Generation is both absurd and conventional, attempting to "suck a kind of non-life from such aged lemons" as the evils of materialism and politics. *Howl* is "only a shrill yap — Walt Whitman multiplied by Jean Genet and divided to a fraction by the personality of a masturbatory child," while *On the Road* is "a somewhat inspired gush." The Beats serve "no purpose commensurate with that human condition in which we all forever move, suffer and dream."

Parkinson, Thomas. "Phenomenon or Generation," in Parkinson, *Casebook on the Beat* (New York: Crowell, 1961), pp. 276-290. Parkinson's introduction to the *Casebook*, which appears with the essays in the volume so that the comments will appear "not as editorial views," remains one of the best early discussions of the Beats. Centers the flowering of the Beat Generation in San Francisco with discussion of Rexroth, *Circle*, the Poetry Center at San Francisco State College, KPFA, etc. Beat poetry attempts "notation of the actual movement of mind and voice in full vernacular."

Scott, James F. "Beat Literature and the American Teen Cult," *American Quarterly*, 14 (Summer, 1962), pp. 150-60. "The Beats have brought only the sensibility of an adolescent to bear upon a problem which requires the courage and mental stamina of a man."

Rexroth, Kenneth. "The New American Poetry," *Harper's Magazine*, 230 (June, 1965), pp. 65-71. In this assessment of the state of contemporary American verse, Rexroth withdraws his support from what he sees as a degeneration of the Beat impulse: "At the height of their notoriety there were never more than two Beat poets, Allen Ginsberg and Gregory Corso. Our reflexes tired early in

the PR racket raised by the Beats." The Beat imitators "can't get beyond an in-fantile acting-out of their defiance in free-verse doggeral full of dirty words....
Race poetry, 'protest poetry,' self-evidently can say nothing new."

Holmes, John Clellon. *Nothing More to Declare*. New York: Dutton, 1967. Col-lects three key articles on the Beats: "This Is the Beat Generation" (written in 1952; Beat "implies the feeling of having been used, of being raw. It involves a sort of nakedness of mind, and, ultimately, of soul; a feeling of being re-duced to the bedrock of consciousness"), "The Philosophy of the Beat Gen-eration" (1958; "though they rushed back and forth across the country on the slightest pretext ... their real journey was inward"), and "The Game of the Name" (1965; discussion of the shifting meaning of "Beat").

Fauchereau, Serge. *Lecture de la Poésie Américaine*. Paris: Editions de Minuit, 1968. A now standard French study of 20th-century American writing, the book devotes a chapter to "la révolte beatnik." The principal quality of Beat poetry is that it is in the oral tradition. Allen Ginsberg is "the most important of the Beat poets," Gregory Corso makes the most use of autobiography, Lawrence Ferlinghetti's primary influence is Prevert, Michael McClure is the only Beat to create a new form, and Bob Kauffman (with LeRoi Jones) is the most interesting black poet after the war.

Sutton, Walter. *American Free Verse: The Modern Revolution in Poetry*. New York: New Directions, 1973. "The Beats advocated a withdrawal from reality into an inner world of surrealistic vision." Continues with short discussions of Ginsberg, Ferlinghetti, Rexroth, and Snyder.

Dickey, R.P. "The New Genteel Tradition in American Poetry," *Sewanee Review*, 82 (Fall, 1974), pp. 730-39. A hostile and sometimes ill-informed review. "The New Genteel tradition is made up of those American poets living at the present who tend to present in the attitudes of their work a simplistic image of the poet as a nice guy.... Among these poets are Allen Ginsberg, Robert Bly, Gary Snyder, and Robert Creeley. The clown prince of the court is Lawrence Ferlinghetti."

Burns, Jim. "*Yugen*" *Poetry Information* (London), 16 (Winter, 1976-77), pp. 39-41. Discussion of Leroi Jones' *Yugen* magazine as "an archetypal publication of the Beat years, spanning the 1958-62 period and printing most of the im-portant members of the movement, plus some of the minor ones."

"The Little Magazine in America: A Modern Documentary History," *Tri-Quarterly*, 43 (Fall, 1978). A *Tri-Quarterly* symposium on the modern little magazine. Contains articles by Seymour Krim ("A Backward Glance o'er Beatnik Roads," a personal essay on Krim's experience while conducting "am-bassadorial negotiation from the downtown world to the uptown one"), Ted Wilentz and Bill Zavatsky ("Behind the Writer, Ahead of the Reader: A Short History of Corinth Books"), Clayton Eshleman ("Doing *Caterpillar*"), Richard Grossinger ("A History of *Io*"), Peter Michelson ("On *Big Table*, *Chicago Review*, and *The Purple Sage*), David Ossman ("Leroi Jones: An Interview on *Yugen*"), and Cid Corman ("*Origin*").

Part Two. The Individuals

WILLIAM BURROUGHS

Works

Junkie (as William Lee). New York: Ace Books, 1953. Reprinted ("the first complete and unexpurgated edition") with an introduction by Allen Ginsberg by Penguin Books, 1977.

Naked Lunch. Paris: Olympia Press, 1959.

Minutes to Go. Paris: Two Cities Editions, 1960.

The Exterminator. San Francisco: Auerhahn Press, 1960.

The Soft Machine. Paris: Olympia Press, 1961.

The Ticket That Exploded. Paris: Olympia Press, 1962.

Dead Fingers Talk. London: John Calder, 1963.

The Yage Letters. San Francisco: City Lights Books, 1963.

Roosevelt After Inauguration. New York: Fuck You Press, 1964. Reprinted as *Roosevelt After Inauguration and Other Atrocities* by City Lights Books, 1979.

Nova Express. New York: Grove Press, 1964.

Time. New York: 'C' Press, 1965.

Health Bulletin: APO-33, A Metabolic Regulator. New York: Fuck You Press, 1965.

So Who Owns Death TV?. San Francisco: Beach Books Texts & Documents, 1967.

The Dead Star. San Francisco: Nova Broadcast Press, 1969.

The Last Words of Dutch Schultz. London: Cape Golliard Press, 1970.

Jack Kerouac (with Claude Pelieu, in French). Paris: L'Herne, 1971.

Ali's Smile. Brighton: Unicorn Books, 1971.

The Wild Boys. New York: Grove Press, 1971.

Electronic Revolution. Cambridge, Mass.: Blackmoor Head Press, 1971.

Brion Gysin Let the Mice In. West Grover, Vt.: Something Else Press, 1973.

Exterminator!. New York: Viking Press, 1973.

White Subway. London: Aloes seolA, 1973.

Mayfair Acadamy Series More or Less. Brighton, England: Urgency Press Rip-Off, 1973.

Port of Saints. London/Ollon: Covent Gardens/Am Here, 1973.

The Book of Breeething. Berkeley, Calif.: Blue Wind Press, 1975.

The Third Mind (with Brion Gysin). New York: Viking Press, 1978.

Blade Runner (a movie). Berkeley, Calif.: Blue Wind Press, 1979.

Doctor Benway. Santa Barbara, Calif.: Bradford Morrow, 1979.

Interviews

Corso, Gregory, and Allen Ginsberg. "Interviews with William Burroughs," *Journal for the Protection of All Beings*, No. 1 (1961), pp. 79-83. Discussion of politics, narcotics, and language: "Words are built into you — in the soft typewriter of the womb you do not realize the word armor you carry."

Knickerbocker, Conrad. "William Burroughs: An Interview," *Paris Review*, Vol. 9 (Fall, 1965), pp. 12-49. Discussion of much biographical material, as well as drugs, politics, and the origin of the cut-up technique.

"The Hallucinatory Operators Are Real," *SF Horizons*, No. 2 (1965), pp. 3-12. Centers on Burroughs' interest in science fiction: "It seems to me that the future of science fiction is practically unlimited." Burroughs is an admirer of C.S. Lewis, H.G. Wells, Arthur C. Clarke, and others.

Odier, Daniel. *The Job: Interviews with William S. Burroughs*. New York: Grove Press, 1970. Translation ("revised and enlarged edition") of *Entretiens avec William Burroughs* by Daniel Odier (Paris: Editions Pierre Belfond, 1969). The major interview with Burroughs, book-length, this covers the whole range of his thought on sex, the police, drugs, Reich, cut-ups, and his novels. Also includes Burroughs' "Playback from Eden to Watergate" and "Electronic Revolution."

Graham Masterton and Andrew Rossabi. *"Penthouse* Interview: William Burroughs," *Penthouse*, 3 (March, 1972), pp. 44-52. A discussion focusing on "the mental engineering which can make or break mankind."

Malanga, Gerard. "An Interview with William Burroughs," *The Beat Book*, 4 (1974), pp. 90-112. Burroughs discusses his friendships with Paul Bowles, Brion Gysin, Richard Seaver, and Terry Southern; also comments on the media and writing.

Tytell, John. "An Interview with William S. Burroughs," *The Beat Diary (the unspeakable visions of the individual*, 5) (1977), pp. 35-49. Conducted in 1974, this interview centers mainly on biography; in addition, some discussion of the novels and cut-ups.

Bibliography

Goodman, Barry. *William S. Burroughs: An Annotated Bibliography of His Works and Criticism*. New York: Garland Publishing, 1975. Useful in conjunction with Mynard and Miles (following entry) primarily for its annotations of Burroughs' articles, essays, and stories, its listing of reviews of Burroughs' books, its annotations of Burroughs criticism, and its descriptions of Burroughs' letters owned by Columbia University and materials in the Grove Press Collection in the George Arents Research Library for Special Collections at Syracuse University.

Maynard, Joe and Barry Miles. *William S. Burroughs: A Bibliography, 1953-73*. Charlottesville: Bibliographical Society of the University of Virginia/University of Virginia Press, 1978. This full-scale descriptive bibliography (with a foreword by Burroughs and an introduction by Allen Ginsberg) covers all of Burroughs' books, pamphlets, contributions to books and anthologies, contributions to periodicals, foreign editions, interviews, records, tapes, and some ephemera. Compiled with the assistance of Burroughs, the bibliography also includes reproductions of all book dust-jackets and wrappers, as well as the covers of many magazines.

Criticism — Full Length Studies

Mottram, Eric. *William Burroughs: The Algebra of Need*. Toronto: Coach House Press, 1971. Revised and greatly expanded edition published in 1977 by Marion Boyers (London). Although this book received mixed reviews, it remains an important discussion of Burroughs' work from *Junkie* to *The Book of Breething*. Burroughs is "within the modern tradition initiated by Joyce, Gertrude Stein, 'The Wasteland,' the methods of cubism and surrealism, and the techniques of montage, superimposition and cutting evolved by the master film-makers since Eisenstein." He understands that "once the human assumes divinity, Control is rife for evil, for total need, for the rabid return of the repressed, for anarchically individualist or group assassination."

Lemaire, Gérard-Georges. *Colloque de Tanger*. Paris: Christian Bourgois Editeur, 1976. From September 24 to 28, 1975, Burroughs and Brion Gysin took part in a colloquium on their work in Geneva; this volume emerged from that event, and it is substantial, a benchmark in Burroughs studies. The edition is in French and has not, unfortunately, been translated into English. Contents: "Hypercollocution" (Interview) by Gérard-Georges Lemaire, "La Chute du Mot" and "Le Conditionnement Sexuel" by William Burroughs (translated from the English by Philippe Mikriammos), "Le Déchet" by Gaetan Brûlotte, "Voix off" by Henri Chopin, "Coupes/coupures" by Françoise Collin, "Une langue monstre" by Catherine Francblin, "Songs" by Brion Gysin, "Ne Crachez pas sur Ce Trottoir" by Gérard-Georges Lemaire, "Le Modele Minutes to go" by Gérard-Georges Lemaire, "Vox Williami, vox Monstrorum" by Philippe Mikriammos, "Le Sourire d'Ali" by Jean-Christophe Ammann (translated from the German by Philippe Mikriammos). "*" by Marc Dachy, "Une Aube Malade" by Ariel Denis, "Trash Dance" by Patrick Eudeline, "Télé-scripteur" by Jean-Joseph Goux, "Un Regard Retro-Prospectif sur William S. Burroughs" by Richard Kostelanetz (translated from the English by Gérard-Georges Lemaire), "Au commencement" by Gérard-Georges Lemaire, "Ready Made & Cup-up" by Jean-Jacques Schuhl, "Snaked Punch" by Philippe Sollers, "Portofolio" (poem and photographs) by François Lagarde and Daniel Mauroc, "Abrégé," "Talons lointains," "Ah Pook Is Here," "Cités de al Nuit Carminée" by William Burroughs (translated from the English by Philippe Mikriammos), "Le Feu — Images Diurnes — Mots Nocturnes" by Brion Gysin (translated from the English by Gérard-Georges Lemaire), "Radio Nova," "Duplicata," "Castelli Romani" by Jean-Noel Vuarnet (with photographs by Françcois Legarde), "Le Sourire de Luciano — Le Sourire d'Ali" by Jean-Christophe Ammann (translated from the German by Philippe Mikriammos), "Ali's Smile" (photographs) by Luciano Castelli, "Tanger — Entretien entre Gérard-Georges Lemaire et Brion Gysin" (Interview), "L'Ecriture du silence" by William Burroughs (translated from the English by Gérard-Georges Lemaire), "Horizontalité/Verticalité" (Interview) by Gérard-Georges Lemaire and Brion Gysin, "Dreamachine I" by Brion Gysin (translated from the English by Jean Chopin), "Dreamachine II" by William Burroughs (translated from the English by Gérard-Georges Lemaire and Anne-Christine Taylor), "Dreamachine III" by Ian Sommerville (translated from the English by Gérard-Georges Lemaire), "Dreamachine IV" (interview) by Gérard-Georges Lemaire and Brion Gysin, "Le K" by Gérard-Georges Lemaire, and interviews with Chambas, Patrick Eudeline, John Giorno and Brion Gysin, Bernard Heidsieck, and Steve Lacy.

Criticism — Shorter Studies

Bowles, Paul. "Burroughs in Tangier," *Big Table*, No. 2 (Summer, 1959), pp. 42-44. Brief memoir of Burroughs, Ginsberg, and Bowles in Tangier.

Ansen, Alan. "Anyone Who Can Pick Up a Frying Pan Owns Death," *Big Table*, No. 2 (Summer, 1959), pp. 32-41. Discussion of Burroughs' "importance as a mentor and example in the lives and works" of the Beat Generation. His "closest parallel is Genet."

Wain, John. "The Great Burroughs Affair," *New Republic*,147 (December 1, 1962), pp. 21-23. *Naked Lunch* is "the merest trash." While Henry Miller is "an affirmative writer," Burroughs is "on the side of death."

McCarthy, Mary. "Burroughs' *Naked Lunch*," *Encounter*, 20 (April, 1963), pp. 92-98. Expanded and revised in *The Writing on the Wall* (New York: Harcourt, 1970). *Naked Lunch* is a "new kind of novel, based on statelessness ... Like a classical satirist, Burroughs is dead serious — a reformer."

Hassan, Ihab. "The Subtracting Machine: The Work of William Burroughs," *Critique*, 6 (Spring, 1963), pp. 4-23. In his discussion of *Junkie, Naked Lunch, Exterminator!, Soft Machine,* and *The Ticket That Exploded*, Hassan argues that "the work of Burroughs takes its nauseous sense of life from our moment."

Abel, Lionel. "Beyond the Fringe," *Partisan Review*, 30 (Spring, 1963), pp. 109-112. *Naked Lunch* fills a "metaphysical need in many people which cannot nowadays be satisfied by the 'high' experiences of ethical decision, speculative wonder, communion with nature or with others."

Gysin, Brion. "Cut-ups: A Project for Disastrous Success," *Evergreen Review*, 32 (April/May, 1964), pp. 56-61. Discussion of the writing of *Naked Lunch*, development of Gysin and Burroughs' "cut-up" theory.

McLuhan, Marshall. "Notes on Burroughs," *The Nation*, 199 (December 28, 1964), pp. 517-19. *Finnegans Wake* is a precedent to Burroughs' novels. Burroughs is not "asking merit marks as a writer; he is trying to point to the shut-off button of an active and lethal environmental process."

Hoffman, Frederick J. *The Mortal No: Death and the Modern Imagination*. Princeton, N.J.: Princeton University Press, 1964, pp. 486-489. Burroughs is "entirely a destructive expression, without joy in destruction or anxiety over the search for an alternative."

Hassan, Ihab. "The Novel of Outrage: A Minority Voice in Postwar American Fiction," *American Scholar*, 34 (Spring, 1965), pp. 239-253. In Burroughs, "action and reaction merge in that apocalyptic destruction of creation that is the complete metaphor of outrage."

Fiedler, Leslie A. "The New Mutants," *Partisan Review*, 32 (Fall, 1965), pp. 505-525. Burroughs is "the chief prophet of the post-male post-heroic world"; *Naked Lunch* is a vision of "post-Hummanist sexuality."

Kostelanetz, Richard. "From Nightmare to Serendipity: A Retrospective Look at William Burroughs," *Twentieth Century Literature*, 9 (1965), pp. 123-130. In his discussion of *Naked Lunch*, Kostelanetz argues that Burroughs is a minor writer because his "subsequent creative works are distinctly less realized and less affecting – indeed, less significant."

Tanner, Tony. "The New Demonology," *Partisan Review*, 30 (Fall, 1966), pp. 547-572. A discussion of Burroughs' work from *Junkie* to *Nova Express*. The novels convey the "feeling of unnameable, unanalyzable malign pressures moving in on the individual."

Lodge, David. "Objections to William Burroughs," *Critical Quarterly*, 8 (Autumn, 1966), pp. 203-212. Burroughs is "deeply confused and ultimately unsatisfying."

Ballard, J.G. "Terminal Documents: Burroughs Reviewed by Ballard," *Ambit*, no. 27 (1966), pp. 46-48. *Junkie, Naked Lunch, Soft Machine*, and *The Ticket That Exploded* give us "the first definitive portrait of the inner landscape of our mid-century."

Hassan, Ihab. "The Literature of Silence: From Henry Miller to Beckett and Burroughs," *Encounter*, 28 (January, 1967), pp. 74-82. The "framework of [Burroughs'] books is science fiction, the new map of our hell, the nightmare that our machines dream when they dream of history."

Adam, Ian W. "Society as Novelist," *Journal of Aesthetics and Art Criticism*, 25 (Summer, 1967), pp. 375-86. A discussion of "the social context of Thackery's *Vanity Fair* and *Naked Lunch* with an eye to its effect on the radically different techniques and conventions of the works."

Mudrick, Marvin. "Sarroute, Duras, Burroughs, Barthelme, and a Postscript," *Hudson Review*, 20 (Autumn, 1967), pp. 473-486. Compares Burroughs to Lenny Bruce; Burroughs has become "progressively stuffier and more static since *Naked Lunch*."

McConnell, Frank D. "William Burroughs and the Literature of Addiction," *Massachusetts Review*, 8 (1967), pp. 665-680. *Naked Lunch* is "set like a depth charge within the inmost form of a cash-and-carry culture, an eminent prefabrication to subvert prefabricators and all their works." It is in the tradition of DeQuincey, Wilde, Coleridge, Lowry, and Algren.

Elliott, George P. "Destroyers, Defilers, and Confusers of Men," *Atlantic Monthly*, 222 (December, 1968), pp. 74-80. "In Swift's satire the ugliness is in the evil attacked"; in *Naked Lunch* the ugliness is "mostly in the style of the attack itself, and the primary object of the attack is not capital punishment but the reader." *Naked Lunch* is an "anti-book."

Michelson, Peter. "Beardsley, Burroughs, Decadence and the Poetics of Obscenity," *Tri-Quarterly*, 12 (1968), pp. 139-155. Beardsley (an "early" Decadent) was celebratory; Burroughs is analytic, his novels "a paradigmatic instance of the later Decadence."

Fox, Hugh. "Cut-up Poetry and William Burroughs," *West Coast Review*, No. 4 (Fall, 1969), pp. 17-19. Burroughs' cut-ups break away "from the fundamental grammar-thought structure of English," thus liberating the mind "from the rationale of western civilization."

Kerouac, Jack and Neal Cassady. "First Night of the Tapes," *Transatlantic Review*, No. 33/34 (Winter, 1969/70), pp. 115-125. Transcript of a taped conversation between Kerouac and Cassady in 1952 centering on Cassady's life with Burroughs in Texas.

Solotaroff, Theodore. "The Algebra of Need," in *The Red Hot Vacuum* (New York: Atheneum, 1970), pp. 247-253. Discussion of *Nova Express, Soft Machine*, and *The Ticket That Exploded* as a "depiction of the endemic lusts of body and mind which prey on men, hook them, and turn them into beasts: The pushers as well as the pushed."

Bryant, Jerry H. *The Open Decision: The Contemporary American Novel and Its Intellectual Background*. New York: Free Press, 1970, pp. 199-228. Discussion of *Naked Lunch* and *Nova Express*. For Burroughs, drug addiction "is both a literal example of human imprisonment and thought control and a figurative representation of similar forces at work in human society at large."

Tanner, Tony. *City of Words: American Fiction, 1950-70*. New York: Harper & Row, 1971, pp. 109-140. Burroughs is "an addict turned diagnostician, a victim of sickness now devoted to the analysis of diseases." Discussion of the cut-up method.

Beml, Maxy. "William Burroughs and the Invisible Generation," *Telos*, No. 13 (Fall, 1972), pp. 125-131. "Chaos and derangement are more integral to the system of integration than the goals of the system itself," and it is to this end that Burroughs' fiction moves.

Bowles, Paul. *Without Stopping*. New York: Putnam, 1972. General biographical material concerning Burroughs in Tangier and his relationship to Bowles.

Vernon, John. *The Garden and the Map: Schizophrenia in Twentieth Century Literature and Culture*. Urbana: University of Illinois Press, 1973, pp. 85-109. For Burroughs "the world has flown into two opposing principles, a labyrinthine external, mechanical structure and a reified organic content." Discussion of fragmentation and the cut-up method.

Kazin, Alfred. *Bright Book of Life*. Boston: Atlantic-Little, Brown Books, 1973, pp. 262-271. Discussion of Burroughs, Thomas Pynchon and Donald Barthelme. "Outside, the planets and constellations reel to prove that life has no meaning, that there is not and cannot be anything but our own sacred consciousness."

Burroughs, William Jr. *Kentucky Ham*. New York: E.P. Dutton, 1973. Memoir of childhood with his father and time spent with him in Tangier. Appeared in an earlier form in "Life with Father," *Esquire*, 76 (September, 1971), pp. 113-115, 140-141, 144-145.

Le Vot, Andre. "Disjunctive and Conjunctive Modes in Contemporary American Fiction," *Forum*, 14 (1976), pp. 44-55. With Hawkes, Coover, and Barthelme, Burroughs is part of a new "Lost Generation," with Nathaniel West as its prophet.

Scheer-Schazler, Brigitte. "Language at the Vanishing Point: Some Notes on the Use of Language in Recent American Literature," *Revue des Langues Vivantes*, 42 (1976), pp. 497-508. Like Barth, Pynchon, and Nabokov, Burroughs thinks language is "a control instrument," calls for its destruction as "diseased."

Tanner, James E. Jr. "Experimental Styles Compared: E.E. Cummings and William Burroughs," *Style*, 10 (1976), pp. 1-27. While both Cummings and Burroughs experiment with language, Cummings is the more revolutionary, as Burroughs "retreats from the word."

GREGORY CORSO

Works

The Vestal Lady on Brattle and Other Poems. Cambridge, Mass.: Richard Brunkenfeld, 1955.

Gasoline. San Francisco: City Lights Books, 1958.

Bomb. San Francisco: City Lights Books, 1958.

A Pulp Magazine for the Dead Generation: Poems, with Henk Marsman. Paris: Dead Language, 1959.

The Happy Birthday of Death. New York: New Directions, 1960.

Minutes to Go (with William Burroughs and Brion Gysin). Paris: Two Cities Editions, 1960.

The American Express. Paris: Olympia Press, 1961.

The Minicab War, with Anselm Hollo, Tom Raworth. London: Matrei Press, 1961.

Long Live Man. New York: New Directions, 1962.

Selected Poems. London: Eyre & Spottiswoode, 1962.

The Mutation of the Spirit. New York: Death Press, 1964.

There Is Yet Time to Run Back Through Life and Expiate All That's Been Sadly Done. New York: New Directions, 1965.

10 Times a Poem. New York: Poets Press, 1967.

Elegiac Feelings American. New York: New Directions, 1970.

Ankh. New York: Phoenix Book Shop, 1971.

Way Out/A Poem in Discord. Kathmandu: Bardo Matrix, 1974.

Earth Egg. New York: Unmuzzled Ox, 1974.

Interviews

King, Robert. "Gregory Corso: An Interview," *The Beat Diary (the unspeakable visions of the individual)*, 5 (1977), pp. 4-24. A major interview, focusing on biography, poetry, and Corso's relationship to the other Beat writers. "I think I am called an original and also very much a primitive type, too, in poetry.... I know the sestina, I know the sonnets, I know the old sources of the information that I lay out."

Bibliography

Wilson, Robert A. *A Bibliography of Works by Gregory Corso*. New York: Phoenix Bookshop, 1966. Description of Corso's books, pamphlets, broadsides, and periodical appearances through 1965.

Criticism

Howard, Richard. *Alone with America*. New York: Atheneum, 1969. Corso's is "a poetry of fragments, of scatterings, even of droppings ... regenerative, seminal, fertilizing, but without sequence or lineal order." It contains "the elements of a giant art."

Dullea, Gerard J. "Ginsberg and Corso: Image and Imagination," *Thoth,* 11 (1971), pp. 17-27. The Beats are "completely anti-Establishment and completely proself." Of the two poets, Corso is the more conventional, using his experience *in* poems rather than (Ginsberg) *as* poems.

Cook, Bruce. *The Beat Generation.* New York: Scribner's, 1971. Cook devotes a chapter to Corso, "the urchin Shelley." "Corso is Saul Bellow's Eugene Henderson, running through the frozen fields of Newfoundland, chanting '*I want, I want, I want'* to himself." Includes much biographical material and part of an interview with Corso.

WILLIAM EVERSON (BROTHER ANTONINUS)

Works

These Are the Ravens. San Leandro, Calif.: Greater West Publishing, 1935.
San Joaquin. Los Angeles: Ward Ritchie Press, 1939.
The Masculine Dead. Prairie City, Iowa: Press of James A. Decker, 1942.
X War Elegies. Waldport, Ore.: Untide Press, 1943.
The Waldport Poems. Waldport, Ore.: Untide Press, 1944.
War Elegies. Waldport, Ore.: Untide Press, 1944.
The Residual Years. Waldport, Ore.: Untide Press, 1944.
Poems MCMXLII. Waldport, Ore.: Untide Press, 1945.
The Residual Years (enlarged edition). New York: New Directons, 1948.
A Privacy of Speech. Berkeley, Calif.: Equinox Press, 1949.
Triptych for the Living. Berkeley, Calif.: The Seraphim Press, 1951.
An Age Insurgent. San Francisco: Blackfriars Publications, 1959.
The Crooked Lines of God. Detroit: University of Detroit Press, 1959.
There Will Be Harvest. Berkeley, Calif.: Kenneth J. Carpenter, 1960.
The Year's Declension. Berkeley, Calif.: Kenneth J. Carpenter, 1961.
The Hazards of Holiness. Garden City, N.Y.: Doubleday, 1962.
The Poet Is Dead. San Francisco: Auerhahn Press, 1964.
The Blowing of the Seed. New Haven, Conn.: Henry W. Wenning, 1966.
Single Source. Berkeley, Calif.: Oyez, 1966.
The Rose of Solitude. Garden City, N.Y.: Doubleday, 1967.
In the Fictive Wish. Berkeley, Calif.: Oyez, 1967.
A Canticle to the Waterbirds. Berkeley, Calif.: Eizo, 1968.
Robinson Jeffers: Fragments of an Older Fury. Berkeley, Calif.: Oyez, 1968.
The Springing of the Blade. Reno, Nev.: Black Rock Press, 1968.
The Residual Years, Poems 1934-1948. New York: New Directions, 1968.
The City Does Not Die. Berkeley, Calif.: Oyez, 1969.
The Last Crusade. Berkeley, Calif.: Oyez, 1969.
Who Is She That Looketh Forth as the Morning. Santa Barbara, Calif.: Capricorn Press, 1972.
Tendril in the Mesh. San Francisco: Cayucos Books, 1973.
Black Hills. San Francisco: Didymus Press, 1973.
Man-Fate. New York: New Directions, 1974.
Archetype West. Berkeley, Calif.: Oyez, 1976.
River-Root. Berkeley, Calif.: Oyez, 1976.
The Veritable Years. Santa Barbara, Calif.: Black Sparrow Press, 1978.
Rattlesnake August. Northridge, Calif.: Santa Susana Press, 1978.

Blame It on the Jet Stream. Santa Cruz, Calif.: Lime Kiln Press, 1979.

Interviews

Earth Poetry: Selected Essays and Interviews of William Everson, ed. by Lee Bartlett. Berkeley, Calif.: Oyez, 1979. This volume collects many of Everson's major interviews.*

Barry, Colman. O.S.B. "The Artist and Religious Life," *Benedictine Review,* 9 (September/December, 1960), pp. 223-38. Included as part of a symposium, "The Catholic and Creativity," this piece focuses on the role of the poet as a spiritual figure. (In *EP.*)

Gelpi, Albert; Sidney Goldfarb, and Robert Dawson. "A Conversation with Brother Antoninus," *Harvard Advocate,* 97 (spring/summer, 1963), pp. 32-46. Explores Everson's ideas on poetry and rhetoric, with reference to modern poetry; some autobiographical discussion. As collected in *Earth Poetry,* the interview includes extensive (and previously unpublished) notes by Everson. (In *EP.*)

Cargas, Harry J. "An Interview with Brother Antoninus," *Renascence,* 18 (spring, 1966), pp. 137-145. Everson discusses his relationship with his second wife, his poetry, and his spiritual experience.

"The Presence of the Poet," *Windmill,* 10 (January, 1967), np. "An informal discourse given before the University of Oklahoma Philosophy Club, Oct. 26, 1962," with questions by the audience. As collected in *Earth Poetry,* includes a previously unpublished section of the discussion. (In *EP.*)

Burns, Jerry. "If I Speak Truth," *Bay Podium,* I (January, 1968). Reprinted as *If I Speak Truth* (San Francisco: Goliards Press, 1968). Extended, though very casual, discussion of poets and poetry, politics, and the publication of Everson's books. "If I speak truth and have truth to say, God will not long permit me to remain silent."

Teiser, Ruth and Catherine Harroun, eds. *Printing as a Performing Art.* San Francisco: Book Club of California, 1970. Includes an interview focusing on Everson's emergence as a handpress printer. Discussion of the *Psalter.* (In *EP.*)

Meltzer, David; ed. *The San Francisco Poets.* New York: Ballantine, 1971. Reprinted as *Golden Gate* (Berkeley, Calif.: Wingbow Press, 1976). A major interview, focusing primarily on biography, influences, the Beat Generation ("out here in San Francisco we were ready for it long before the rest of the country"), and Everson's life as brother Antoninus.

Gelpi, Albert. "William Everson: The Poet As Prophet," *Sequoia,* 22 (Autumn, 1977), pp. 37-46. Extended discussion of the poet's prophetic function: "I aspired to the prophetic in terms of the Hebraic tradition evoking divine inspiration." (In *EP.*)

Palandri, Guido. "Waldport: An Interview with William Everson," *Imprint: Oregon,* 5 (Fall-Spring, 1978-79), pp. 2-27. Very extensive discussion of Everson's life as a conscientious objector (to military service) in Waldport internment camp from 1943 to 1946.

Bibliography

Bartlett, Lee, and Allan Campo. *William Everson: A Descriptive Bibliography,*

Of the remaining selections in the Interviews, *several appear in* Earth Poetry. *These are noted as* "(In EP.)" *at the end of the annotation.*

1934-1976. Metuchen, N.J.: Scarecrow Press, 1977. Contains descriptions of Everson's books, pamphlets, broadsides, contributions to books and periodicals, and ephemera; also includes discussion of unpublished manuscripts. With checklist of selected criticism. According to William Stafford, the publication of the poet's work has created an "elaborate puzzle" in bibliography; the editors of this volume have attempted to "cut the Gordian Knot." Compiled with the assistance of William Everson.

Criticism — Full Length Studies

Stafford, William E. *The Achievement of Brother Antoninus.* Glenview, Ill.: Scott, Foresman, 1967. Primarily an introductory anthology of Everson's poetry; in his extended preface, Stafford calls the poet "one of the most notable, extreme, jagged figures of modern American poetry." Stafford uses Everson's anarcho-pacifism to bring his witness into focus, and he does a fairly close (though concise) reading of a number of poems.

Campo, Allan; David A. Carpenter, and Bill Hotchkiss. *William Everson: Poet from the San Joaquin.* Newcastle, Calif.: Blue Oak Press, 1978. Following two poems by Everson ("We Walk the Young Earth" and "The Summer of Fire") are essays by Allan Campo ("The Sensous Awakening: 1934-1938" — a close analysis of Everson's early poems collected in *These Are the Ravens*), David A. Carpenter ("Taproot of Instinct: The Western Regional Archetype in the Pre-Catholic Poetry" — a discussion of the poet's early poetry, pantheism, and the West), and Bill Hotchkiss ("The Roots of Recovery: The Poetry of William Everson" — ten "contemplations" on subjects ranging from *River-Root* and "Canticle to the Waterbirds" to the influence of Robinson Jeffers). Photographs.

Bartlett, Lee; ed. *Benchmark & Blaze: The Emergence of William Everson.* Metuchen, N.J.: Scarecrow Press, 1979. Contains 22 essays published between 1958 and 1978 on various aspects of Everson's life and work as a poet and printer. Includes a chronology of the poet's life and a selected bibliography.*

Criticism — Shorter Studies

Stiehl, Harry. "At the Edge," *San Francisco Bay Window* (October 29, 1958). "Perhaps no other modern Catholic writer has more profitably used the depth psychology of Jung to drag into the light the hidden and recurring terrors of men." (In *BB.*).

Mazzaro, Jerome. "Antoninus: Trihedral Poet," *Fresco* (Winter, 1958), pp. 4-10. "The Bill Everson who begins the metaphysical sprouting with an alliance of a man and nature becomes increasingly important as a poet when viewed from the later Everson who resolves the growth first by the realization that nature is responsible to a larger force and then by the realization that this force is God." (In *BB.*).

"The Beat Friar," *Time* (May 25, 1959), pp. 59-61. Profile of Brother Antoninus as the "Beat Friar." (In *BB.*)

McDonnell, Thomas P. "The Poetry of Brother Antoninus," *Spirit*, 28 (May, 1961), pp. 54-60. Everson's "quarrel with the world is not that of the whining anti-materialist, but of a man who knows something of our human alienation in a world resplendent with beauty and terror." (In *BB.*).

*Of the shorter studies in criticism, following, several appear in Benchmark & Blaze. *These are noted as* "(In BB.)" *at the end of the annotation.*

Stiehl, Harry. "Achievement in American Catholic Poetry," *Ramparts*, 3 (November, 1962), pp. 26-38. Discussion of a number of Catholic poets. "Buttressed by moral theology and by depth psychology, Brother Antoninus' massive investigation of the Ecstasy and the Anguish of the life wholly given to God is of incalculable value to our age."

Krebs, A.V. "Brother Antoninus: Poet of Insurgence," *Way: Catholic Viewpoints*, 19 (January-February, 1963), pp. 46-51. Focuses on biography. "As a Dominican oblate he is still deeply committed to the struggle of re-interpreting life and working to solidify the link between the visionary and the institutional." (In *BB*.)

McDonnell, Thomas P. "Poet from the West," *The Commonweal*, 78 (March 29, 1963), pp. 13-4. "When this order of poetry reading is given by a poet of abundantly authentic gifts, it is not too presumptuous to say that it is nothing less than a breakthrough." A summary of Everson's first East Coast reading tour. (In *BB*.)

Cavanaugh, Brendon, O.P.; Alfred Camillus Murphy, O.P., and Albert Doshner, O.P. "Brother Antoninus: A Symposium," *Dominicana*, 68 (Spring, 1963), pp. 33-53. The first extended discussion of Everson's work (as Antoninus) by his co-religionists. "The poet has not just thrown off before an audience some psychic material of his, but has transformed his inner conflicts in commanding, tough, and vibrating language." (In *BB*.)

Mills, Ralph J. Jr. *Contemporary American Poetry*. New York: Random House, 1965. Discussion of Everson's work through *The Hazards of Holiness*. "He resembles an existential philosopher, a Heidegger or a Sartre, who tries to wrest new and difficult meanings from his experience." (In *BB*.)

Cargas, Harry. "The Love Poet," *Marriage*, 51 (February, 1969), pp. 44-8. Discussion of *The Rose of Solitude* in the tradition of the erotic mysticism of St. John of the cross. (In *BB*.)

Rizzo, Fred. "Brother Antoninus: Vates of Radical Catholicism," *Denver Quarterly*, 3 (Winter, 1969), pp. 18-38. "Throughout his canon, from the devastating introspection of *The Residual Years*, the first false fervor of conversion seen in *Prodigious Thrust*, the deepening psychological exploration in *Crooked Lines*, through the radical inward expedition in *The Rose of Solitude*, the poet Everson, and the poet-religious Antoninus wrestle against the herd-mentality latent in Institutionalism, and against the unreturnable ventures into chaos that are possible in the state of freedom."

Charters, Samuel. *Some Poems/Poets: Studies in American Underground Poetry Since 1945*. Berkeley, Calif.: Oyez, 1971. An analysis of Everson's *In the Fictive Wish*. The poet has a closer affinity to Vaughn, Crabshaw, Alabaster ... than he does to the insistent objectivity of Robert Creeley or Denise Levertov." *In the Fictive Wish* is "brilliantly sustained." (In *BB*.)

Hoyem, Andrew. "The Poet as Printer," *The Book Club of California Quarterly News-Letter*, 37 (Winter, 1971), pp. 2-17. Discussion of Everson's career as a hand-press printer.

Lacey, Paul A. *The Inner War*. Philadelphia: Fortress Press, 1972. An extended discussion of Everson's Catholic poetry. "*The Hazards of Holiness* is a flawed but powerful book. The flaws seem the greatest where the poet cannot let experiences—dreams, temptations, sins, insights—stand by themselves and make their own meanings." (In *BB*.)

Childress, William. "William Everson," *Poetry Now*, I (Fall, 1974), pp. 21-2. A profile article focusing on biography. Includes passages from an interview with Everson.

Gentry, Linnea. "On William Everson as Printer," *Fine Print* (July, 1975). Discussion of Everson as a hand-press printer; he "is a man of wide vision, who believes in idealism and the passionate creativity of the human spirit." (In *BB.*)

Dill, Vicky Schrieber. "The Books of William Everson," *Books at Iowa* (1978). An extended discussion of the range of Everson's work as collected in The University of Iowa Libraries. "As a poet-printer, he has sought to make the book as printed artifact speak a single and unequivocal truth." (In *BB.*)

Ross, Cliff. "William Everson: Witness of the Incarnation," *Radix*, 11 (September/ October, 1979), pp. 25-7. An extended review of *The Veritable Years*. Everson is "one of the most energetic living influences in modern Christian poetry, who has sparked a new generation of poets." He "has the remarkable gift of transcending established forms through vision."

LAWRENCE FERLINGHETTI

Works

Pictures of the Gone World. San Francisco: City Lights, 1955.
Tentative Description of a Dinner Given to Promote the Impeachment of President Eisenhower. San Francisco: Golden Mountain Press, 1958.
A Coney Island of the Mind. Norfolk, Conn.: New Directions, 1958.
Her. Norfolk, Conn.: New Directions, 1960.
Berlin. San Francisco: Golden Mountain Press, 1961.
Starting from San Francisco. Norfolk, Conn.: New Directions, 1961.
Dear Ferlinghetti (with Jack Spicer). San Francisco: White Rabbit Press, 1962.
Unfair Arguments with Existence. New York: New Directions, 1963.
Routines. New York: New Directions, 1964.
To Fuck Is to Love Again. New York: Fuck You Press, 1965.
After the Cries of Birds. San Francisco: Dave Haselwood Books, 1967.
An Eye on the World. London: MacGibbon & Kee, 1967.
The Secret Meaning of Things. New York: New Directions, 1969.
Tyrannus Nix?. New York: New Directions, 1969.
The Mexican Night. New York: New Directions, 1970.
Back Roads to Far Towns after Basho. San Francisco: Privately published, 1970.
The Illustrated Wilfred Funk. San Francisco: City Lights Books, 1971.
Open Eye, Open Heart. New York: New Directions, 1973.
Who Are We Now? New York: New Directions, 1976.
Northwest Ecolog. San Francisco: City Lights, 1978.
Landscapes of Living and Dying. New York: New Directions, 1979.

Interviews

Meltzer, David, ed. *The San Francisco Poets*. New York: Ballantine Books, 1971. Reprinted as *Golden Gate* (Berkeley, Calif.: Wingbow Press, 1976). A major, extended interview, conducted in 1969. "I don't feel myself to be part of any scene now.... The Cuban Revolution was the Spanish Civil War of my generation.... The surrealist poets were some of my earliest sources." Discussion of biography, City Lights, the Beats, etc.

Bibliography

There is no separate bibliography of Ferlinghetti's work. See Kherdian's and Lepper's works (on pages 195 and 196).

Criticism — Full Length Studies

Cherkovski, Neeli. *Ferlinghetti: A Biography*. Garden City, N.Y.: Doubleday, 1979. A full-length, though popular, biography of Ferlinghetti drawn from "more than sixty hours of taped conversations and nontaped conversations with Lawrence Ferlinghetti." Includes much discussion of Ferlinghetti's association with other members of the Beat Generation, City Lights, and Ferlinghetti's work. Photographs.

Criticism — Shorter Studies

Charters, Samuel. *Some Poems/Poets: Studies in American Underground Poetry Since 1945*. Berkeley, Calif.: Oyez, 1971. Analysis of "One Thousand Fearful Words for Fidel Castro." The technique "is persistent inner logic of rhetorical device, the structure covered up with a loose, casually idiomatic poetic language." Although the poem is angry, it is "only another expression of the intense idealism that has shaped the poetry."

Hopkins, Crale D. "The Poetry of Lawrence Ferlinghetti: A Reconsideration," *Italian Americana*, 1 (Autumn, 1974), pp. 59-76. Discussion of *Pictures of the Gone World* ("poems of lyric observation"), *A Coney Island of the Mind* ("more surrealistic and has more satiric social observation"), and *Starting from San Francisco* ("primitive, earthy, Lawrentian sort of love that Ferlinghetti sees as salvation in the unreal world"). Annotated by Ferlinghetti.

Skau, Michael. "Toward Underivative Creation: Lawrence Ferlinghetti's *Her*," *Critique: Studies in Modern Fiction*, 19 (1978), pp. 40-6. In Ferlinghetti's *Her*, "the relationship between the author, frustrated in his attempt at autobiography, and his created character, prevented from asserting a measure of autonomous independence, symbolizes Ferlinghetti's view of the human predicament. He shows man as the inadvertent operator of the machinery of associations, frustrated in his attempts at 'underivative creation'."

ALLEN GINSBERG

Works

Howl for Carl Solomon. San Francisco: Martha Rexroth, San Francisco State College, 1955.

Siesta in Xbalba and Return to the States. Icy Cape, Alaska: Privately published, 1956.

Howl and Other Poems. San Francisco: City Lights Books, 1956.

Empty Mirror: Early Poems. New York: Totem Press/Corinth Books, 1961.

Kaddish and Other Poems, 1958-1960. San Francisco: City Lights Books, 1961.

The Change. London: Writers' Forum Booklets, 1963.

The Yage Letters. San Francisco: City Lights Books, 1963.

Reality Sandwiches. San Francisco: City Lights Books, 1963.

Mystery in the Universe: Notes on an Interview with Allen Ginsberg (with Edward Lucie-Smith). London: Turret Books, 1965.

Prose Contribution to the Cuban Revolution. Detroit: Workshop Press, 1966.

Witchita Vortex Sutra. San Francisco: Coyote Books, 1967.

Planet News. San Francisco: City Lights Books, 1968.

T.V. Baby Poems. New York: Grossman, Orion Press, 1968.

Ankor Wat. London: Fulcrum Press, 1968.

Airplane Dreams. San Francisco: Anansi/City Lights Books, 1968.

Indian Journals. San Francisco: David Haselwood/City Lights Books, 1970.

Improvised Poetics. Buffalo, N.Y.: Anonym Press, 1971.
The Gates of Wrath: Rhymed Poems. Bolinas, Calif.: Four Seasons Found., 1972.
The Fall of America, Poems of These States. San Francisco: City Lights Books, 1973.
Iron Horse. San Francisco: Coach House Press/City Lights Books, 1974.
Gay Sunshine Interview (with Allen Young). Bolinas, Calif.: Grey Fox Press, 1974.
Allen Verbatim (ed. by Gordon Ball). New York: McGraw-Hill, 1974.)
The Visions of the Great Rememberer. Amherst, Mass.: Mulch Press, 1974.
First Blues. New York: Full Court Press, 1975.
Chicago Trial Testimony. San Francisco: City Lights Books, 1975.
Sad Dust Glories. Berkeley, Calif.: Workingman's Press, 1975.
To Eberhardt from Ginsberg. Lincoln, Mass: Penmaen Press, 1976.
Journals Early Fifties Early Sixties (ed. by Gordon Ball). New York: Grove Press, 1977.
As Ever: The Collected Correspondence of Allen Ginsberg & Neal Cassady (ed. by Barry Gifford). Berkeley, Calif.: Creative Arts, 1977.
Mind Breaths, Poems 1972-1977. San Francisco: City Lights Books, 1977.
Poems All Over the Place—Mostly Seventies. New York: Cherry Valley Editions, 1978.
Composed on the Tongue (ed. by Donald Allen). Bolinas, Calif.: Grey Fox Press, 1980.

Interviews

Of all the Beat Generation writers, Allen Ginsberg has probably been the most frequently interviewed. A few interviews have been recently collected by Donald Allen in Composed on the Tongue (Bolinas, Calif.: Grey Fox Press, 1980). * In addition, many of Ginsberg's "lectures" (with questions posed by audiences) have been collected in Allen Verbatim, edited by Gordon Ball (New York: McGraw-Hill, 1974); included in that volume are discussions on "Identity Gossip," "Eternity," "Words and Consciousness," "Addition Politics, 1922-1970," "Crime in the Streets Caused by Addiction Politics," "Narcotics Agents Peddling Drugs," "CIA Involvement with Opium Traffic," "Advice to Youth (with Robert Duncan)," "Early Poetic Community (with Robert Duncan)," "Kerouac," "Poetic Breath, and Pound's Usura," "The Death of Ezra Pound," "War and Peace: Vietnam and Kent State," and "Myths Associated with Science." Following is a selective list of some of the most important interviews:*

Clark, Thomas. "Allen Ginsberg: An Interview," *Paris Review*, 10 (Spring, 1966), pp. 13-55. A major interview. Discussion of Bunting, Burroughs, Kerouac, Corso, and Blake. "Part II of *Howl* was written under the influence of peyote.... *Kaddish* was written with amphetamine injections."
Colbert, Alison. "A Talk with Allen Ginsberg," *Partisan Review*, 38 (1971) pp. 289-309. Discussion of Blake, Williams, Kerouac, and the entry of Buddhist ideas into the literature of the early fifties.
Aldrich, Michael, Edward Kissam, and Nancy Blecker. *Improvised Poetics.* Buffalo, N.Y.: Anonym Press, 1971. Discussion of technique: "my basic measure is a unit of thought, so to speak." Influence of Pound and Kerouac on Ginsberg's style. (In *CT*.)
Le Pellec, Yves. "The New Consciousness," in *CT*, pp. 63-93. First English translation of Le Pellec's *Entretiens* interview with Ginsberg. See page 197 above. Centers on biographical matters, Kerouac, Burroughs, Snyder, and Cassady.

Several interviews appear in Composed on the Tongue. *They are noted hereafter as* "(In *CT*.)."

Tytell, John. "A Conversation with Allen Ginsberg," *Partisan Review*, 61 (1974), pp. 253-62. Discusses Ginsberg's relationship to Burroughs and the impact of Burroughs on the work of Ginsberg and Kerouac.

Geneson, Paul. "A Conversation with Allen Ginsberg," *Chicago Review* (Summer, 1975), pp. Of Naropa Institute, "What we're thinking of setting up is something run by poets.... It would involve poetics based on classical principles of open form ... or the American tradition of the improvised blues." (In *CT*.)

McKenzie, James. "Interview," *The Beat Journey (the unspeakable visions of the individual)*, 8 (1978), pp. 3-45. Conducted in 1974, contains much biographical information and discussion of the Beats. *Howl* "was a return to the vocalization of the poem, a return from the page to the voice."

Portuges, Paul. *The Visionary Poetics of Allen Ginsberg*. Santa Barbara, Calif.: Ross-Erikson, 1979. Includes three "conversations" with Ginsberg — on drugs, mantras, and Tibetan Buddhism. Extensive, with much discussion of religion, politics, and the poetry.

Bibliography

Dowden, George. *A Bibliography of Works by Allen Ginsberg, October, 1943 to July 1, 1967*. San Francisco: City Lights Books, 1971. A detailed catalog of Ginsberg's work (books, pamphlets, broadsides, anthologies, contributions to periodicals, recordings, films, paintings and drawings, translations). Includes a separate chronology of Ginsberg's first appearance. Extremely useful, though now greatly out-of-date.

Kraus, Michelle P. *Allen Ginsberg: An Annotated Bibliography, 1969-1977*. Metuchen, N.J.: Scarecrow Press, 1980. A major work that aims to bring the Dowden up to date.

Criticism — Full Length Studies

Ehrlich, J.W., ed. *Howl of the Censor*. San Carlos, Calif.: Nourse Pub. Co., 1961. A history of the trial of Ginsberg's *Howl and Other Poems*. Includes a complete transcript of the trial (with testimony for the defense by Kenneth Rexroth, Mark Schorer, and Walter Van Tilberg Clark), the decision, and *Howl* itself.

Merrill, Thomas S. *Allen Ginsberg*. New York: Twayne, 1969. Volume 161 in the Twayne United States Authors Series, the first Twayne study of a Beat Generation writer. "The task of this volume is to avoid the carnival aspects of Ginsberg's career as much as possible and to focus upon the question of his worth as a poet." Includes a good opening discussion of the Beat Generation, followed by analysis of *Empty Mirror, Howl, Kaddish, Reality Sandwiches*, "Wichita Vortex Sutra," and "The Change." A fine introduction.

Kramer, Jane. *Allen Ginsberg in America*. New York: Random House, 1969. An informal and popular, albeit interesting and useful, biography of Ginsberg, expanded from Kramer's earlier *New Yorker* profile of the poet. Much discussion of Ginsberg's relationships with other Beat Generation writers.

Mottram, Eric. *Allen Ginsberg in the Sixties*. Brighton, England: Unicorn Bookshop, 1972. A monograph, with an emphasis on the sixties, wherein the "theme of power and paranoia is the center of Ginsberg's concern.... The Beat had a violent freshness which barely concealed a suicidal retreat into self-exploration and cosmic consciousness."

Tysh, Christine. *Allen Ginsberg*. Paris: Seghers, 1974. Volume 221 in Seghers'

"Poètes d'Aujourd'hui" series, in French. Contains an extended introduction by Tysh (discussing biography, influences, and technique), Tom Clark's *Paris Review* interview, a selection of poems, and a bibliography. Photographs.

Criticism — Shorter Studies

Rosenthal, M.L. "Poet of the New Violence," *The Nation*, 184 (February 23, 1957), p. 162. In *Howl*, "Ginsberg has brought a terrible psychological reality to the surface with enough originality to blast American verse a hair's-breadth forward in the process... This is poetry of genuine suffering."

Dickey, James. "From Babel to Byzantium," *Sewanee Review*, 65 (Summer, 1957), pp. 509-10. Reprinted in *Babel to Byzantium* (New York: Grosset, 1968). Hostile reviews of *Howl* and (in *Babel*) *Kaddish*. "Confession is not enough, and neither is the assumption that the truth of one's experience will emerge if only one can keep talking long enough in a whipped-up state of excitement."

Rumaker, Michael. "Allen Ginsberg's *Howl*," *Black Mountain Review* (Autumn, 1957), pp. 228-37. Review of *Howl*. "It's a 'bad' poem — it's not *said* right.... The hysteria distorts, preventing emergences of images."

Trilling, Diana. "The Other Night at Columbia," *Partisan Review*, 26 (Spring, 1959), pp. 214-30. Description of Ginsberg at Columbia, along with Trilling's reactions to his performance at a reading. "When Ginsberg forgot himself in the question period and said that something or other was bull-shit, I think he was more upset than his listeners."

Oppen, George. "Review," *Poetry*, 100 (August, 1961), p. 329. Review of *Kaddish and Other Poems*. While most of the poems are minor, "Kaddish" is "firm and sure."

Glaser, Alice. "Back on the Open Road for Boys," *Esquire*, 60 (July, 1963), pp. 48-9, 115. An affectionate account of Glaser's visit in Benares with "probably the only two Beats on the road," Ginsberg and Peter Orlovsky. Photographs.

Hunsberger, Bruce. "Kit Smart's Howl," *Wisconsin Studies in Contemporary Literature*, 6 (Winter/Spring, 1965), pp. 34-44. Traces the similarities between Smart's life and Beat themes: religious fervor, the madhouse, nonconformity, and the monkish ideal. *Jubilato Agno* and *Howl* use long lines and repetition which gives them a "liturgical form."

Rosenthal, M.L. *The New Poets*. New York: Macmillan, 1967. Discussion of Ginsberg as a "confessional poet." "The program he announces in 'Howl' is after all an aestheticist one, echoing that of Stephen Dedalus in *A Portrait*." Extended discussion of "Kaddish," a "remarkable utterance" which "seems to have brought Ginsberg to a point beyond which he cannot advance through further drawing on literal memory recollected in manic or hysterical frenzy."

Holmes, John Clellon. *Nothing More to Declare*. New York: E.P. Dutton, 1967. In "The Consciousness Widener," Holmes reflects on his friendship with Ginsberg. *Howl* "was the first statement of a point of view that was uniquely ours, and it was also far better poetry than most of us realized."

Stepanchev, Stephen. *American Poetry Since 1945*. New York: Harper Colophon Books, 1967. Allen Ginsberg is the most important Beat writer, "a sort of Theodore Dreiser of American poetry." *Howl* expresses "some of the themes and attitudes of the whole group: their aspiration towards holiness and blessedness, their attacks on the establishment from a generally leftist but unprogrammatic point of view, and their sense of the inter-relationship between madness, sex, drug addiction, and poverty." Short discussion of *Kaddish and Reality Sandwiches*.

Carroll, Paul. *The Poem in Its Skin*. Chicago: Follett, 1968. An extended analysis

of "Wichita Vortex Sutra." The poem is "a major work" which "embodies and
sustains throughout the statement of Ginsberg's complex desire to assume the
function of poet as priestly legislator and as Baptist announcing the dispensa-
tion of peace." Concludes with extensive notes to the poem by Ginsberg.
Howard, Richard. "Allen Ginsberg: O Brothers of the Laurel, Is the World Real?
Is the Laurel a Joke or a Crown of Thorns?" *Minnesota Review*, 9 (1969),
pp. 50-6. "It is Ginsberg's *presence* — quick-witted, slow-moving, imperturb-
ably amiable — which allows his *prophecy* its full function." Discussion of
"the fate of prophecy as self-consumption" and the poem as "discovery."
Parkinson, Thomas. "Reflections on Allen Ginsberg as a Poet," *Concerning Poetry*,
2 (1969), pp. 21-4. Discussion of response to destruction in *Planet News* and
C.S. Lewis' *Out of the Silent Planet*. Where Lewis responds with indignation,
Ginsberg responds with "sad, lost affection." Ginsberg is "one of the most im-
portant men alive on the planet."
Charters, Samuel. *Some Poems/Poets: Studies in American Underground Poetry
Since 1945*. Berkeley, Calif.: Oyez, 1971. Analysis of "American Change":
"The openness of Ginsberg's response to the pocketful of loose change has the
simplicity of a medieval poet's symbolic imagery of flowers and plants,"
though "in Ginsberg the language and the attitudes are entirely personal."
Cargas, Harry J. *Daniel Berrigan and Contemporary Protest Poetry*. New Haven,
Conn.: College & University Press, 1972. Contains a short chapter, "Allen
Ginsberg: The Shock of Despair," in which Cargas argues that the protest in a
poem like "Wichita Vortex Sutra" is "one against the abuse of language." The
notion of personal responsibility is central to his work."
Mersmann, James F. *Out of the Vietnam Vortex: A Study of Poets and Poetry
Against the War*. Lawrence: University Press of Kansas, 1974. A major discussion of Ginsberg as an antiwar poet. "A study of the protest poetry of the
sixties properly begins with Allen Ginsberg.... Though his poetry and poetic
creed may still be at the periphery of general poetic practice, he seems to express the *Zeitgeist*." Discussion of *Empty Mirror*, *Howl*, *Ankor Wat*, and
"Wichita Vortex Sutra."
Gertmenian, Donald. "Remembering and Rereading *Howl*," *Ploughshares*, 2
(1975), pp. 151-63. "For me, reading it again after fifteen years, the poem
genuinely evoked sorrows of human limitation." In *Howl*, Ginsberg "reopens
a vein of Romantic experience that has seemed more or less closed in American
poetry."
Ginsberg, Allen, and Richard Eberhart. *To Eberhart from Ginsberg*. Lincoln,
Mass.: Penmaen, 1976. Contains "a letter about 'Howl' 1956: an explanation
by Allen Ginsberg of his publication *Howl* and Richard Eberhart's *New York
Times* article 'West Coast Rhythms,' together with comments by both poets."
Hahn, Stephen. "The Prophetic Voice of Allen Ginsberg," *Prospectus: Annual of
American Cultural Studies*, 2 (1976), pp. 527-67. Extended discussion of Ginsberg's poetry as self-revelation and self-creation. "The prophetic voice is not
the personal voice of the poet, but the one used to enact the universal or the
historical dilemma of the soul in a particular nation."
Simpson, Louis. *A Revolution in Taste*. New York: Macmillan, 1978. In his chapter "The Eye Altering Alters All," Simpson discusses Ginsberg's work in terms
of his life. *Howl* "is as full of moral attitudes as a sermon by a Baptist
preacher, only in this case morals have been stood on their head." While *Kaddish* is a poem "in the Modernist sense, with characters and a plot, 'Howl' is
post-Modernist, a direct expression of the writer's personality."
Molesworth, Charles. *The Fierce Embrace: A Study of Contemporary American*

Poetry. Columbia: University of Missouri Press, 1979. Contains a chapter on the poetry of Ginsberg and Robert Lowell, "arguably the best poets of their generation.... Ginsberg's poetry has developed out of an aesthetic of immediacy," relying on "paratactical orderings." Both Ginsberg and Lowell "have advanced beyond the psychological mire of 'confessionalism' by continuing to enunciate a historical and social dimension in their work."

JOHN CLELLON HOLMES

Works

Go. New York: Scribner's, 1952.
The Horn. New York: Random House, 1958.
Get Home Free. New York: E.P. Dutton, 1964.
Nothing More to Declare. New York: E.P. Dutton, 1967.
The Bowling Green Poems. California, Pa.: the unspeakable visions of the individual, 1977.

Interviews

Tytell, John. "An Interview with John Clellon Holmes," *The Beat Book (the unspeakable visions of the individual)*, 4 (1974), pp. 37-52. Discussion of Holmes' relationship to Kerouac, Burroughs, and Ginsberg, with an emphasis on his own work and its place in the Beat Generation.

Hunt, Tim. "John Clellon Holmes: Interview," *The Beat Journey (the unspeakable visions of the individual)*, 8 (1978), pp. 147-66. Detailed discussion of *Go* and *The Horn*: while *Go* is a *roman à clef*, *The Horn* "is not reportorial in any way." "American artists who are serious can never get complacent, and that's why the best poetry in the English language in this century has been written by Americans."

Bibliography

Ardinger, Richard K. *An Annotated Bibliography of Works by John Clellon Holmes.* Pocatello: Idaho University Press, 1979. A descriptive bibliography of books, pamphlets, contributions to newspapers and periodicals, anthologies, translations, and ephemera of John Clellon Holmes. Holmes has provided annotations to many entries; also included is a description of the Holmes Collection of manuscripts deposited at Boston University.

Criticism

Aside from dissertations, and occasional reviews of individual volumes as they appear, no critical work has been attempted as yet on Holmes' work.

JACK KEROUAC

Works

The Town and the City. New York: Harcourt, Brace, 1950.
On the Road. New York: Viking Press, 1957.

The Subterraneans. New York: Grove Press, 1958.
The Dharma Bums. New York: Viking Press, 1958.
Doctor Sax. New York: Grove Press, 1959.
Maggie Cassidy. New York: Avon Books, 1959.
Mexico City Blues. New York: Grove Press, 1959.
Visions of Cody. New York: New Directions, 1959.
The Scripture of the Golden Eternity. New York: Totem Press/Corinth Books, 1960.
Tristessa. New York: Avon Books, 1960.
Lonesome Traveler. New York: McGraw-Hill, 1960.
Book of Dreams. San Francisco: City Lights Books, 1961.
Pull My Daisy. New York: Grove Press, 1961.
Big Sur. New York: Farrar, Straus & Cudahy, 1962.
Visions of Gerard. New York: Farrar, Straus, and Company, 1963.
Desolation Angels. New York: Coward-McCann, 1965.
Satori in Paris. New York: Grove Press, 1966.
Vanity of Duloz. New York: Coward-McCann, 1968.
Scattered Poems. San Francisco: City Lights Books, 1971.
Visions of Cody. New York: McGraw-Hill, 1973.
Old Angel Midnight. [London?]: Booklegger, 1973.
Two Early Stories. New York: Aloe Editions, 1973.
Trip Trap. Bolinas, Calif.: Grey Fox Press, 1973.
Home at Christmas. New York: Privately published, 1973.
Heaven & Other Poems. Bolinas, Calif.: Grey Fox Press, 1977.

Interviews

"The Art of Fiction XLI," *Paris Review*, 43 (Summer, 1968), pp. 61-105. A major interview, conducted by Ted Berrigan, Aram Saroyan, and Duncan McNaughton. Discussion of technique ("I got the idea for the spontaneous style of *On the Road* from seeing how good old Neal Cassady wrote his letters to me"), the novels, poetry ("haiku is best reworked and revised"), Zen ("what's really influenced my work is Mahayana Buddhism"), drugs, the Beat Generation.

McClintock, Jack. "This Is How the Ride Ends," *Esquire*, 73 (March, 1970), pp. 138-39, 188-89. An article, with extensive quotes from an interview with Kerouac. "If Kerouac had a hero, it was William F. Buckley, Jr." For Kerouac, Thomas Wolfe was the greatest American writer, "after me, of course."

Twardowicz, Sanley. "Excerpts from an Interview with Jack Kerouac," *Street Magazine*, 1 (Spring, 1975), n.p. Conducted in 1964, this interview deals with Kerouac's hitchhiking in France, Corso, Ginsberg, Cassady, Mailer, Hemingway, and etc. "They changed the name from Walt Whitman Bridge to Joyce Kilmer Bridge because Walt Whitman was a queer. But Joyce Kilmer was a hundred times worse."

Bibliography

Charters, Ann. *A Bibliography of Works by Jack Kerouac*. New York: Phoenix Bookshop, 1967. Revised and expanded edition, 1975. A good descriptive bibliography compiled by Kerouac's biographer, with Kerouac's assistance. Lists books, pamphlets, and broadsides by Kerouac, his contributions to periodicals and anthologies, translations of his work, recordings and musical settings of his work, and interviews and articles with quotations by Kerouac. Unfortunately the bibliography includes no discussion of critical materials available or unpublished work by Kerouac.

Criticism — Full Length Studies

Burroughs, William; Jack Kerouac and Claude Pelieu. *Jack Kerouac.* Paris: L'Herne, 1971. A memorial volume, containing an essay by Burroughs ("if Fitzgerald was the writer of the Jazz Age, Kerouac is the writer of a generation of travelers on the road"), Alfred G. Aranowitz's interview with Kerouac, "Notes" on the publication of his works by Kerouac, a long poem ("mosaiques electriques indigo off soft zoom Jack Kerouac et la radio-nuit-de-l'en-fance") by Claude Pelieu, "Notes" on Kerouac by Pelieu (with an epilogue poem — "Jack Kerouac est mort"), a poem ("Jack Kerouac est mort le 21 octobre 1969") by Allen Ginsberg, photographs, and two newspaper clippings on Kerouac's death. In French.

Charters, Ann. *Kerouac: A Biography.* San Francisco: Straight Arrow Books, 1973. Reviews of this biography were mixed, but on the whole a fascinating and useful book. Essentially a full-scale biography, Charters also attempts some criticism of individual novels. Contains valuable information about many of the Beats — Ginsberg, Burroughs, Corso, and Neal Cassady in particular — as well as a bibliographical chronology and an identity key to Kerouac's works. Photographs.

Gifford, Barry. *Kerouac's Town.* Santa Barbara, Calif.: Capra Press, 1973. Revised and expanded edition, Berkeley, Calif.: Creative Arts Book Co., 1977. A monograph. Short journal of Gifford's trip to Lowell, Mass., in 1971, on the second anniversary of the death of Kerouac. Contains some biographical information. The revised edition adds a description of Gifford's visit with Stella Kerouac, Jack's wife, who explains her unhappiness over Charters' *Biography* due to its "inaccuracies." Photos by Marshall Clements of various scenes in Lowell.

Jarvis, Charles. *Visions of Kerouac.* Lowell, Mass.: Ithaca Press, 1975. A biography of Kerouac written by a man who, like Kerouac, was born in Lowell, Massachusetts. Jarvis knew Kerouac at school, knew his family and friends, and spent time with him when Kerouac returned to Lowell before his death. Less useful than Charters in describing the Beat years, but fills in many gaps in its discussion of Kerouac's early and late years in Lowell.

Cassady, Carolyn. *Heart Beat: My Life with Jack & Neal.* Berkeley, Calif.: Creative Arts Book Co., 1976. A memoir of Carolyn Cassady's life with Kerouac and Neal Cassady in the San Francisco Bay Area, 1952-53. Much gossip and some interesting biographical information, with letters from Kerouac, Cassady, and Allen Ginsberg (including an interesting one from Ginsberg giving his reactions to an early draft of *On the Road*). Photographs.

Hipkiss, Robert A. *Jack Kerouac: Prophet of the New Romanticism.* Lawrence, Kansas: Regents Press, 1976. Kerouac wrote "novels about the Beat quest for meaning and place in a seemingly mad universe, becoming more despairing of man's future in the world and concomitantly more attracted to mysticism." Discussion of the major works, spontaneous prose, and Kerouac's relationship to Salinger, Purdy, Knowles, and Kesey.

Montgomery, John. *Kerouac West Coast: A Bohemian Pilot Detailed Navigational Instructions.* Palo Alto, Calif.: Fels & Fern Press, 1976. A memoir of Kerouac and other Beat Generation writers. "The physical, sports, movement, action is I think a distinguishing characteristic of Beat Prose and in a sense Beat is a misnomer." Discussion of Kerouac's relationship with Burroughs, Cassady, and Snyder.

Gaffie, Luc. *Jack Kerouac: The New Picaroon.* New York: Postillon Press, 1977. Monograph study of picaresque elements in Kerouac's novels, with emphasis on *On the Road, The Dharma Bums,* and *Desolation Angels.* Argues that the picaresque allows Kerouac "to display a Rabelaisian fullness" which redeems "the blemishes resulting from the lack of technical skill and coherent thinking."

Gifford, Barry, and Lawrence Lee. *Jack's Book: An Oral Biography of Jack Kerouac.* New York: St. Martin's Press, 1978. A biography which intends "to provide the framework of a first or fresh reading of Kerouac as a man who succeeded in giving us his one vast book, but in the bits and pieces the marketplace demanded." The commentary is interspersed with passages from interviews with numerous of Kerouac's friends and associates, including Ginsberg, Snyder, Corso, Burroughs, Ferlinghetti, and Stella Kerouac. Concludes with a very detailed character key to the "Duluoz Legend."

Criticism — Shorter Studies

"Blazing and the Beat," *Time,* 71 (February 24, 1958), p. 104. Review of *The Subterraneans,* a novel "about an oddball fringe of social misfits who conceive of themselves as 'urban Thoreaus' in an existential state of passive resistance to society."

Mahoney, Stephen. "The Prevalance of Zen," *The Nation* (November 1, 1958), pp. 311-15. In *The Dharma Bums,* Kerouac's "Zen is expressed in the richness of natural detail and in the naivete and bouyancy of his language.... Zen will enrich our formal culture. It will polish the surface of our minds."

Amis, Kingsley. "The Delights of Literary Lecturing," *Harper's Magazine,* 219 (October, 1959), pp. 181-82. Amis recounts his experiences with Kerouac while the two sat on a New York panal discussing, "Is there a Beat Generation?" Hostile, but amusing.

Tallman, Warren. "Kerouac's Sound," *Evergreen Review,* 4 (January-February, 1960), pp. 153-69. "It is the Bop influence ... which has been the shaping spirit of" Kerouac's work. "The principle of spontaneous creative freedom ... has freed jazz from the tedium of banal melodies." Discussion of the early novels. In *Casebook of the Beats.*

Widmer, Kingsley. "The American Road: The Contemporary Novel," *University of Kansas City Review,* 26 (Summer, 1960), pp. 309-17. Study of "the road" as a literary device, a "lyric image of American yearning," in the work of Kerouac, Bellow, Malamud, Salinger, Algren, and Gold.

Leer, Norman. "Three American Novels and Contemporary Society," *Wisconsin Studies in Contemporary Literature,* 3 (Fall, 1962), pp. 67-86. Discussion of Malamud's *The Assistant,* Morris' *The Field of Vision,* and Kerouac's *Dharma Bums* as "novels of inquiry." In *Dharma Bums,* the Zen Buddhist seeks "identity through submission to intuitive experience."

Duffy, Bernard. "The Three Worlds of Jack Kerouac," in *Recent American Fiction: Some Critical Views,* ed. by Joseph J. Waldmeir (Boston: Houghton Mifflin, 1963). Kerouac's first "world" is his identification with the Beat Generation; his second is rhapsody; his third, "the process of fiction" (spontaneous prose and "Romantic comedy").

Feied, Frederick. *No Pie in the Sky: The Hobo As American Cultural Hero in the Works of Jack London, John Dos Passos, and Jack Kerouac.* New York: Citadel Press, 1964. While for London and Dos Passos the hobo problem was a concrete fact of American life born of economic crises, for Kerouac the hobo became a symbol of conscious rejection of contemporary values. In *On the Road*, Dean Moriarty emerges as "an unconscious caricature of Nietzsche's superman"; in *The Dharma Bums*, Japhy Ryder is a "natural descendent of the vanishing wobbly."

Webb, Howard W., Jr. "The Singular Worlds of Jack Kerouac," in *Contemporary American Novelists*, ed. by Harry T. Moore (Carbondale: Southern Illinois University Press, 1964). Kerouac has two worlds: the world of Lowell, Mass., and the world of "the road." His "Beat" values are actually the values of his early life in Lowell.

Holmes, John Clellon. *Nothing More to Declare*. New York: E.P. Dutton, 1967. Chapter four is an account of Holmes' first meeting with Kerouac: "he was so evidently on his way toward some accomplishment, or some fate, that it was impossible not to warm to him immediately." Chapter six, "The Great Rememberer," remains a key article: Kerouac is "the kind of writer that only America could produce, and that only America could so willfully misunderstand." His work is "not so much concerned with events as it is concerned with consciousness, in which the *ultimate* events are images."

Krim, Seymour. *Shake It for the World, Smartass*. New York: Dial Press, 1970. In his chapter "The Kerouac Legacy," Krim argues that "the significant thing about Kerouac's creation of the Beat Generation, what made it valid and spontaneous enough to leave a lasting wrinkle on history and memorialize his name, was that there was nothing calculated or phoney about the triumph of his style."

Vopat, Carole G. "Jack Kerouac's *On the Road*: A Re-evaluation," *Midwest Quarterly*, 14 (1973), pp. 385-407. Kerouac's characters are not questing for "identity," but attempting to escape from it.

Hart, John E. "Future Hero in Paradise: Kerouac's *The Dharma Bums*," *Critique: Studies in Modern Fiction*, 14 (1973), pp. 52-62. Kerouac's hero is in the tradition of Odysseus, Don Quixote, Rasselas, and Nick Adams in his "pilgrimage of organized spontaneity."

Dardess, George. "The Logic of Spontaneity: A Reconsideration of Kerouac's 'Spontaneous Prose Method,'" *Boundary* 2, 3 (Spring, 1975), pp. 729-45. Although Emerson and Thoreau are proponents of spontaneous writing as an entry into their subject (an entry which is later subject to revision), for Kerouac "spontaneous writing is both the final phase and the end-product of mental activity rather than its raw material."

Gelfant, Blanche. "Residence Underground: Recent Fictions of the Subterranean City," *Sewanee Review*, 83 (Summer, 1975), pp. 406-38. Discussion of the "subterranean city novel" with reference to Kerouac, Burroughs, Pynchon, and Reed.

Hull, Keith N. "A Dharma Bum Goes West to Meet the East," *Western American Literature*, 11 (Winter, 1977), pp. 321-29. *Dharma Bums* is more "carefully composed" than Kerouac let on. "The surprisingly subtle structure of the novel depends on the slow, backsliding progress that Ray makes toward achieving the Zen ideal which Japhy holds out for him."

Note: Moody Street Irregulars—A Jack Kerouac Newsletter, *edited by Joy Walsh and Michael Basinski, prints short pieces on Kerouac (stories, memoirs, book reviews, news, poems, letters); a recent issue (#5, Summer/Fall, 1979) contains, for example, "The Delussons and the Martins: Some Family Resemblances" by Maurice Poteet, "The 'Little (Known) Literature' of Kerouac's 'Little Canada,'" by*

Poteet, "A Catholic's View of Kerouac" by Father Armand Morrissette, "Heart Beat Goes to Hollywood," and "First Reader of On the Road in Manuscript: An Excerpt from the Journals of John Clellon Holmes."

Michael McClure

Works

Passage. Big Sur, Calif.: Jonathan Williams, 1956.
For Artaud. New York: Totem Press, 1959.
Hymns to St. Geryon. San Francisco: Auerhahn Press, 1959.
!The Feast! San Francisco: Batman Press, 1960.
The New Book/The Book of Torture. New York: Grove Press, 1961.
Pillow. New York: New York Poets Theatre, 1961.
Dark Brown. San Francisco: Auerhahn Press, 1961.
Meat Science Essays. San Francisco: City Lights Books, 1963.
Ghost Tantras. San Francisco: privately published, 1964.
The Blossom; or Billy the Kid. New York: American Theatre for Poets, 1964.
13 Mad Sonnets. Milan, Italy, privately published, 1965.
The Beard. Berkeley, Calif.: Oyez, 1965.
Poisoned Wheat. Berkeley, Calif.: Oyez, 1965.
Unto Caesar. San Francisco: Dave Haselwood, 1965.
Mandalas. San Francisco: Dave Haselwood, 1966.
Love Lion Book. San Francisco: Four Seasons Foundation, 1966.
Freewheelin Frank, Secretary of the Angels. New York: Grove Press, 1967.
Hail The Who Play. Los Angeles: Black Sparrow Press, 1968.
Little-Odes, Jan-March 1961. New York: Poets Press, 1968.
The Sermons of Jean Harlow & The Curses of Billy the Kid. San Francisco: Four
    Seasons Foundation/Dave Haselwood Books, 1968.
Muscled Apple Swift. Topanga, Calif.: Love Press, 1968.
The Surge. Buffalo, N.Y.: Frontier Press, 1969.
Plane Pomes. New York: Phoenix Bookshop, 1969.
Little Odes & The Raptors. Los Angeles: Black Sparrow Press, 1969.
The Cherub. Los Angeles: Black Sparrow Press, 1970.
The Mad Club. New York: Bantam Books, 1970.
Star. New York: Grove Press, 1970.
The Adept. New York: Delacorte Press, 1971.
Gargoyle Cartoons. New York: Delacorte Press, 1971.
The Mammals. San Francisco: Cranium Press, 1972.
Solstice Blossom. Berkeley, Calif.: Arif Press, 1973.
The Book of Joanna. Berkeley, Calif.: Sand Dollar, 1973.
Rare Angel. Los Angeles: Black Sparrow Press, 1974.
Fleas 189-195. New York: Aloe Editions, 1974.
September Blackberries. New York: New Directions, 1974.
Organism. Canton, N.Y.: Institute of Further Studies, 1974.
Flea 100. New York: Frank Hallman, 1975.
Two Plays. San Francisco: privately published, 1975.
Jaguar Skies. New York: New Directions, 1975.
Man of Moderation. New York: Frank Hallman, 1975.
Antechamber & Other Poems. New York: New Directions, 1978.
The Grabbing of the Fairy. San Francisco: Truck Press, 1978.

Interviews

Meltzer, David, ed. *The San Francisco Poets*. New York: Ballantine Books, 1971. Reprinted as *Golden Gate* (Berkeley: Wingbow Press, 1976). A major interview. Much biographical material; discussion of influences, poetry and drama, philosophy ("What I am most concerned with now is the river within ourselves. The biological energy of ourselves is extrusions or tentacles of the universe of meat").

McAllister, Mick. "Interview with Michael McClure," *The Beat Journey (the unspeakable visions of the individual)*, 8 (1978), pp. 93-111. Discussion of influences, *Fleas* ("250 spontaneously written, rhymed electric typewriter poems about my childhood"), *The Beard* and *The Blossom* ("the Kid is a prophet of death"), *Rare Angel* ("seems really Oriental, not anything in subject matter or appearance, but *linguistically*"), etc.

Bertholf, Robert J. "A Conversation with Joanna and Michael McClure," in *Robert Duncan: Scales of the Marvellous*, ed. by Robert J. Bertholf and Ian W. Reid (New York: New Directions, 1979). Discussion of the McClures' friendship with Robert Duncan. ("Robert was the first poet I knew who showed me that one could use poetry as a vehicle of thought without disengaging it from feeling").

Bibliography

Clements, Marshall. *A Catalogue of Works by Michael McClure, 1956-1965*. New York: Phoenix Book Shop, 1965. A description of McClure's books, pamphlets, broadsides, contributions to periodicals, recordings, and translations, through 1965.

Criticism

Aside from reviews of McClure's work as it appears, and mention of him in most of the longer studies of Beat Generation writers (see Charters' Kerouac and Cherkovski's Ferlinghetti, for example), the Thurley essay reprinted in this volume is the only analysis yet attempted of the poet's oeuvre. Two reviews:

MacSweeney, Harry. "The Mammal and the Stars Are Equal," *Poetry Information*, 12/13 (Spring, 1975), p. 74. In McClure's 99 *Theses*, "we find certain finely honed statements, keys which aid us to enter McClure's work-body.... THE UNIVERSE IS THE MESSIAH, EACH MAMMAL DESERVES, MEAT IS THOUGHT."

Lynch, Michael. "A Broad Silk Banner," *Parnassus*, 4 (Spring/Summer, 1976), pp. 156-65. Extended review of *September Blackberries* and *Rare Angel*. McClure is an exponent of "hip zoological primitivism." "McClure's language operates much as his fellow Californian Professor Hayakawa sees language operating: it is a map ... to something beyond itself. This gives the lie to his, McClure's, claim that 'poetry is not a system but it is real events spoken of, or happening, in sounds'."

GARY SNYDER

Works

Riprap. Ashland, Mass.: Origin Press, 1959.

Myths & Texts. New York: Totem Press, 1960. Reprinted with a new preface by Snyder by New Directions, 1978.

Ryosen-An: Zendo Practices. Kyoto: First Institute of America in Japan, 1960.

The Wooden Fish; Basic Sūtras and Gathās of Rinzai Zen (with Gutetsu Kanet-suki). Kyoto: First Institute of America in Japan, 1961.

Riprap, & Cold Mountain Poems. San Francisco: Four Seasons Foundation, 1965.

Six Sections from Mountains and Rivers without End. San Francisco: Four Seasons Foundation, 1965. Reprinted as *Six Sections from Mountains and Rivers without End Plus One* by Four Seasons Foundation, 1970.

A Range of Poems. London: Fulcrum Press, 1966.

Three Worlds, Three Realms, Six Roads. Marlboro, Vt.: Griffin Press, 1966.

The Back Country. London: Fulcrum Press, 1967. Reprinted in an expanded edition in 1968 by New Directions.

The Blue Sky. New York: Phoenix Book Shop, 1969.

Earth House Hold: Technical Notes & Queries to Fellow Dharma Revolutionaries. New York: New Directions, 1969.

Regarding Wave. Iowa City: Windhover Press, 1969. Reprinted in an expanded edition in 1970 by New Directions.

Cold Mountain Poems. Portland, Ore.: Press-22, 1970.

Manzanita. Bolinas, Calif.: Four Seasons Foundation, 1972.

The Fudo Trilogy. Berkeley, Calif.: Shaman Drum, 1973.

Turtle Island. New York: New Directions, 1976.

The Old Ways. San Francisco: City Lights Books, 1977.

He Who Hunted Birds in His Father's Village. Bolinas, Calif., 1979.

Interviews

"Changes," *San Francisco Oracle*, 7 (1967), pp. 1-3, 6-17, 29-34, 40-1. Reprinted in *Notes from the New Underground*, ed. by Jesse Kornbluth (New York: Viking Press, 1968). A discussion among Alan Watts, Timothy Leary, Allen Ginsberg, and Gary Snyder centering on politics, drugs, consciousness, and so on.

Grahm, Dom Aelred. "LSD and All That," in *Conversations: Christian and Buddhist; Encounters in Japan* (New York: Harcourt, Brace & World, 1968). Discussion with Snyder in Japan; centers on Zen and Catholicism, Jung, drugs. "The LSD world is best understood in the language and mythology of Hinduism and Vajrayana Buddhism."

Tarn, Nathaniel. "From Anthropologist to Informant: A Field Record of Gary Snyder," *Alcheringa*, 4 (Autumn, 1972), pp. 104-11. Centers on biography, influences, and friendships. "I always felt that Olson was an apologist for Western Culture.... [Robert] Duncan is possibly my favorite poet, now."

Bartlett, Lee. "Interview: Gary Snyder," *California Quarterly*, 9 (Spring, 1975), pp. 43-50. Discussion of poetic craft and the oral tradition, shamanism, language, and energy.

McKenzie, James. "Moving the World a Millionth of an Inch," *The Beat Diary (the unspeakable visions of the individual)*, 5 (1977), pp. 140-57. An extended discussion of the Beats, Gregory Corso, *Mountains and Rivers Without End*.

Bibliography

Norton, David. "Gary Snyder Checklist," *Schist* (Willimantic, Conn.), 2 (Summer, 1974), pp. 58-66. A substantial checklist, including books, chapbooks, broadsides, some ephemera and nonprint material, and prose in periodicals, through 1973.

Note: *A full-length, descriptive bibliography of the work of Gary Snyder has been announced for publication by the Phoenix Press.*

Criticism — Full Length Studies

McCord, Howard. *Some Notes to Gary Snyder's Myths & Texts.* Berkeley, Calif.: Sand Dollar, 1971. A useful compilation of sources and allusions in *Myths & Texts.* Snyder provided many of the notes.
White, Kenneth. *The Tribal Dharma: An Essay on the Work of Gary Snyder.* Dyfed: Unicorn, 1975. A revision of an essay which first appeared in *Raster* (Amsterdam) in 1971, under the title "Poetry and the Tribe." Rather slight and padded with quotes (130 footnotes in an essay of 36 pages), this sympathetic piece begins with a discussion of the San Francisco Renaissance, then continues with sections on "rules of poetic wandering," "the Indian background," "in the steps of Han Shan," "return to the West," "the Great Subculture," and "the Tribe."
Steuding, Bob. *Gary Snyder.* Boston: Twayne, 1976. A volume in Twayne's United States authors series, this is the first full study of Snyder's life and work. Includes a biographical introduction and chapters on the major work through *Turtle Island,* emphasizing the poetry. An interesting and very useful book.

Criticism — Shorter Studies

Sward, Robert W. "Poetry Chronicle," *Poetry,* 94 (July, 1960), pp. 244-46. First major review of *Riprap.* "Though they do not attempt very much, at least three of these poems are fully convincing."
Dickey, James. "First Five Books," *Poetry,* 97 (February, 1961), pp. 316-20. In his review of *Myths & Texts,* Dickey sees Snyder as the most interesting of the Beats. Snyder owes a debt to Pound; his style is "sharp-edged, vivid, detached."
"Crunk." "The Work of Gary Snyder," *The Sixties,* 6 (Spring, 1962), pp. 25-42. Snyder's "is essentially a Western imagination." His poetry "is very different from 'Beat' poetry." His orientalism is, unlike other Beats, genuine.
Howard, Richard. "To Hold Both History and Wilderness in Mind: The Poetry of Gary Snyder," *Epoch: A Magazine of Contemporary Literature,* 15 (Fall, 1965), pp. 88-96. Reprinted (expanded) in Howard's *Alone with America* (New York: Atheneum Publishers, 1969). Discussion of *Riprap, Myths & Texts,* and *Rivers and Mountains without End.* "These poems are tough, sharp-edged, concentrated on the thing shown."
Lyon, Thomas J. "Gary Snyder, a Western Poet," *Western American Literature,* 3 (Fall, 1968), pp. 207-16. Like John Muir, Robinson Jeffers, and Frank Waters, Snyder has "a certain feeling for Western nature that shapes his ultimate philosophical view of reality." Nature is "their standard."
Zahniser, Edward. "Poet in Today's Wilderness," *Living Wilderness,* 33 (Spring, 1969), pp. 34-36. With emphasis on *The Back Country,* Zahniser discusses Snyder's poetry in terms of the conservation movement.
Scott, Robert Ian. "Gary Snyder's Early Uncollected Mallory Poem," *Concerning Poetry,* 2 (1969), pp. 33-37. Snyder "seems to have started turning away from myths ... in 1950-52, when he re-wrote this early uncollected poem about

George Leigh Mallory's disappearance on Everest." Two drafts of the poem are included.

Paul, Sherman. "From Lookout to Ashram: The Way of Gary Snyder," *Iowa Review*, 3/4 (Spring & Fall, 1970), pp. 76-91; 70-85. A major essay on Snyder's work to 1970. "I know of no one since Thoreau who has so thorougly espoused the wild as Gary Snyder — and no one who is so much its poet." "Poetry and the Primitive" is Snyder's "most important statement and the resolution of much of his work."

Berry, Wendell. "A Secular Pilgrimage," *Hudson Review*, 23 (1970), pp. 401-24. Discussion of nature poetry and the work of Snyder, Denise Levertov, and A.R. Ammons. Of the three, Snyder "is the most austere, the one willing to venture farthest from the human assumptions and enclosures."

Rexroth, Kenneth. *American Poetry in the Twentieth Century.* New York: Herder & Herder, 1971. "Snyder is probably the most influential — on the young — poet of his generation ... [and] an accomplished technician who has learned from the poetry of several languages and who has developed a sure and flexible style."

Parkinson, Thomas. "The Theory and Practice of Gary Snyder," *Journal of Modern Literature*, 2 (1971-72), pp. 448-52. Extended review of *Earth House Hold* and *Regarding Wave.* Snyder's "concern with the primitive is not romanticism but an effort to find basic common human elements, principles rather than subjects that he can undergo and explore."

Lewis, Peter Elfred. "Robert Creeley and Gary Snyder: A British Assessment," *Stand*, 13 (1972), pp. 42-7. Discussion of Snyder as an "idiom" poet; both Snyder and Creeley "are gifted but undeniably minor poets."

Paul, Sherman. "Noble and Simple," *Parnassus*, 3 (1975), pp. 217-25. Extended review of *Turtle Island.* "'I Went into the Maverick Bar' does for Snyder some of the things 'The Desert Music' does for Williams: it permits him to confront his present self as well as an earlier self and world, to acknowledge their continuing existence, and in its resolution to transcend them again and continue his work."

Williamson, Alan. "Gary Snyder: An Appreciation," *New Republic*, (November 1, 1975), pp. 28-30. "Snyder seems to me one of the two or three best craftsmen among poets under 50, and the most impressive moral thinker." Discussion of "Burning the Small Dead," "This Tokyo," and "The Bath."

Rothberg, Abraham. "A Passage to More than India: The Poetry of Gary Snyder," *Southwest Review*, 61 (Winter, 1976), pp. 26-38. Snyder "is both a symbolic and symptomatic figure in contemporary letters." His sources are Whitman and the Transcendentalists, and, "like Emerson, Snyder understands that nature can be approached and understood not by reason but only by intuition."

Kern, Robert. "Recipes, Catalogues, Open Form Poetics: Gary Snyder's Archetypal Voice," *Contemporary Literature*, 18 (Spring, 1977), pp. 173-97. Snyder is a poet "for whom wilderness is not only a precious source of value but something like a metaphysical ground." Snyder's catalogs "transcend their appearance and become expressive not only in general, but in terms of an apotheotic quest."

Goldstein, Laurence. "Wordsworth and Snyder: The Primitivist and His Problem of Self-Definition," *The Centennial Review*, 21 (1977), pp. 75-86. Discussion of Snyder as a romantic poet who believes that "the word comes to us as the essential expression" of being, yet who recognizes "that language betrays its originating spirit."

Almon, Bert. "Buddhism and Energy in the Recent Poetry of Gary Snyder,"
    Mosaic, 11 (1977), pp. 117-25. Focuses on Buddhist elements in Snyder's later
    poetry, with emphasis on his movement within Buddhism from Zen to
    Vajrayana.
Chung, Ling. "Whose Mountain Is This? — Gary Snyder's Translation of Han
    Shan," *Renditions*, 7 (1977), pp. 93-102. In translating *Cold Mountain Poems*,
    Snyder "experimented with the English language by deliberately adopting
    Chinese grammatical and metrical patterns."
Altieri, Charles. *Enlarging the Temple*. Lewisburg, Pa.: Bucknell University Press,
    1979. In his chapter "The Poetry of Gary Snyder and Robert Duncan," Altieri
    argues that Snyder "repeats the central strategies of Dante and Donne."
    Snyder and Duncan "share a fundamental model for correlating style and
    religious belief."

PHILIP WHALEN

Works

Self-Portrait from Another Direction. San Francisco: Auerhahn Press, 1959.
Memoirs of an Interglacial Age. San Francisco: Auerhahn Press, 1960.
Like I Say. New York: Totem Press, 1960.
Monday in the Evening: 21 viii 61. Milan: East 128, 1964.
Everyday. Eugene, Ore.: Coyote's Journal, 1965.
Highgrade. San Francisco: Coyote's Journal, 1966.
You Didn't Even Try. San Francisco: Coyote, 1967.
The Invention of the Letter. New York: Irving Rosenthal, 1967.
T/O. San Francisco: David Haselwood, 1967.
On Bear's Head. New York: Harcourt, Brace & World/Coyote, 1969.
Severance Pay. San Francisco: Four Seasons Foundation, 1970.
Scenes of Life at the Capital. San Francisco: Maya, 1970.
Imaginary Speeches for a Brazen Head. Los Angeles: Black Sparrow Press, 1972.
The Kindess of Strangers. Bolinas, Calif.: Four Seasons Foundation, 1977.
Decompressions: Selected Poems. Bolinas, Calif.: Grey Fox Press, 1978.

Interviews

   Philip Whalen's interviews have been collected in Off the Wall: Interviews
with Philip Whalen *[OW below], edited by Donald Allen (Bolinas, Calif.: Four
Seasons Foundation, 1978), and are as follows:*

Waldman, Ann. "Tiger Whiskers," *The World*, 30 (1976). In *OW*, pp. 5-37. The
    longest published interview with Whalen, this focuses primarily on biographi-
    cal material, with much reference to Gary Snyder and Lew Welch.
Saroyan, Aram. "Interview," *Strange Faeces* (1972). In *OW*, pp. 38-49. Biog-
    raphy; discussion of inspiration, writing techniques, art.
Le Pellec, Yves. "Zen Poet," *Entretiens* (1975). In *OW*, pp. 51-67. Originally pub-
    lished in French, this interview focuses on Snyder, Ginsberg, and Kerouac,
    Zen Buddhism, and literary influences.
Bartlett, Lee. "Interview" (previously unpublished). In *OW*, pp. 68-78. Discussion
    of Zen and the San Francisco Zen Center, writing techniques, and the publica-
    tion history of some early Beat work.

Gifford, Barry, and Larry Lee, "Remembering Jack Kerouac" (previously unpublished). In *OW*, pp. 80-88. Whalen's memories of Kerouac; Gifford and Lee included some of this material in *Jack's Book* (see Kerouac bibliography).

Bibliography

There is no separate bibliography of Whalen's work. See Kherdian's and Lepper's works on pages 195-196 for checklists of primary and secondary materials.

Criticism

Aside from the Thurley article included in this volume, and occasional reviews of individual volumes as they appear, no critical work has been attempted as yet on Whalen's work.

There is included here no separate bibliography for Bob Kaufman. He has published only two books (*Golden Sardine*, San Francisco: City Lights Books, 1967, and *Solitudes Crowded with Loneliness*, New York: New Directions, 1965) and, aside from a few reviews of these books and the Christian essay in the present volume, the editor has been unable to unearth any criticism of his work. New Directions has announced a volume of Kaufman's collected poems (including new work) for publication late in 1981.

Three important items were received by the editor too late to be included in the bibliography proper:

Faas, Ekbert, ed. *Towards a New American Poetics: Essays & Interviews*. Santa Barbara, Calif.: Black Sparrow Press, 1978. Contains short essays on, and very detailed and extended interviews with, Allen Ginsberg and Gary Snyder.

Ferlinghetti, Lawrence, and Nancy J. Peters. *Literary San Francisco*. San Francisco: City Lights Books/Harper & Row, 1980. A popular photo-history of "literary San Francisco" from 1493 to the present, with the bulk of the book given over to the Beats, their precursors, and their followers. Particularly interesting in that it establishes a literary line of which the Beats are the proper inheritors.

McNally, Dennis. *Desolate Angel: Jack Kerouac, the Beat Generation, and America*. New York: Random House, 1979. With Charters' *Kerouac* and Tytell's *Naked Angels*, McNally's extended study becomes a key text. Primarily a biography of Kerouac (as such it fills many gaps in Charters' book), *Desolate Angel* also contains much new information about other members of the Generation. According to John Clellon Holmes, this "is the best book on Jack Kerouac so far."

Index

"A. J." 25
Abomunism 112
Abraham 116
Adam 186
Adonis 23
"Ahab" 131
Algren, Nelson 7
"Alice" 30
Allen, Donald 9
Anaximander 16
Apollo 41, 115, 120, 121, 125, 181-194
Arhat 92, 93
Aristotle 117
Arnold, Matthew 150
Ashbery, John 6
"Assassins" 24
Auden, W.H. 177
Autry, Gene 123

Bartlett, Lee 186-194
Basho 136
Basie, Count 6
Bate, Walter Jackson 148
Baudelaire, Charles 72, 76, 177
Beat Generation 2, 3, 4, 5, 6, 44, 72, 99, 107, 108, 112, 115, 166, 172, 177, 178, 179, 180, 181-194
The Beatles 12
Beethoven, Ludwig van 27
Bellow, Saul 166; *Herzog* 165, 177
"Dr. Benway" 24, 25, 36
Bergson, Henri 151
Saint Bernadette of Lourdes 184
Berryman, John 41, 165, 166; *Dream Songs* 165
Black Mountain 6, 8, 173, 190
Blake, William 10, 76, 85, 145, 166, 171, 178
Bloom, Harold 148

Blythe 10
Boehme, Jakob 166
Bosch, Hieronymus 36
"Bradley the Buyer" 24
Bradstreet, Anne 41
Brown, Norman O. 37; *Life Against Death* 37
Buber, Martin 71
Buckley, William F. 3
Buddha 176
Bukowski, Charles 191
Burroughs, William S. 3, 9, 14-29, 30-39, 90, 122, 123, 124, 167, 176; "Atrophied Preface" 17, 26, 27, 28, 35; "The Black Meat" 24, 25; "The Conspiracy" 19, 27; "The County Clerk" 25; "Deposition: Testimony Concerning a Sickness" 16, 19, 23, 24; *The Exterminator* 17; "Hassan's Rumpus Room" 25; "In Search of Yage" 16, 18, 20, 22, 26; "Islam Incorporated and the Parties of Interzone" 25; *The Job* 16, 17; *Junkie* 16, 18, 20, 21, 22, 23, 24, 25, 26; *Naked Lunch* 9, 16, 17, 18, 19, 20, 26, 27, 30-39, 90; "Ordinary Men and Women" 25; "Playback from Eden to Watergate" 16, 18; "Seven Years Later" 17, 18; *The Soft Machine* 16, 19; *The Ticket That Exploded* 19; *The Yage Letters* (with Allen Ginsberg) 18, 22
Burrows, Vinnie 108
Buson 10
Byron, George Gordon, Lord 176

Caen, Herb 141
Cage, John 177
Campbell, Joseph 20, 21, 25, 26, 27

231